LATE STAGE DEMENTIA CARE
A Basic Guide

Edited by

Christine R. Kovach
College of Nursing
Marquette University
Milwaukee, Wisconsin

Taylor & Francis
Publishers since 1798

USA	Publishing Office:	Taylor & Francis 1101 Vermont Avenue, N.W., Suite 200 Washington, DC 20005-3521 Tel: (202) 289-2174 Fax: (202) 289-3665
	Distribution Center:	Taylor & Francis 1900 Frost Road, Suite 101 Bristol, PA 19007-1598 Tel: (215) 785-5800 Fax: (215) 785-5515
UK		Taylor & Francis Ltd. 1 Gunpowder Square London, EC4A 3DE Tel: 0171 583 0490 Fax: 0171 583 0581

LATE-STAGE DEMENTIA CARE: A Basic Guide

1 2 3 4 5 6 7 8 9 0   BRBR   9 8 7 6

This book was set in Times Roman by Brushwood Graphics, Inc. The editors were Christine Williams and Kathleen Sheedy. Cover design by Michelle Fleitz.

A CIP catalog record for this book is available from the British Library.
∞The paper in this publication meets the requirements of the ANSI Standard Z39.48-1984 (Permanence of Paper)

Library of Congress Cataloging-in-Publication Data
Late-stage dementia care : a basic guide / edited by C. R. Kovach.
   p.   cm.
   Includes bibliographical references.

   1. Dementia—Nursing.   2. Dementia—Patients—Care.   I. Kovach,
C. R. (Christine R.)
   [DNLM: 1. Dementia—nursing.   2. Nursing—methods.   WY 152 L351 1997]
RC521.L38   1997
616.8′3—dc20
DNLM/DLC
for Library of Congress   96-35127
                                                 CIP
ISBN 1-56032-514-3 (case)
ISBN 1-56032-515-1 (paper)

To our patients with dementia, who remind us to live in the present and have taught us so much about humanity, life, and living, and to their families and caregivers, who are exemplars of courage and moral strength.

Contents

Contributors

ALISON BARNES, J.D.
Assistant Professor of Law
Marquette University
Milwaukee, Wisconsin

MARILYN J. BONJEAN, Ed.D.
President, ICF Consultants, Inc.
Milwaukee, Wisconsin

RONALD D. BONJEAN, Ph.D.
Clinical Assistant Professor
Marquette University
Milwaukee, Wisconsin

MARGARET P. CALKINS, M. Arch.
President, IDEAS Inc.
Cleveland, Ohio

MARY COHAN, M.D.
Assistant Professor of Medicine
Medical College of Wisconsin
Director Geriatric Evaluation
    Unit/Medical Service
Clement J. Zablocki Veteran's
    Administration Medical Center
Milwaukee, Wisconsin

ROXANNE DEPAUL, Ph.D.
Associate Professor
Department of Communicative Disorders
University of Wisconsin-Whitewater
Department of Neurology
Waisman Center
University of Wisconsin-Madison
Madison, Wisconsin

EDMUND H. DUTHIE, JR., M.D.
Professor of Medicine
Chief, Geriatrics and Gerontology
Medical College of Wisconsin
Clement J. Zablocki Veteran's
    Administration Medical Center
Milwaukee, Wisconsin

CARLY R. HELLEN, OTR/L
Executive Director
The Wealshire
Lincolnshire, Illinois
Nursing Home Services
Rush Alzheimer's Disease Center
Chicago, Illinois

ANN C. HURLEY, R.N., D.N.Sc.
Associate Director
Geriatric Research Education Clinical
    Center
E.N. Rogers Memorial Veteran's Hospital
Associate Professor of Nursing
Northeastern University
Boston, Massachusetts

CHRISTINE R. KOVACH, Ph.D., R.N.
Associate Professor
College of Nursing
Marquette University
Milwaukee, Wisconsin

JANET WESSEL KREJCI, Ph.D., R.N.
Assistant Professor
Marquette University
Milwaukee, Wisconsin

JUDITH I. KULPA, M.S., CCC-SLP
Department of Otolaryngology & Human
   Communication
Medical College of Wisconsin
Froedtert Lutheran Hospital
Milwaukee, Wisconsin

JILL S. MAGLIOCCO, Art Therapist
Special Care Unit Coordinator
St. Camillus Health Center
Milwaukee, Wisconsin

E. MAHONEY, Ph.D., R.N.
Associate Professor
Boston College School of Nursing
Chestnut Hill, Massachusetts

PATRICIA E. NOONAN, M.S.N.,
R.N., C.S.
Clinical Nurse Specialist
St. Camillus Health Center
Milwaukee, Wisconsin

MARILYN J. RANTZ, Ph.D., R.N.
Assistant Professor
University Hospital and Clinics
Professor of Nursing
University of Missouri-Columbia
Columbia, Missouri

SANDRA A. STEARNS, M.S.N., R.N.
Director of Nursing
St. Camillus Health Center
Milwaukee, Wisconsin

LADISLAV VOLICER, M.D., Ph.D.
Professor of Pharmacology and
Psychiatry
University School of Medicine
Boston University School of Medicine
Clinical Director, GRECC
Boston, Massachusetts

THELMA J. WELLS, R.N., Ph.D.,
F.A.A.N., F.R.C.N.
Nurse Researcher
University of Wisconsin-Madison
William S. Middleton Memorial
   Veteran's Hospital
Madison, Wisconsin

SARAH A. WILSON, Ph.D., R.N.
Assistant Professor
Marquette University
Milwaukee, Wisconsin

MARY ZWYGART-STAUFFACHER,
Ph.D., R.N.
Gerontological Nurse Practitioner
Red Cedar Clinic/Mayo Health System
Associate Professor
College of St. Catherine
St. Paul, Minnesota

Preface

A caregiver exclaimed recently about the care she was giving a person with late-stage dementia, "It's not supposed to be like this." This book attempts to answer the question, "What is care supposed to be like?" Our efforts were spurred by a demographic imperative that can no longer be ignored and by frequent questions and expressions of frustration from caregivers regarding late-stage dementia care.

Little is definitively known about the best care for people with late-stage dementia. The research that is available is scant and suffers from methodological problems frequently found when studying a population that is difficult to research. Everything that is presented in this book is written by experts in their field who have extensive experience providing dementia care. Everything that is presented in this book requires further research, clarification, and evaluation. The book, however, is based on a strong premise that even if we are uncertain about what constitutes best care, we have strong anecdotal reports and some empirical evidence that something can be done to improve the lives of people with dementia. Thus, this book presents what is at least better care than that which is now provided in many settings.

Chapter 1 presents a brief overview of stages of dementia. There are already many excellent resources that examine the pathophysiology and clinical course of Alzheimer's disease and other illnesses associated with dementia. Because the focus of this book is on practical care delivery and interventions, issues involved in staging the course of dementia and basic science research are not addressed. There is debate over what constitutes late-stage dementia, what signs and symptoms differentiate stages, and the duration of each stage. We chose to broadly divide stages into early, middle, and late phases. Many patients in the late stage have a Mini-Mental State Examination score of 5 or lower, have severely compromised mobility, are totally incontinent, and have major communication and functional impairments.

In a society in which productivity and intellect are highly valued, it is easy for people to view a dementing illness with a horror beyond reason and to devalue and cast aside those afflicted. The ways in which a society cares for its vulnerable groups says a lot about that society. This book encourages humane and dignified care by focusing on maintaining personhood, comfort, quality of life, and human dignity. Many of these concepts emerge from the hospice movement, and chapter 2 provides some background on the hospice movement and hospice concepts. Our work is not, however, based on the traditional hospice model of the National Hospice Organization because of the different needs of people with late-stage dementia. Chapter 3 discusses a core challenge in late-stage dementia—maintaining personhood—and presents a philosophy and goals that begin to make a bridge between conceptualizing a palliative care model for late-stage dementia and operationalizing the model in the form of goals and actions. Chapter 4 contains practical suggestions for opening a late-stage dementia care unit, including staffing and program guidelines.

Chapters 5–12 each present guidelines for understanding and treating an array of common needs. Assessment, prevention, and judicious treatment of physical needs and illnesses, as presented in chapters 5 and 6, promote comfort and conserve health care resources. Use of the comprehensive mealtime suggestions described in chapter 7 will help caregivers prevent aspiration of food and fluid, maintain adequate nutrition, and promote more pleasant mealtime experiences. Results of a survey presented in chapter 8 advance understanding of features in the environment that are particularly important for this population. An examination of both micro- and macro-level environmental features provides many suggestions for creating a supportive environment.

Unique strategies for assisting patients with common physical needs such as bathing, dressing, and shaving are found in chapter 9. Techniques such as bridging and rescuing are particularly effective when an activity such as bathing begins to exceed the person's stress threshold. Chapters 10 and 11 focus on behaviors commonly associated with late-stage dementia. Identification of when a behavior should and should not be considered a problem is delineated, and detailed interventions for preventing many common behavior problems are described. Successful pharmacologic and nonpharmacologic interventions to treat behavioral symptoms of dementia are outlined. Multiple ideas for planning activities for the low-functioning person with dementia are presented in chapter 12. Step-by-step instructions facilitate easy and successful implementation of these therapeutic activities.

Chapters 13–17 each deal with special issues in late-stage dementia care. Chapter 13 discusses approaches to providing family-centered care, including how to conduct a family meeting and a terminal-stage care conference. This chapter advances understanding of normal grief, and the many practical suggestions will help caregivers to provide families with the help needed before, during, and after death. Inclusion of chapter 14 on change strategies in this compilation was prompted by a strong belief that when attempts are made to implement change in long-term care or other systems, education of staff is never enough. Smart administrators, before embarking on any change or innovation, have a thorough understanding of human beings' natural discomfort with change.

Understanding people's responses to change, and planning strategies for successfully initiating and sustaining change are needed for implementation of any real and lasting improvements in late-stage dementia care.

Chapter 15 highlights the thorny and complex legal and ethical issues often encountered when a person is incapacitated, and provides an overview of legal rules and specific examples from law cases. Chapter 16 provides guidelines for assessing the quality of a late-stage dementia program, including establishing measurement criteria and evaluating processes and outcomes of care. Finally, Chapter 17 poses some of the challenges and opportunities for the future of late-stage dementia care.

As this book aptly demonstrates, palliative care does not mean little or no intervention. Case studies presented throughout the book highlight the idea that people with dementia are heterogeneous in disability, clinical course, and treatment success. The interventions suggested will work for some but not for others, and what works today for one person may no longer be effective next week or next month.

Perhaps above all else, this book presents a moral challenge to a society that finds great discomfort dealing with loss of control, loss of mental abilities, and the interdependence of humans. People do not consist of memory alone, and human worth cannot, and should not, be based on one's IQ or cognitive ability. Hope for the future of people with dementia, and for other vulnerable groups, rests in our ability to value the essential unity of humanity and our concerted effort to journey together on a path toward competent, humane, and dignified care.

Christine R. Kovach

Acknowledgments

We would like to thank the Helen Bader Foundation for their support of this work and other efforts in the field of dementia care. We also would like to thank Barb Alioto and K-K Reyes for their efforts in preparing the manuscript, and the staff of Taylor & Francis for their work on this book. Finally, heartfelt thanks to family and friends for the constancy of their support, encouragement, and presence.

Part One

Foundations and Options for Program Development

Chapter 1

Stages of Dementia: An Overview

Mary Cohan

Caring for a relative or patient with a dementing illness is challenging. A framework for thinking about specific behaviors and symptoms can help caregivers anticipate and deal with new problems. This chapter will briefly review the diagnosis, prognosis, and stages of dementia to help develop that framework. Other chapters will address more detailed strategies targeted to specific medical and behavioral issues.

Fortunately, increased research has been dedicated to Alzheimer's disease and other illnesses associated with dementia. There is an increased awareness of the devastating effects of these illnesses on quality of life, life expectancy, family dynamics, and the cost of health care. There is hope that research will improve the ability to diagnose dementia of the Alzheimer type (DAT) and understand the causal factors that contribute to these illnesses. Research is complicated by heterogeneity in early symptoms and in rate of decline and by difficulties sorting neurobiological changes seen in normal aging from those seen when disease is present. More basic and applied research is needed in virtually all areas under study.

DIAGNOSIS OF DEMENTIA

Diagnosis of DAT often occurs over a period of time when reversible causes of dementia are being eliminated as the factor responsible for manifested changes in memory, behavior, or function. Often, persons with dementia will not present themselves to the physician's office for diagnosis. Family members, friends, or concerned neighbors often make the initial contact with the health care system when memory impairment is suspected. It is not known if people with early dementia are unaware of the seriousness of their problem, lack the judgment to seek help, or are in a state of denial (Ham, 1992). Older adults who do express concern about their own memory losses usually have benign forgetfulness, depression, or are experiencing one of the reversible causes of dementia. In fact, diagnosis of dementia is often impaired by the plethora of complicating factors that may explain or contribute to cognitive losses. Common reversible causes of dementia include medication side effects, thyroid and other endocrine abnormalities, vitamin B_{12} deficiency, alcohol ingestion, trauma, depression, and infection.

DSM–IV diagnostic criteria for a clinical diagnosis of dementia are listed in Table 1.1. There must be a decline in two or more areas of cognition significant enough to interfere with job or social functioning to establish the diagnosis. Areas of cognitive decline may include memory, language, visual–spatial perception, construction, calculations, judgment, abstraction, and personality changes.

There are a number of causes of dementia, but Alzheimer's disease accounts for 50–60% of cases. Other common causes are vascular problems such as multi-infarct dementia, Parkinson's disease, and dementia associated with chronic alcoholism. Clinical history, a thorough medical diagnostic workup, and neuro-psychological testing are needed to arrive at a probable clinical diagnosis of DAT. Repeated assessments are typically needed to distinguish the persistence or reversibility of the impairments.

Alzheimer's disease continues to be definitively diagnosed only on autopsy. Autopsy studies have confirmed the clinical diagnoses of possible and probable Alzheimer's disease in the majority of cases diagnosed according to the criteria

Table 1.1   DSM–IV Criteria for Dementia of the Alzheimer's Type

A. The development of multiple cognitive deficits manifested by both:
  1) Memory impairment
  2) One or more of the following:
    Aphasia
    Apraxia
    Agnosia
    Disturbance in executive function
B. The cognitive deficits in Criteria A1 and A2 each cause significant impairment in social or occupational functioning and represent a significant decline from a previous level of functioning
C. The course is characterized by gradual onset and continuing cognitive decline
D. The cognitive deficits in Criteria A1 and A2 are not due to any of the following:
  1) Other central nervous system conditions
  2) Systemic conditions known to cause dementia
  3) Substance inducted conditions
E. The deficits do not occur exclusively during the course of a delirium
F. The disturbance is not better accounted for by another Axis 1 disorder

Note. From Diagnostic and Statistical Manual of Mental Disorders (4th ed., pp. 142–143). Washington, DC: American Psychiatric Association, 1994. Reprinted by permission.

developed by the National Institute of Neurological and Communicative Disorders and Stroke and the Alzheimer's Disease and Related Disorders Association (NINCDS–ADRDA).

Computer tomography (CT) and magnetic resonance imaging (MRI) scans are not sensitive enough to confirm a diagnosis of Alzheimer's disease. The degree of atrophy shown in these tests is greater for patients with Alzheimer's disease than for controls, but a large number of patients with Alzheimer's disease show no more atrophy than expected for age alone (Albert & Stafford, 1988; LaRue, 1992). CT and MRI scans are used more successfully to screen for vascular problems associated with dementia. Progress is being made in the development of antemortem diagnostic tests through positive emission tomography (PET) scan procedures, blood testing, and other laboratory analyses.

Some formal cognitive testing is helpful for establishing a probable diagnosis of DAT and following the course of illness. Two brief commonly used screening tools are the Mini-Mental State Exam (MMSE) and the Blessed Dementia Scale. These tools are easily administered in the course of a physical exam, and use of these tools can detect early cognitive problems and improve the objectivity of repeated assessments. Most tools assess orientation, registration, attention and calculation, recall, language, and construction abilities. However, people with dementia can score in the normal range on these tests, and a variety of factors can cause scores to be inaccurately low or reflect more cognitive loss than is true. Factors that may contribute to false low scores are acute illness (e.g., infection), sensoriperceptual deficits (e.g., hearing loss or impaired vision), depression, impaired effort on the part of the person responding to the tool, impaired communication, inability to read or write, and administration conditions.

PATHOLOGY

Brains of people with Alzheimer's disease show atrophy of the cerebral cortex that is usually diffuse but may be more pronounced in the frontal, parietal, and temporal lobes. Atrophy is also seen in normal aging, and the degree of atrophy does not correlate with the degree of cognitive impairment. Microscopic neurofibrillary tangles and senile plaques are seen. The number of senile neuritic plaques per microscopic field correlates with cognitive losses. Biochemically, there is a 50–90% reduction in the activity of choline acetyltransferase, an enzyme found only in cholinergic neurons. It appears that there is a selectively greater loss of cholinergic neurons in the brains of individuals with Alzheimer's disease. Other neurotransmitters in the cholinergic, noradrenergic, and serotonergic systems are reduced. Forty to 60% of large corticoneurons may be destroyed, and there is additional loss of neurons in other portions of the brain (Terry, Peck, DeTeresa, Schecter, & Horoupian, 1981). The fact that pathological changes are distributed selectively in various parts of the brain explains the predominance of cognitive declines in early and mid-stage dementia, with relatively fewer sensory and motor impairments.

STAGES OF ALZHEIMER'S DISEASE

Alzheimer's disease is a progressive disorder with an average duration of 9 years (range 1–16 years) from symptom onset to death. The rate of progression is highly variable, and some patients may progress to the late-stage in one year. One study (Walsh, Welch, & Larson 1990) found that a lower MMSE score and the combination of falls and wandering were associated with decreased survival. Comorbid medical conditions were not associated with decreased survival. Particularly early in the illness, there is large variability in symptoms associated with Alzheimer's disease. Authors have classified the stages of Alzheimer's disease in various ways. A common classification system divides the disease into three stages: early, mid, and late.

Early-stage dementia

- Memory loss
- Time and spatial disorientation
- Poor judgment
- Personality changes
- Withdrawal or depression
- Perceptual disturbances

Mid-stage dementia

- Recent and remote memory worsens
- Increased aphasia (slowed speech and understanding)
- Apraxia
- Hyperorality
- Disorientation to place and time
- Restlessness or pacing
- Perseveration
- Irritability
- Loss of impulse control

Late-stage dementia

- Incontinence of urine and feces
- Loss of motor skills, rigidity
- Decreased appetite and dysphagia
- Agnosia
- Apraxia
- Communication severely impaired
- May not recognize family members or self in mirror
- Loss of most or all self-care abilities
- Cognition severely impaired
- Immune system depressed

Regardless of how the stages are delineated, there is significant overlap in symptoms between stages. The staging is, in essence, an arbitrary marker of progression through a syndrome notable for extensive variability. Staging has a variety of uses, including assisting in communicating and comparing findings between researchers and health care professionals.

Early-Stage Dementia

Alzheimer's disease has an insidious onset of symptoms, whereas with vascular causes of dementia, cognitive declines may present more abruptly. The initial problem in Alzheimer's disease is the inability to learn new information. During the early stage, memory loss, time and spatial disorientation, and poor judgment become evident. Patients may be unable to reason through problems and may have difficulty functioning outside of established routines. Personality changes, suspiciousness, and depression are common. Depression is present in up to 25% of these patients. Visuospatial skills are affected, and the patient may become lost in familiar surroundings or while driving. Language disturbance starts with poor word list generation and progresses to anomia. Family members may notice personality and mood changes, as well as difficulty with numbers involved in phone use, paying bills, and money handling. Delusions, usually of a persecutory nature, are present in up to half of dementia patients at some point during the illness. Patients commonly think that their belongings are being stolen or that their spouse is unfaithful. Illusions that are misinterpretations of real events are also common. Shadows or television voices may be misinterpreted. The physical exam is usually normal at this stage.

Mid-Stage Dementia

In the middle or moderate stage of dementia, remote and recent memory decline. Patients are disoriented to place and time and may no longer recognize family members. As aphasia progresses, their conversation takes on a vacant quality. Apraxia effects the ability to perform activities of daily living. These are usually lost in descending order from bathing, dressing, mobility, and toileting to eating. Patients may develop increased muscle tone or extrapyramidal symptoms that affect gait and may contribute to falls.

Behaviors are manifested during this stage that may reflect decreased impulse control or responses to fear and frustration. Indifference and irritability increase. Wandering and pacing become evident. Wandering may have different underlying etiologies that need to be addressed: restlessness, stress, delusions about the past, or need for exercise. Aggression, repetition in movement and verbalizations, and socially inappropriate behavior may be present. Hyperorality, placing inappropriate objects in the mouth, may become a problem.

Hallucinations are found in up to one third of patients with Alzheimer's disease, and the majority of these are visual (Lerner, Koss, Patterson, Ownby, Hedera, Friedland, & Whitehouse 1994). Lerner et al. found that patients with visual hallucinations had more behavioral symptoms such as verbal outbursts, delusions, and paranoia.

Sleep disturbance is present in early dementia and worsens with advancing Alzheimer's disease. Loss or damage to the neuronal pathways responsible for sleep initiation and maintenance lead to impaired sleep. This may be manifested as increased daytime napping and nighttime wakefulness. The daytime napping is mainly Stage 1 and 2 sleep, resulting in a loss of the more restorative REM and Stages 3 and 4 sleep. *Sundowning* is a clinical term that caregivers and health care professionals use to describe the exacerbation of agitated or disruptive behaviors in the evening. It is seen as a significant burden in caring for patients, but the etiology of this clinical syndrome is unclear. Little data are available, but some hypothesize a link between the disturbed sleep–wake cycle and sundowning behavior.

Late-Stage Dementia

During the late stage of dementia the person becomes more bed or chair bound and develops increased rigidity. Extrapyramidal symptoms and primitive reflexes develop. Paratonia, a primitive reflex, is the involuntary resistance in an extremity in response to a sudden passive movement. Clinically this means that if a caregiver moves the arm of a patient quickly, the patient may automatically resist the movement. Other primitive release signs (sucking and grasp reflexes) return. Myoclonus is present in 10–15% of patients and is associated with increased disease severity. Seizures are uncommon but may occur. Contractures, pressure ulcers, urinary tract infections, and pneumonia may develop from immobility.

Appetite decreases, and the patient loses the ability to chew and swallow because of severe apraxia. Weight loss is nearly universal. Speech deteriorates, and patients become unable to communicate. Some patients are mute, and others scream repeatedly. Bowel and bladder incontinence are present. Urinary incontinence associated with dementia may be multifactorial. There is loss of sphincter control associated with cognitive impairment and detrusor muscle instability with periodic uninhibited bladder contractions.

By the end stage of dementia, the sleep–wake cycle is markedly disturbed, and up to 40% of time in bed is spent awake, with many of the daytime hours spent sleeping (Vitiello, Bliwise, & Prinz, 1992). Hallucinations persist. Death is often the result of infectious complications such as pneumonia or urinary tract sepsis.

CASE EXAMPLE

Mrs. Jones is an 80-year-old woman who lives with her husband in their own home. They have no children but have contact with nieces and nephews. Over the past 3 years her husband had noted increased forgetfulness. Gradually he had taken over the cooking, cleaning, shopping, and laundry because Mrs. Jones was unable to perform the tasks. He needed to remind her about bathing and dressing, but she was then able to complete the tasks independently. She was very sociable and loved family gatherings, where her nieces and nephews noticed only some repetition.

That winter Mr. Jones was hospitalized for congestive heart failure. Mrs. Jones went to stay with her nephew and his wife because she was afraid to be alone. She was restless and confused, asking repeatedly about her husband. One day she insisted on going out for a walk, and the nephew's wife was unable to dissuade her. Police eventually found her nearly 10 miles from her home, unharmed.

Her medical evaluation at that time revealed a woman in good health. She had a history of hyperlipidemia but no other chronic health problems. Laboratory, x-ray, and computed axial tomography (CAT scan) of the head were all normal. She scored 18/30 on the Mini-Mental Status Exam. Her neurologic exam was nonfocal, and her gait was normal.

She was admitted to a nursing home on an emergency basis.

During the first few months in the nursing home, she worried about her husband and inquired about him many times a day. She was easily redirected and was very social. She chatted with staff and other residents but was very repetitive and had word-finding difficulties. She went into other residents' rooms and put on their clothing and jewelry. In the late afternoon and evening she paced, attempted to leave the facility, and was often awake at night.

Over the next few years, she became more irritable and anxious, paced almost continuously, and had visual hallucinations. She began losing weight and falling. She became incontinent of urine and could no longer participate in group activities for more than a few minutes. Different medications were tried that either did not relieve her symptoms or left her somnolent during the daytime.

Eventually all medications were stopped. She remained in a wheelchair, and her speech and appetite deteriorated. She spoke in strings of words that had no content and became resistive to bathing, dressing, eating, and taking medications. Six months later she was chair or bed bound, incontinent of bowel and bladder, and became dependent on the staff for all of her care. She could not communicate her needs, although she still spoke a few words. Her family decided to provide comfort measures and limit medical interventions for any acute illnesses.

CASE DISCUSSION

Mrs. Jones illustrates many of the features of the different stages of Alzheimer's disease. She did not come to the attention of health care professionals until the middle stage of her illness—a time of crisis for her caregiver. Initially, perhaps because her social skills remained intact, her husband was able to compensate for many of her deficits so that other family members were unaware of the extent of her problems. Her husband took over care of the home, but she was able to maintain personal cares with cueing and an established routine. With her husband's hospitalization, she was thrust into a stressful situation away from her caregiver and her home.

On evaluation, her history, physical exam, and mental status testing were consistent with dementia. The normal screening exam, laboratory, and diagnostic testing suggested a diagnosis of probable Alzheimer's disease.

In the nursing home she exhibited classic signs of mid-stage dementia. Wandering, pacing, and sleep disturbance became prominent as her communication skills deteriorated. Multiple interventions were used by the staff: redirection, finger foods, activities on the unit, rest periods, and a safe place to wander. During periods of pacing, extra attention was paid to her physical and emotional needs. A medical evaluation was conducted when her symptoms escalated to rule out any acute illness affecting her function. Medications were used when the visual hallucinations and anxiety became increasingly disturbing to the patient. Target symptoms and side effects were monitored, but in her case it was difficult to find the appropriate dose of a medication to treat the symptoms and minimize side effects. Despite these difficulties, a time-limited trial of medications with careful monitoring is warranted.

In the late stage of dementia, her behavior was less of a problem, and the focus shifted to comfort with incontinence management, skin care, and feeding. The weight loss and difficulties with hand feeding were expected. Food and fluids were not forced, and she did better with more frequent small feedings. No means of artificial nutrition with a gastric feeding tube or intravenous feeding were used in accordance with her own and her family's wishes.

As her illness progressed, Mrs. Jones' caregivers managed different symptoms. The focus on maintaining safety and independence was appropriate during the early and middle phases of her illness. As she entered the terminal phase of Alzheimer's disease, many of the other symptoms abated and the focus of care shifted to meeting her basic needs and providing comfort.

CONCLUSION

Much is left to be learned regarding the diagnosis, prognosis, and clinical course of irreversible dementia. Work is progressing in all of these areas, but the clinician is left to use available resources for making assessments and a working diagnosis. Families need information to understand the nature of a presenting problem. The diagnosis of Alzheimer's disease or irreversible dementia is not welcome and should never be made prematurely. Once the family has an established diagnosis, however, considerable actual and anticipatory work can begin, including grieving, attention to financial matters, and making living arrangements.

Throughout the rest of this book, chapters focus on the issues, care, and treatment facing this population—a population typically represented by a client such as Mrs. Jones.

BIBLIOGRAPHY

Albert, M. S., & Stafford, J. L. (1988). Computed tomography studies. In M. S. Albert & M. B. Moss (Eds.), *Geriatric neuropsychology* (pp. 211–227). New York: Guilford Press.

Cummings, J. L., & Benson, D.F. (1992). *Dementia: A clinical approach* (2nd ed.). Boston: Butterworth-Heinemann.

Franssen, E. H., Kluger, A., Torossian, C. L., & Reisberg, B. (1993). The neurologic syndrome of severe Alzheimer's disease. *Archives of Neurology, 50,* 1029–1039.

Hall, G. R. (1994). Caring for people with Alzheimer's disease using the conceptual model of progressively lowered stress threshold in the clinical setting. *Nursing Clinics of North America, 29*(1), 129–141.

Ham, R. J. (1992). Confusion, dementia, and delirium. In R. J. Ham & P. D. Sloan (Eds). *Primary care geriatrics: A case-based approach* (pp. 259–312). St. Louis, MO: Mosby-Yearbook.

LaRue, A. (1992). *Aging and neuropsychological assessment.* New York: Plenum Press.

Lerner, A. J., Koss, Patterson, M. B., Ownby, R. L., Hedera, P., Friedland, R. P., & Whitehouse, P. J. (1994). Concomitants of visual hallucinations in Alzheimer's disease. *Neurology, 44,* 523–527.

Mayeux, R., & Chun, M. R. (1995). Acquired and hereditary dementias. In L. P. Rowland (Ed.), *Merritt's textbook of neurology* (9th ed.). Baltimore: Williams & Wilkins.

Terry, R. D., Peck, A., DeTeresa, R., Schecter, R., & Horoupian, D. S. (1981). Some morphometric aspects of the brain in senile dementia of the Alzheimer type. *Annals of Neurology, 10,* 184–192.

Tierney, M. C., Fisher, R. H., Lewis, A. J., Zorzitto, N. L., Snow, W. G., Reid, D. W., & Nieuwstraten, P. (1988). The NINCDS–ADRDA work group criteria for the clinical diagnosis of probable Alzheimer's disease: A clinicopathologic study of 57 cases. *Neurology, 38,* 359–364.

Viticllo, M. V., Bliwise, D. L., & Prinz, P. N. (1992). Sleep in Alzheimer's disease and the sundown syndrome. *Neurology, 42* (Supplement 6), 83–93.

Walsh, J. S., Welch, G., & Larson, E. B. (1990). Survival of patients with Alzheimer's type dementia. *Annals of Internal Medicine, 113,* 429–434.

Williams, L. (1986). Alzheimer's: The need for caring. *Journal of Gerontological Nursing, 12*(2), 21–28.

Chapter 2

Palliative Care for Late-Stage Dementia

Sarah A. Wilson

Alzheimer's disease is the most common form of dementing illness, affecting approximately 4 million Americans (National Institutes of Health, 1995). This number will continue to increase with the growth of the population over 65 years of age and the expected quadrupling of the 85-years-old and older group. The National Institute on Aging has projected that 14 million people will be affected by the year 2050 (Austin & Melbourne, 1990). Alzheimer's disease is the fourth leading cause of death in persons age 65 and older (Brechling & Kuhn, 1989). It is a progressive disorder lasting anywhere from 1 to 16 years.

Persons with Alzheimer's disease are cared for in a variety of settings: home, adult day care, group homes, nursing homes, and special care units within nursing homes. The majority of these settings are most appropriate for persons with early-to mid-stage dementia. As the disease progresses to later stages a new level of care is more appropriate. A brief overview of the settings of care for mid-stage dementia care is presented in this chapter, followed by an in-depth discussion of an innovative approach to the care of persons with late-stage or terminal dementia.

SETTINGS OF CARE FOR PERSONS WITH EARLY- AND MID-STAGE DEMENTIA

Home

The majority of persons with Alzheimer's disease are cared for at home by family members. It is estimated that there are 6–8 million family caregivers (Richards, 1990). Caring for a person with Alzheimer's disease can be a physical, emotional,

13

and financial burden for many families. Families and friends provide countless hours of care without any reimbursement, taking time off from work without pay, and using vacation time to devote to caregiving (Max, Webber, & Fox, 1995). The caregiver is most often a spouse who is also older and may have one or more chronic illnesses or an adult daughter who may also have family or work responsibilities (or both). Home care has been described as a 36-hr per day responsibility (Brechling & Kuhn, 1989). Families need supportive services that are often unavailable and not covered by Medicare. The risk of institutionalization increases as families expend personal and economic resources (Paveza, 1993).

Adult Day Care

Specialized adult day care programs emerged in the 1980s as a number of states provided funds for Alzheimer's disease services. These programs provided the family with some respite, making it possible for persons to remain at home longer. Most adult day care programs are designed to serve persons with mild cognitive impairment and are limited in their ability to serve clients with moderate to severe cognitive impairment. Transportation to adult day care may be difficult to arrange and expensive. Although adult day care provides families with a temporary respite, as the disease continues to progress, nursing home placement may be the only alternative.

Group Homes

Group homes and retirement centers have developed special facilities for persons with Alzheimer's disease. These facilities were developed to increase census, improve revenue, and respond to family demands for a more homelike environment (Orr-Rainey, 1994). Group homes are appropriate for persons who are at an early stage in the disease process and need little medical attention or intervention. As the disease progresses, most retirement centers and group homes are not able to provide the continuum of care that is needed. Families are then faced with the additional stress of relocation.

Special Care Units

Long-term care facilities have responded to the increasing numbers of residents with Alzheimer's disease and other types of dementia by creating special care units. It is estimated that at least 50% of the nursing home population has Alzheimer's disease or some other condition that causes dementia (Maslow, 1994). Special care units (SCUs) emerged in the 1980s as a new model of care to address the needs of this population. By 1991, 10% of U.S. nursing homes had some type of SCU (Maslow, 1994). The growth in SCUs occurred in response to a need but without the benefit of research on the efficacy of these units (Berg, 1994; Cohen, 1994; Green, Asp, & Crane, 1985; Orr-Rainey,

1994). There is no agreed upon definition of what an SCU is, and considerable variation exists in philosophy, goals, design, patient/staff ratios, and activity programming (Kutner & Wimberley, 1994). The U.S. Office of Technology Assessment issued a report that identified six principles of SCUs: (a) something can be done for the person with dementia; (b) quality of life and disability may be improved by identifying causative factors; (c) people with dementia have residual strength; (d) behaviors may represent feelings and needs the person is unable to express; (e) physical and social environment affects functioning; and (f) family and the person with dementia are an integral unit (Maslow, 1994). Most SCUs provide a low-stimulus environment in which residents may interact with others who have similar problems. Staff in SCUs receive special education and are selected for working in this type of environment. SCUs are designed for residents who are able to participate in some activity programming and who have few physical problems. The person with late-stage dementia often does not qualify for these units because of an inability to participate in group programming and deterioration in physical status or increased physical care needs. Residents may be discharged from SCUs and transferred to a regular nursing home unit as their disease progresses (Riter & Fries, 1992). The goals of a general nursing home unit may be cure, rehabilitation, maintenance, or comfort. These goals may compete with one another, and the person with late-stage dementia may have his or her needs sacrificed for the person who has curative or rehabilitation needs. A continuum of care is needed for persons with dementia. Currently, a gap exists in services for the growing number of persons who have late-stage dementia.

This book is based on the notion that the primary focus of care for persons with late-stage dementia is palliative care with the goal of maintaining personhood. The traditional medical model of delivering care in most nursing homes is based on cure and rehabilitation. This is no longer appropriate for the person with late-stage dementia. The hospice model of care delivery, with an emphasis on holistic life affirming care is more congruent with the needs of this patient population.

HOSPICE CARE FOR TERMINALLY ILL PERSONS AND FAMILIES

The hospice movement has provided many strategies for treating persons who are no longer candidates for curative or rehabilitation services; however, the implementation of these services has been fragmented and cursory. Health care providers in long-term care facilities need an array of clinical protocols and interventions to promote comfort and maintain quality of life in the late stages of a dementing illness. Orr-Rainey (1994) stated that "if providers are truly committed to a continuum of care, the focus must include a quality of life philosophy that encompasses hospice" (p.142). This book is based on the belief that quality of life can be improved for persons with dementia, that persons consist of more than memory, and that caring communities can be created that transcend the human condition of dementia.

Research and program descriptions in the literature support the idea of applying hospice concepts in long-term care for residents who are in the later stages of a dementing illness (Austin & Melbourne, 1990; Kovach, Wilson, & Noonan, 1996; Luchins & Hanrahan, 1993; Volicer, Volicer, & Hurley, 1993; Volicer, Rheaume, Brown, Fabiszewski, & Brady, 1986). The appropriate level of care for persons in the late stage of a dementing illness has not, however, been examined in any known large-scale studies (Luchins & Hanrahan, 1993). Luchins and Hanrahan surveyed all 819 physician members and 1,000 randomly selected nonphysician members of the Gerontological Society of America, along with 500 family members of demented relatives from the Alzheimer's Association, to determine what kind of care is considered appropriate for end-stage dementia patients. The majority of physicians (61%), gerontologists from other professions (55%), and family members (71%) chose palliative care only. The increased age of the respondent and knowledge of terminal care choices were associated with the choice of palliative care. The majority of health professionals (91%) and family members (90%) agreed that hospice care was appropriate for persons with a late-stage dementing illness. Health professionals and family members differed on the setting for hospice care. Health professionals were asked whether, if a family caregiver was available and had adequate support, they would prefer home or institutional care. The majority of health professionals chose home care. Family members were asked whether they would prefer their relative receive hospice care at home or in an institutional setting. The majority of families chose an institutional setting for hospice care. Families are perhaps more aware of caregiving responsibilities and the physical and economic cost of assuming this role.

HISTORY OF HOSPICE

The origins of hospice are in antiquity. However, the modern hospice program did not take shape until the mid-1960s with the founding of St. Christopher's Hospice in England (Gentile & Fello, 1990). The modern word *hospice* is derived from the Latin root word *hospec,* meaning both host and guest, and symbolizes the mutual caring of people for each other. The National Hospice Organization (NHO) defined hospice as a program of palliative and supportive services that provides physical, psychological, social, and spiritual care for dying patients and their families (1991). Hospice is based on the belief that through a supportive and caring community, patients and families will be free to obtain a degree of mental and spiritual preparation for death.

Philosophy and Purpose of Hospice

The philosophy of hospice as described by the NHO includes the following beliefs: Patient and family know the terminal condition; death is openly talked about; treatment and interventions should be supportive only; pain control should be available to prevent discomfort as needed; an interdisciplinary team is essential to provide hospice services; families and friends should be supported in death and bereavement; and trained volunteers may provide additional support.

The primary purpose of hospice care is to provide comfort and support to patients and families in the final stages of an incurable illness so they may live as fully and as comfortably as possible. Hospice affirms life. "Dying is not considered a medical problem, but a significant part of life's journey that involves the patient, family, and community" (Brechling, Heyworth, Kuhn, & Peranteau, 1989, p. 22). Death is neither hastened nor postponed. Interventions are palliative and are directed at relief of symptoms and meeting the psychosocial needs of patients and their family members.

The rapid growth of the hospice movement in the United States, from one hospice in 1974 to over 1,700 in 1989, occurred in response to consumers' dissatisfaction with the care of the terminally ill and demands for death with dignity. The hospice movement was essentially a grassroots effort with community volunteers. Consumers were especially concerned about the overuse of technology and the right to participate in decisions affecting their care. One of the major goals of a hospice program is to maintain the person's quality of life. Hospice has been described as a high touch, low technology approach to care of dying persons. Public support for the hospice movement was so strong that it became a benefit covered under Medicare only 8 years after the first hospice was founded. It was thought that hospice care would result in significant savings by providing supportive services rather than inappropriate costly and curative services.

Hospice Programs and Requirements

Hospice is a program of care and does not refer to a specific place. Three basic models of hospice organizational structure have evolved, with some variations. The three models are (a) hospices affiliated with a hospital, with or without a home care program, (b) hospices affiliated with home health agencies, with or without an inpatient program, and (c) hospices serving exclusively the terminally ill, with or without a special inpatient unit (Mor & Masterson-Allen, 1987). Hospices are required to provide some type of respite care for families and continuous home care in times of crisis. Hospice care is based on an interdisciplinary team approach. Four core services must be provided directly by the hospice: nursing, medicine, social work, and counseling. Nursing and medical services must be available on a 24-hr basis. The hospice is also required to use volunteers and furnish documentation of cost saving. The patient and family are considered the unit of service and contribute to the plan of care. Bereavement counseling must also be available to family members.

Eligibility Requirements

Patients must meet certain requirements to be eligible for care under the hospice Medicare benefit. A physician must certify that the person is terminally ill and has a limited prognosis—usually 6 months or less. Over 90% of the patients in the National Hospice Study had a primary diagnosis of cancer, which had progressed to affect their functioning, and were close to death (Mor & Masterson-Allen, 1987). Dementia, the fourth leading cause of death, has not been listed as a diagnosis in hospice studies (Mor, Greer, & Kastenbaum, 1988). The ideal patient from the standpoint of the economic survival of hospice is one who the physician can predict with some certainty will die in 6 months or less and who has few complications. Inherent in such program, some argue, is the notion that patients have an obligation to die "on time." The length of time for survival and intensity of illness contribute to hospice costs.

The hospice patient must also sign a release that explains the person has a noncurable illness, what services will be provided by the hospice, and the patient and family role in contributing to the plan of care and decision making. Hospices differ in what types of treatments and interventions are permitted; however, in all cases the patient must agree that no cardio-pulmonary resuscitation be initiated. For example, some programs may not treat infections with antibiotics but keep patients as comfortable as possible with the use of analgesics and antipyretics (Volicer et al., 1986).

As a statutory requirement, 80% of a hospice program's aggregated enrollment days must be spent in home care. This requirement in effect shifted the burden of care to families and resulted in hospice being primarily a home care program in the United States (Wilson, 1994). Hospice home care patients must also have a primary care provider. The Department of Health and Human Services has defined a primary care provider as a responsible person who lives in the home of the patient and is available at least 19 hr a day (Kaplan & O'Connor, 1987). The requirement of a primary care provider who can assume virtually around-the-clock care and who has the resources to sacrifice the time is likely to exclude many elderly individuals, low-income groups, and minorities (Wilson, 1994). This requirement places a significant burden on the elderly, many of whom have one or more chronic illness and may be living alone. A strong family support system is a requirement for hospice home care.

HOSPICE CARE FOR PERSONS WITH LATE-STAGE DEMENTIA

The application of hospice concepts to the care of persons with dementia is a recent development. Hospice has traditionally been associated with cancer patients. Home care hospice services for Alzheimer's patients and their families may be provided by organizations such as the Visiting Nurses Association and other hospice home care programs. Austin and Melbourne (1990) described a hospice home care program that was a joint effort by the Visiting Nurse/Hospice Atlanta and Alzheimer's Care Program. By merging the two services, families were provided with needed respite care that otherwise would not have been available in a traditional hospice home care program.

Volicer, Volicer, and Hurley (1993) stated that "inclusion of patients with end-stage dementia in a hospice program would provide compassionate care not offered in other settings" (p. 55). However, they noted that persons with Alzheimer's disease differ from most hospice patients in two ways: They are not able to participate fully in decisions regarding the program of care because of loss of cognitive abilities, and it is difficult to predict the length of survival. Volicer, Volicer, and Hurley designed a scale to predict disease severity and probability of death after an infection.

Volicer et al. (1986) discussed a hospice approach for care of patients with advanced dementia and the process used to make decisions regarding the withholding of treatment in a study of patients on an intermediate medical unit. Five levels of care were identified, ranging from aggressive diagnostic workup and treatment of infections with antibiotics to supportive care only. The two most common complications of dementia, pneumonia and urinary tract infections, were treated with liberal use of antipyretion and annlgonia to onouro comfort An optimal level of care was assigned by staff, and this correlated highly with the severity of dementia. Family members met with the multidisciplinary team to discuss care options. Care levels assigned in meetings with families correlated poorly with staff recommendations and severity of dementia. Families were able to make changes in the choice of treatment at any time. Preliminary results from the study indicated that mortality did not increase even though medical treatment was limited and the majority of the patients were not treated with antibiotics for urinary tract infections or pneumonia.

The person with Alzheimer's disease or other dementing illness differs from the typical hospice patient with terminal cancer in several ways. Alzheimer's is a progressive disease lasting a period of years. The terminally ill cancer patient has a limited survival rate that can be predicted from disease statistics. The terminally ill cancer patient is usually not cognitively impaired and can participate in the decision to seek hospice care, but the person with late-stage dementia is cognitively impaired and unable to participate in this decision. The person with cancer often has problems with pain and needs large doses of analgesics, usually narcotics. People with late-stage dementia illnesses usually do not need aggressive treatment with narcotics for pain control and may benefit more from nonpharmacological interventions. Both groups of patients may benefit from hospice care.

In summary, hospice is an effective intervention for terminally ill patients and their families. However, requirements for third party reimbursement may have altered and limited the original intent of hospice care. Hospice care may be applied in any setting. Components of hospice care that may be applied in long-term care facilities for persons with dementing illnesses include creating caring communities in which the emphasis is on living, caring, and connecting with others; individualizing care; providing symptom relief and promoting comfort; and being honest with residents and families. Staff may empower residents and families by giving permission to express negative feelings and providing choices. Families may be assisted with maintaining hope, finding meaning, and meeting spiritual needs. Finally, staff need to recognize that the care they provide does make a difference. The following case is an example of applying hospice concepts to the care of a person with late-stage dementia in a long-term care facility.

CASE EXAMPLE

Mrs. Williams is an 88-year-old widow who has been living at Riverview Nursing Home for 4 years. Mrs. Williams lived at home by herself after the death of her husband. She has one adult child, Jean, who is married and has three children. Jean visited her mother daily and began noticing changes in her mother that were a concern. Mrs. Williams started becoming forgetful, she did not know what day it was, often left the stove on without realizing it, stopped visiting her friends, and wanted to stay at home. Jean started spending more time at her mother's home doing the wash, cleaning, and preparing meals. She noticed her mother often neglected her hygiene, and Jean was more concerned about her safety. Jean felt torn between her own family's needs and her mother. She finally decided it would be best if her mother were in a nursing home where she would be given 24-hr care. Jean felt somewhat guilty because, as she reflected on her mother, she realized that some of these changes were occurring when her father was sick. After some time Mrs. Williams adjusted to the nursing home, but her condition deteriorated over the years to the point that she was confused, unable to communicate with intelligible speech, and became incontinent. Mrs. Williams was not able to participate in group activities and spent most of her time wandering up and down the halls. The staff at the nursing home noted that Mrs. Williams had repetitive behavior, such as holding one arm up and repeating one-syllable words (e.g.,"put, put, put"). As Mrs. Williams became more agitated, her verbalizations became more intense.

One of the staff suggested that Mrs. Williams be considered for admission to a new unit for Alzheimer's residents that was incorporating hospice concepts in care. The approach to care was explained to Mrs. Williams' daughter. Jean agreed to have her mother participate in this program of care and hoped it would be of benefit to her. The nurse and nursing assistant who worked with Mrs. Williams in this program discussed her behavior and explored ways to decrease her agitation. They discovered that consistent caregivers were able to notice changes that otherwise might be overlooked. When Mrs. Williams became agitated, they took her to a quieter environment and her agitation decreased; the "put" sounds diminished. Sometimes they assisted Mrs. Williams in going to her room or to a lounge. The nursing assistant often took Mrs. Williams to a window where they could watch the birds. The aide would often talk about the birds. She noticed that Mrs. Williams would follow commands with her eyes. One day, to the aide's surprise, Mrs. Williams pointed to a bird and said "Look!" This was the first time staff had any idea Mrs. Williams could speak. A human connection had been established. After that, Mrs. Williams uttered occasional words that had some meaning for staff. Mrs. Williams did well on this unit until the staff noticed she was getting weaker and refusing to eat. She frequently tried to get out of bed. Mrs. Williams started having high temperatures and was diagnosed with pneumonia. The nurse discussed treat-

ment options with Jean. She explained that Mrs. Williams could be transferred to the hospital and given intravenous antibiotics and other intravenous fluids or could remain at the nursing home. The nurse explained that every effort would be made to keep Mrs. Williams comfortable and that she would receive oral antibiotics and medications for fever and discomfort. Jean was reluctant to have her mother experience the stress of relocation and new caregivers. After meeting with the physician, nurse, and the chaplain, Jean decided to have her mother stay at the nursing home. "This is her home, this is where she would want to be," Jean answered. The nurse continued to assess Mrs. Williams' condition and provided her with comfort measures. Mrs. Williams was given oral antibiotics until she could no longer swallow. The nursing assistant sat with Mrs. Williams and held her hand. Mrs. Williams died when the nursing assistant was holding her hand. She was not alone.

CASE DISCUSSION

This case illustrates how hospice concepts may be applied to the care of a person with a late-stage dementing illness. Mrs. Williams was admitted to a nursing home from her home. She had one adult daughter who assumed responsibility for her care. The daughter was very concerned about her mother and wanted to do what she could to help her. However, the daughter had family responsibilities and a job and could not fulfill the criteria for a primary caregiver under the Medicare definition for hospice home care. Because Mrs. Williams was confused, she was not able to participate in the decision to enter a nursing home or the subsequent decision about her preferences for care with a life threatening illness. This is something that Jean and her mother could have discussed prior to this event. However, it was one of those things they just put off talking about. Unlike most hospice patients, Mrs. Williams was not able to participate in the decision-making process. The staff in the nursing home were able to provide a caring environment for Mrs. Williams and her daughter Jean. They supported Jean's decision to have Mrs. Williams cared for in the nursing home and to have her remain in the nursing home when she was diagnosed with pneumonia. Relocating Mrs. Williams to a hospital would have been stressful for both her and her daughter. The diagnostic workup and treatment of pneumonia in the hospital might have increased discomfort and most likely would not have changed the eventual outcome. Comfort measures were provided through the use of antipyretics and analgesics and the presence of a caring staff. Mrs. Williams was a unique person with special characteristics that the staff came to appreciate. She had abilities that staff were unaware of prior to this program of care.

CONCLUSION

The program described in this chapter makes use of the concepts of personhood, comfort, quality of life, and human dignity. These concepts are operationalized in a practical model of care. The resulting model of care delivery is designed to meet the unique needs of persons with late-stage dementia who have low functional abilities and a variety of physical, behavioral, physiological, spiritual, and emotional needs. No attempt was made to conform to the hospice guidelines set forth by the National Hospice Organization or the regulations set forth to meet requirements for reimbursement by Medicare as a hospice program. Regulations cannot guide interventions. Attempting to fit this program into standards set for a population that generally has a diagnosis of cancer, is not cognitively impaired, and is experiencing problems with pain control would result in a program that, at the core, does not meet the needs of a person with late-stage dementia. The foundation of care for the unique situation and sequelae resulting from being severely cognitively impaired is maintaining personhood. Although more needs to be learned about dementia, few would disagree that the severe cognitive impairment and resulting sequelae of late-stage dementia constitute a unique set of needs that call for new, innovative, and challenging interventions.

BIBLIOGRAPHY

Austin, B., & Melbourne, P. (1990). Hospice services for the terminal Alzheimer's patients. *Caring,* (November), 60–62.

Berg, L. (1994). Commentary: A wish list. *Alzheimer Disease and Associated Disorders, 8*(1), 373–374.

Brechling, B. G., & Kuhn, D. (1989). A specialized hospice for dementia patients and their families. *The American Journal of Hospice Care,* (May/June), 27–30.

Brechling, B. G., Heyworth, J.A., Kuhn, D., & Peranteau, M.F. (1989). Extending hospice care to end-stage dementia patients and families. *The American Journal of Alzheimer's Care and Related Disorders and Research,* (May/June), 21–29.

Cohen, G. D. (1994). Forward: Toward new models of dementia care. *Alzheimer Disease and Associated Disorders, 8*(1), 2–4.

Gentile, M., & Fello, M. (1990). Hospice care for the 1990s: A concept coming of age. *Journal of Home Health Practice, 3*(1), 1–15.

Green, J., Asp, J., & Crane, N. (1985). Specialized management of the Alzheimer's patient: Does it make a difference? A preliminary progress report. *Journal of the Tennessee Medical Association, 78,* 58–63.

Kaplan, M., & O'Connor, P. (1987). The effects of Medicare on access to hospice care. *American Journal of Hospice Care, 4*(6), 34–42.

Kovach, C. R., Wilson, S. A., & Noonan, P. (1996). Effects of hospice interventions on behaviors, discomfort, and physical complications of end-stage dementia nursing home residents. *American Journal of Alzheimer's Disease, 11*(4), 7–15.

Kutner, N. G., & Wimberley, E. T. (1994). Overview of different models of care. *American Journal of Alzheimer's Disease and Associated Disorders, 8*(1), 112–114.

Luchins, D. J., & Hanrahan, P. (1993). What is appropriate health care for end-stage dementia? *American Geriatrics Society, 41,* 25–30.

Maslow, K. (1994). Current knowledge about special care units: Findings of a study by the U.S. Office of Technology Assessment. *Alzheimer Disease and Associated Disorders, 8*(1), 14–39.

Max, W., Webber, P., & Fox, P. (1995). Alzheimer's disease: The unpaid burden of caring. *Journal of Aging and Health, 7*(2), 179–199.

Mor, V. M., & Masterson-Allen, S. (1987). *Hospice care systems: Structure, process, cost, and outcomes.* New York: Springer.

Mor, V. M., Greer, D., & Kastenbaum, R. (Eds). (1988). *The hospice experiment.* Baltimore, MD: Johns Hopkins University Press.

National Hospice Organization. (1991). *Fact sheet.* Arlington, VA: Author.

National Institutes of Health. (1995). *Progress report of Alzheimer's disease 1994.* Bethesda, MD: Author.

Orr-Rainey, N. (1994). Commentary: The evolution of special care units: The nursing home industry perspective. *Alzheimer's Disease and Associated Disorders, 8*(1), 139–143.

Paveza, G. J. (1993). Social services and the Alzheimer's disease patient: An overview. *Neurology, 43*(4), 11–15.

Richards, B. S. (1990). Alzheimer's disease: A disabling neurophysiological disorder with complex nursing implications. *Archives of Psychiatric Nursing, 1*(1), 39–42.

Riter, R. N., & Fries, B. E. (1992). Predictors of the placement of cognitively impaired residents on special care units. *The Gerontologist, 32,* 184–190.

Volicer, B. J., Hurley, A., Fabiszewski, K. J., Montgomery, P., & Volicer, L. (1993). Predicting short-term survival for patients with advanced Alzheimer's disease. *American Geriatrics Society, 41,* 535–540.

Volicer, L., Rheaume, Y., Brown, J., Fabiszewski, K., & Brady, R. (1986). Hospice approach to the treatment of patients with advanced dementia of the Alzheimer type. *Journal of the American Medical Association, 256*(16), 22101–2213.

Volicer, L., Volicer, B. J., & Hurley, A. C. (1993). Is hospice appropriate for Alzheimer's patients? *Caring,* (November), 50–55.

Wilson, S. A. (1994). Hospice and Medicare benefits: Overview, issues, and implications. *Journal of Holistic Nursing, 11*(4), 356–367.

Chapter 3

Maintaining Personhood: Philosophy, Goals, Program Development, and Staff Education

Christine R. Kovach

The primary task in providing care to people with late-stage dementia is to maintain personhood. Several excellent articles on the qualities of self and personhood relative to dementia have been written (Bleathman & Morton, 1988; Kitwood & Bredin, 1992; Sabat & Harre, 1992). Personhood refers to having an "I" reference, a personal identity, or sense of self. Listening to people with late-stage dementia verbalize even such feelings as "I hurt" and "I like ice cream" suggests personhood can be maintained. There are widespread examples of people with late-stage dementia who are nonverbal and do not ever communicate from an "I" perspective. Have these people lost personhood? One argument against loss of personhood is the many examples of people who have been deprived of meaningful human interaction and, when stimulated, seem to come to life, regain some social and verbal skills, and express an "I" orientation (Kovach, Wilson, & Noonan, 1996). Kitwood and Bredin (1992) called this process rementia. Loss of personhood can result, however, if people with late-stage dementia are not allowed to experience, to be, to do, to touch, or to interact and, most important, when their attempts to make human contact are ignored, minimized, or patronized. Clearly personhood can become fragmented and cursory when irreversible dementia exists. Interventions are needed that elicit, restore, and affirm personhood.

LIMIT THE EXPERIENCE, LIMIT THE LIFE

When caregivers work to maintain personhood, it does not mean that they "make it all better." In fact, when caregivers try to make it all better, they may work to define the person's inadequacy and disable and disengage the person further. Being human involves experiencing both good days and bad, as well as a range of emotions and feelings, including pleasure, surprise, frustration, discomfort, and sadness. People with late-stage dementia are able to experience a range of emotions and feelings. In other words, they continue to be able to experience the human condition of living. Although caregivers are interested in quality of life, comfort, and well-being, they should not dilute, limit, and hamper a person's range of positive life experiences by doing everything for him or her in the name of making it better.

CASE EXAMPLE

Mr. Gardner is an 84-year-old man with Parkinson's disease and severe dementia. His last Mini-Mental State Examination (MMSE) score was 1. Mr. Gardner suffers from excessive salivation, drooling, and spitting. Consults with an otolaryngologist, speech therapist, and neurologist have yielded little success in treating his condition. Mr. Gardner enjoys eating in the dining room with others. He eats his salad and other foods with his hands and frequently spits large quantities of saliva on the floor.

Mr. Gardner continues to eat in the dining room. He is permitted to eat his salad and other food as he wishes. The floor and his wheelchair have been draped with towels to contain the saliva.

CASE DISCUSSION

Mr. Gardner should not be shunned from eating in the dining room with others as long as his behavior can be accommodated without causing harm to others. The staff should assess how bothersome Mr. Gardner's behavior is to others so that their rights are not violated. Perhaps Mr. Gardner can sit with a staff member rather than other residents. It is very important for staff to accept the resident's behavior as one facet of the person's illness. It does not facilitate human dignity if Mr. Gardner is shunned, scolded, and forced to eat alone in his room.

Two staff factors work to limit experience for people with late-stage dementia: (a) lack of acceptance and (b) constrained and mistaken beliefs about human dignity. Central to maintaining personhood is the essential task of accepting people as they are. How many interventions are well meaning but communicate a lack of acceptance of the person? For example, if a person is neatly fed rather than allowed to be more independent but messy, this communicates that the person's eating behaviors are not acceptable. If a resident seems to be comforted by rocking back and forth in a chair or repetitively verbalizing the same phrase, interventions that stop the behavior communicate nonacceptance. If the plush pet animal or doll that provides a sense of security but appears childlike is removed, who is being helped?

Family members, health care workers, and administrators express sincere concern for the human dignity of older adults with late-stage dementia but may have constrained views regarding what is meant by human dignity. Some aspects of what people consider human dignity may change and evolve when a person suffers from irreversible dementia. Human experience can be limited by narrowly defining human dignity or by ascribing one set of criteria for what constitutes human dignity to groups with a variety of differing needs. Activities and lifestyles of people with late-stage dementia need to reflect serious consideration of the needs of the person with dementia rather than some rigid views of proper behavior or proper values, likes, dislikes at a specific stage of development.

To maintain personhood, the late-stage dementia program should be designed to balance and meet these needs:

- Satisfying the primary self.
- Satisfying the inner self.
- Satisfying the social self.

SATISFYING THE PRIMARY SELF

Certain basic needs must be satisfied to avoid negative feelings and emotions, such as hunger, thirst, a full bladder, feeling too cold or too hot, pain, and feeling unsafe, uncomfortable, or insecure in the environment. People with late-stage dementia may display behaviors such as anxious restlessness, aggression, or loud verbalization when primary self-needs are not met. It is extremely important to have an individualized care plan that addresses primary self-needs. As the illness progresses, the person needs assistance with all primary self-needs. Several chapters in this book provide helpful suggestions for satisfying primary self-needs.

SATISFYING THE INNER SELF

Personhood is primarily discussed as arising from the social world. But personhood requires both inner self-processes and social self-processes. People with late-stage dementia exhibit more null and somnolent behavior than during earlier stages of the disease. Null behavior may be described as being in a state of physical inactivity, with eyes open but not focused on a particular event or person, and with no apparent purposeful activity. Somnolent behavior is a state in which the person is not deeply sleeping but has his or her eyes closed in apparent sleep for short periods of time and is easily aroused. A logical question regarding this increased withdrawn behavior arises: Is the increased null and somnolent behavior the result of neglect from caregivers or is the behavior a natural part of the disease process? If the change is the result of neglect from caregivers, initiation of meaningful human interaction and satisfaction of primary self-needs should help ameliorate it. If, on the other hand, the increase in disengaged behavior reflects a natural progression of the disease, it is less clear whether caregiver interventions will be effective or are needed. No unequivocal answer to these dichotomous positions is currently available, but anecdotal observation and some research support that both perspectives may have merit.

In a study in which hospice households were set up in three long-term care facilities, residents with late-stage dementia who were provided meaningful human interaction and a full schedule of appropriate activities decreased their null and somnolent behavior (Kovach et al., 1996). In another study, those people with more severe dementia spent more time, when stressed, in an inner retreat state. In this study, behaviors that were not directed toward the outside environment or the caregiver seemed to be attempts by the person to regain a sense of inner equilibrium after losing control over factors occurring in the social context of the bathing experience (Kovach & Meyer-Arnold, 1996). Inner retreat behaviors may include null behavior, somnolence, withdrawing, continued repetition of a meaningless word or phrase, moving legs and feet, picking at one's clothes, fumbling with a towel, and nondirected verbal agitation.

In summary, even though there appears to be a definite need for inner retreat, the person who engages in inner retreat behaviors for large periods of the day may be deprived of social self-needs. Research is clearly needed to more fully understand the relationship between inner self-needs, social self-needs, behaviors associated with dementia, and the maintenance of personhood.

SATISFYING THE SOCIAL SELF

Healthy older adults work to maintain continuity in their inner self and social behavior to maintain their strengths, cope, and adapt to changes in old age (Atchley, 1989). People may be thought of as having a basic psychological and social structure or gestalt that is maintained by continuing to do familiar things from their past, using familiar problem-solving strategies, and engaging in social behaviors and activities from the past. In dementia, these familiar inner psychological strategies and social behaviors become more fragmented. The person has difficulty maintaining a sense of continuity, wholeness, or gestalt. The person with dementia, when compared with the older adult with normal cognition, needs more social input to maintain personhood. The sense of personhood needs to be affirmed, evoked, and replenished. The person needs to be treated with positive regard. In other words, negative reinforcement, such as scolding or withdrawing from a person whose behavior is less desirable, is ineffective and counterproductive.

PROGRAM PLANNING

Program Philosophy

A philosophy is a broad statement that clearly and concisely describes the purpose or mission of the program. It is important for the late-stage dementia program to have a clear identity and focus. The philosophy of the entire facility in which the program will be opened should be discussed, as well as the ideas of palliative care, personhood, quality of life, human dignity, and comfort. A small representative group of staff who will be involved in the late-stage dementia program should come to some shared understanding of these terms and the purpose of the program. An example of a program philosophy is the following:

> *The late-stage dementia household is a home for residents with late-stage Alzheimer's disease and other dementing illnesses. The household provides a nurturing, safe, and stimulating environment with an emphasis on maintaining personhood, comfort, quality of life, and human dignity. Holistic needs of the resident are met through an interdisciplinary therapeutic approach to care. The household is committed to meeting the needs of the resident–family dyad.*

Applying the Program Philosophy

Goals for the households need to be developed from the philosophy and will direct the remainder of the program planning. Below are some useful goals for a late-stage dementia program.

To provide a home for people with late-stage dementia that is safe, therapeutic, dignified, and life-affirming and that provides a sense of security For example, several resident rooms clustered together on a wing of a traditional unit may be used to form a household of 8–12 residents. Stenciling a homelike design around the door of each room could serve to visually distinguish and group these rooms as a separate household. The bedrooms should be in close proximity to a small multipurpose room, which can serve as the hub for most dining and social activities. This multipurpose room should be for the exclusive use of residents in this program. The bedrooms and multipurpose room should be made as homelike as possible through decorations such as pictures, pillows, afghans, plants, and homelike furniture.

Some dementia units can quickly resemble kindergarten classrooms with a lot of art, crafts, and holiday decorations. It will probably create a more homelike and predictable atmosphere and be less visually overwhelming if artwork and activity therapy items are limited to one area. Holiday and seasonal decorations should not create too much visual clutter and should resemble the type and quantity of decorations one would use at home.

To provide therapies and programs that promote comfort, personhood, quality of life, and human dignity For example, compared with persons with mid-stage dementia, individuals with late-stage dementia generally need more one-on-one stimulation and individualized, rather than group, programming. Activities should be prescribed that achieve specific goals of individualized treatment in the following areas: primary self-needs, social self-needs, and inner self-needs. Examples of each type of activity for the person with late-stage dementia are listed in Table 3.1.

Table 3.1   Examples of activities to satisfy needs of the person with late-stage dementia

Type of need	Activities
Primary self-needs	Bathing; dressing; skin care; flannel sheets; plush pillow, animal, or doll; positioning; treatment of discomfort, hunger, or thirst; administration of pain medication
Inner self-needs	Listening to repetitive prayers; rocking in a chair; having a quiet time in bed or a geri-chair; time-limited afternoon nap; decreasing sensory stimulation by turning down lights, eliminating sounds, and tucking in with blankets; allowing repetitive verbalizations such as grunting or calling out (as long as the perseveration does not become intense); facilitating safe, repetitive body movements by decreasing restraints and using padding
Social self-needs	Friendly visiting; observing toddlers at play; pet therapy; sharing an afternoon beverage or snack; small group dining; back massage or hand lotioning; connecting with the world through sensory stimulation; aroma therapy; rummage box; music listening; pictures; kneading dough or clay with another person; painting; patchwork fabric movement with another person

Providing an afternoon glass of nonalcoholic wine has been a successful activity in one late-stage dementia program. The residents express pleasure, the staff provide casual socialization, and residents seem to relax from this shared activity that requires no performance or success. Another successful activity involved having a volunteer make a quilt with the group. Even though the volunteer essentially did the task of creating the quilt, she kept the residents involved moving and folding fabric, "winding" thread, and socializing with her. The residents enjoyed this nonthreatening social activity. In terms of social self-needs, presence is an intervention. Connecting with another person by being there in an engaged and caring manner is very powerful even though few words are needed. Too many words can actually overwhelm and stress the person.

To balance inner retreat activities with socially connected activities so that residents do not become overwhelmed or overburdened   For example, it is extremely important for each resident to have an activity plan developed for each half hour of waking time. Even though this seems like a formidable task and it is unrealistic to expect that the schedule will be rigidly followed, it is a necessary tool for evaluating several components essential to maintaining personhood: (a) the amount of each day that is truly therapeutic, (b) whether the amount of each day that addresses inner self-needs is excessive or deficient, (c) whether the amount of each day that involves social self-needs and one-on-one meaningful human interaction with another person is sufficient, and (d) whether the balance between active times and downtime is correct for that person so that the stress threshold is not exceeded and personhood is nurtured and maintained. An example of a daily activity schedule is provided in Figure 3.1.

Figure 3.1 Daily activity schedule

Time of day	Activity	Responsible discipline
7:00–7:30	Quiet in bedroom	
7:30–8:00	Prayer in cordial room	Pastoral care
8:00–8:30	Breakfast in cordial room	Nursing
8:30–9:00		
9:00–9:30	Toilet	Nursing
9:30–10:00	Quiet in bedroom	
10:00–10:30	One-on-one activity	Recreation and nursing
10:30–11:00	Toilet	Nursing
11:00–11:30	Activity in cordial room	Recreational therapy
11:30–12:00	Exercise	Nursing
12:00–12:30	Lunch	Nursing
12:30–1:00		
1:00–1:30	Toilet	Nursing
1:30–2:00	Music therapy	Recreational therapy
2:00–2:30	Nap	
2:30–3:00		
3:00–3:30	Toilet/range of motion	Nursing
3:30–4:00	Nonalcoholic wine, social activity in cordial room	Recreational therapy
4:00–4:30	Toilet/range of motion	Nursing
4:30–5:00	Music and singing	Volunteers
5:00–5:30	Quiet time	
5:30–6:00	Supper	Nursing
6:00–6:30	Rummaging activities	Recreational therapy
6:30–7:00	Toilet, quiet in bedroom	Nursing
7:00–7:30	Lotion massage	Nursing
7:30–8:00	Bed	

To allow residents to set their own pace and style of participation, whether that is initiating, observing, or actively participating For example, one resident may be able to observe an exercise class but refuse to participate even when someone assists her by moving her arms as the other residents move. Another resident may be able to clap her hands but refuse to mimic the leaders' behavior. The resident can be offered passive range of motion exercises in her room at a later time but should not be excluded from participation. A resident may shun offers of a massage and then later in the day grab the arm of a caregiver and rub it rhythmically. A person may participate in music therapy by grunting and rocking back and forth in a chair. Accept the resident's pace and style of participation unless it compromises health or safety.

To prevent physical iatrogenic problems For example, consider providing nursing staff with more instruction in physical assessment skills and common physical problems of older adults. Because people with late-stage dementia are often unable to communicate needs, more thorough physical assessments should be done. Chapter 6 provides specific guidelines for a nursing assessment, and Chapter 10 presents a physical assessment protocol that can be used when a behavior change is manifested. The nurse should document a thorough physical assessment each week and conduct daily assessments as needed. Also, consistent caregivers are better able to identify when there is a subtle change in the resident that may indicate a physical problem. Residents will need care plans to prevent common physical problems such as skin breakdown, dehydration, weight loss or malnutrition, aspiration, constipation or impaction, and infection. One facility had four cases of urosepsis in 6 months. Staff were then instructed to dipstick urine with a leukocyte esterase dipstick to identify potential urinary tract infection when behavior change presented as a symptom. The urosepsis rate dropped to zero for the subsequent 6-month time period (Wilson, Kovach, & Stearns, 1996).

To maintain, nurture, and value a sense of family ties and positive family involvement   Staff often identify a lack of overt support or reward for social interaction with families. Family interventions should be included on certified nursing assistant (CNA) assignment cards as well as on interdisciplinary care plans. Staff do need to be reminded that watching a loved one change and deteriorate in the late stages of dementia can be exceedingly painful for relatives and friends. Often small interventions such as getting a family member a cup of coffee, sincerely talking to them about how they are, or validating that the situation is difficult are very comforting.

Staff and family can work together to construct biographical sketches and picture collages of the resident's life. Constructing these is a poignant and therapeutic activity for many family members and, after the resident's death, they are a meaningful and treasured gift to the family.

Because people with late-stage dementia need more one-on-one activity, there is optimum opportunity for family volunteers. Many family members are experiencing tremendous grief and loss over the changes they are witnessing in the relative and their relationship with the relative. Staff need to be very aware of this pain and not impose expectations for involvement. Family members enjoy having a bulletin board devoted to their needs. This bulletin board can contain invitations to support group meetings, articles, recipes, prayers, poems, and so forth. Support meetings should be held, and family members should identify the form and agenda of the meetings. Sometimes families desire education and support, and sometimes they would just like to have a social time with staff and other visitors to the unit who are sharing similar life experiences.

To provide the resources and atmosphere needed for staff to be able to actualize the philosophy and goals of the program and to give and receive support from one another   Staff education is an integral part of this program and should begin the process of reflecting on the importance of the work that is done and the meaningfulness of creating a caring community in the household. Experience has demonstrated that concerns about staff being burned out from the heavy demands of late-stage dementia care are unfounded. Staff who were initially assigned 4 residents with late-stage dementia and 4 residents from the general unit with another diagnosis because of concerns about burnout quickly began asking for their entire assignment to come from the late-stage program. CNAs stated that they enjoyed spending a large part of the day in the activity room doing therapies and were able to have more empathy for the residents when their role was expanded to include leading activities such as exercise, clay art, and sensory stimulation (Wilson et al., 1996).

It is very important to keep staffing levels adequate. It is impossible for a program such as this to be successful without consistent adequate staffing. Optimally, CNAs should be allowed to choose their own assignment and should keep this assignment for at least 4 months. If a resident is identified by the CNAs as being particularly stressful to care for, the staff should mutually agree on a system of rotating this assignment.

Admission Criteria

Those working on special care units for mid-stage dementia frequently state that the issue of admission and discharge criteria for the unit is fraught with emotion, confusion, and contradiction. Some people are doing excellent work in attempting to stage people with dementing illnesses more carefully (Reisberg, 1983; Volicer, Hurley, Fabiszewski, Montgomery, & Volicer, 1993; Volicer, Hurley, Lathi, & Kowall, 1994). Some of the procedures for clinical evaluation are lengthy and require a skilled and consistent assessor. The clinical measurements described in the criteria listed below do not require as lengthy or sophisticated an assessment and may be implemented after one training session.

1   Diagnosis of irreversible dementia.
2   MMSE score of 1–7 (Folstein, Folstein, & McHugh, 1975).
3   Functional Behavior Profile (FBP) score below 40 (Baum, Edwards, & Morrow-Howell, 1993; see Table 3.2).
4   Usually unable to engage in group programming designed for residents with dementia.
5   Advanced directive that no cardiopulmonary resuscitation (CPR) be initiated.

Most of the residents in the hospice programs score in the 0–3 range on the MMSE. The FBP was designed specifically for people with dementia and assesses functional abilities in three areas: task performance, social interaction, and problem solving. The FBP, because of its emphasis on identifying remaining abilities, is a useful tool for goal-setting and choosing therapeutic regimes.

The admission criteria related to continuing to benefit from group programming is critical. If a resident has an MMSE score of 7 and an FBP score of 35 but continues to function well and live in harmony with the residents on a mid-stage dementia unit, he or she should remain on that unit. If the resident no longer benefits from the mid-stage dementia programming or his or her physical care needs or behavior abrogate the therapeutic milieu on the unit, then he or she should be moved. Staff can become overzealous in adhering to numerical scores on the MMSE and FBP. These scores can fluctuate for a host of reasons. Clinical judgment by the staff who know the resident may currently be the best predictor of optimum placement. The late-stage dementia program may serve residents with late mid-stage dementia as well as end-stage disease. Experience has shown that people who were classified as end-

Table 3.2   The Functional Behavior Profile: Institutional version

This assessment is designed to record the capacity of an impaired person to engage in tasks, social interactions, and problem solving. The assessment is administered by a staff member who is familiar with the person. All of the questions relate to how the person with impaired cognitive function performs in their daily activities. As a reference the staff should respond based upon the impaired person's behavior during the past week.

The resident _____   Date _____   Score _____

1. Is able to concentrate on a task for:

$|^4$ _____ $|^3$ _____ $|^2$ _____ $|^1$ _____ $|^0$ T__
over 25 min.   5–15 min.   3–5 min.   1–3 min.   <1 min.

2. Finishes the tasks that have been staked.

$|^4$ _____ $|^3$ _____ $|^2$ _____ $|^1$ _____ $|^0$ T__
Always   Usually   Sometimes   Rarely   Never
(100%)   (80%)   (50%)   (20%)   (<10%)

3. Performs work that is neat.

$|^4$ _____ $|^3$ _____ $|^2$ _____ $|^1$ _____ $|^0$ T__
Always   Usually   Sometimes   Rarely   Never
(100%)   (80%)   (50%)   (20%)   (<10%)

4. Can use tools or instruments in performing tasks, (hobby, razor).

$|^4$ _____ $|^3$ _____ $|^2$ _____ $|^1$ _____ $|^0$ T__
Always   Usually   Sometimes   Rarely   Never
(100%)   (80%)   (50%)   (20%)   (<10%)

5. Can manipulate small items (hand work, buttoning, makeup).

$|^4$ _____ $|^3$ _____ $|^2$ _____ $|^1$ _____ $|^0$ T__
Always   Usually   Sometimes   Rarely   Never
(100%)   (80%)   (50%)   (20%)   (<10%)

6. Activities are appropriate to the time of day
   (sleeps at night, alert during the day).

$|^4$ _____ $|^3$ _____ $|^2$ _____ $|^1$ _____ $|^0$ T__
Always   Usually   Sometimes   Rarely   Never
(100%)   (80%)   (50%)   (20%)   (<10%)

7. Performs work that is accomplished within a
   resonable time frame.

$|^4$ _____ $|^3$ _____ $|^2$ _____ $|^1$ _____ $|^0$ T__
Always   Usually   Sometimes   Rarely   Never
(100%)   (80%)   (50%)   (20%)   (<10%)

8. Makes simple decisions independently like what to wear, what to eat,
   what to do around the house.

$|^4$ _____ $|^3$ _____ $|^2$ _____ $|^1$ _____ $|^0$ T__
Always   Usually   Sometimes   Rarely   Never
(100%)   (80%)   (50%)   (20%)   (<10%)

9. Can solve a problem when given repeated assistance.

$|^4$ _____ $|^3$ _____ $|^2$ _____ $|^1$ _____ $|^0$ T__   P__
Always   Usually   Sometimes   Rarely   Never
(100%)   (80%)   (50%)   (20%)   (<10%)

Table 3.2 The Functional Behavior Profile: Institutional version (*continued*)

10. Takes responsibility for basic tasks (maintains their room, bathes, grooms).

|4 _____ |3 _____ |2 _____ |1 _____ |0   T__   P__

Always   Usually   Sometimes   Rarely   Never
(100%)   (80%)   (50%)   (20%)   (<10%)

11. Can respond to a one-step command. (directions to do only one thing, like "sit here" or "take my hand.")

|4 _____ |3 _____ |2 _____ |1 _____ |0   T__   S__

Always   Usually   Sometimes   Rarely   Never
(100%)   (80%)   (50%)   (20%)   (<10%)

12. Shows enjoyment in activities.

|4 _____ |3 _____ |2 _____ |1 _____ |0   T__   S__

Always   Usually   Sometimes   Rarely   Never
(100%)   (80%)   (50%)   (20%)   (<10%)

13. Participates in activities.

|4 _____ |3 _____ |2 _____ |1 _____ |0   T__   S__

Always   Usually   Sometimes   Rarely   Never
(100%)   (80%)   (50%)   (20%)   (<10%)

14. Performs activities without frustration.

|4 _____ |3 _____ |2 _____ |1 _____ |0   T__   S__

Always   Usually   Sometimes   Rarely   Never
(100%)   (80%)   (50%)   (20%)   (<10%)

15. Continues an activity when frustrated.

|4 _____ |3 _____ |2 _____ |1 _____ |0   T__   S__

Always   Usually   Sometimes   Rarely   Never
(100%)   (80%)   (50%)   (20%)   (<10%)

16. Can identify familiar persons.

|4 _____ |3 _____ |2 _____ |1 _____ |0   T__   S__

Always   Usually   Sometimes   Rarely   Never
(100%)   (80%)   (50%)   (20%)   (<10%)

17. Initiates conversation with family or staff.

|4 _____ |3 _____ |2 _____ |1 _____ |0   T__   S__

Always   Usually   Sometimes   Rarely   Never
(100%)   (80%)   (50%)   (20%)   (<10%)

18. Socializes when others initiate the interactions.

|4 _____ |3 _____ |2 _____ |1 _____ |0   T__   S__

Always   Usually   Sometimes   Rarely   Never
(100%)   (80%)   (50%)   (20%)   (<10%)

19. Expresses him or herself appropriate to the situation.

|4 _____ |3 _____ |2 _____ |1 _____ |0   S__

Always   Usually   Sometimes   Rarely   Never
(100%)   (80%)   (50%)   (20%)   (<10%)

20. Isable to make a decision when presented with chokes (menu activity).

|4 _____ |3 _____ |2 _____ |1 _____ |0   S__

Always   Usually   Sometimes   Rarely   Never
(100%)   (80%)   (50%)   (20%)   (<10%)

(*Table continued on next page*)

Table 3.2   The Functional Behavior Profile: Institutional version
(*continued*)

21. Can learn a simple activity without difficulty
    (how to call the nurse, operate T.V.).

|⁴ _____ |³ _____ |² _____ |¹ _____ |⁰   S__   P__

Always   Usually   Sometimes   Rarely   Never
(100%)   (80%)   (50%)   (20%)   (<10%)

22. Can respond to a two-step command. (Directions
    to do two things in sequence like "open the door,
    and get the paper.")

|⁴ _____ |³ _____ |² _____ |¹ _____ |⁰   P__

Always   Usually   Sometimes   Rarely   Never
(100%)   (80%)   (50%)   (20%)   (<10%)

23. Can respond to a three-step command. (Directions
    to do three things in sequence like "open the door,
    and get the paper and if Mary is in the yard tell her
    to come in for dinner.")

|⁴ _____ |³ _____ |² _____ |¹ _____ |⁰   P__

Always   Usually   Sometimes   Rarely   Never
(100%)   (80%)   (50%)   (20%)   (<10%)

24. Can learn a complex activity without difficulty
    (a new activity, directions).

|⁴ _____ |³ _____ |² _____ |¹ _____ |⁰   P__

Always   Usually   Sometimes   Rarely   Never
(100%)   (80%)   (50%)   (20%)   (<10%)

25. Knows the day of the week and/or date.

|⁴ _____ |³ _____ |² _____ |¹ _____ |⁰   P__

Always   Usually   Sometimes   Rarely   Never
(100%)   (80%)   (50%)   (20%)   (<10%)

26. Independently makes complex decisions (activity choices).

|⁴ _____ |³ _____ |² _____ |¹ _____ |⁰   P__

Always   Usually   Sometimes   Rarely   Never
(100%)   (80%)   (50%)   (20%)   (<10%)

27. Can solve a problem without assistance.

|⁴ _____ |³ _____ |² _____ |¹ _____ |⁰   P__

Always   Usually   Sometimes   Rarely   Never
(100%)   (80%)   (50%)   (20%)   (<10%)

Note. From Baum, C., Edwards, D. F., Morrow-Howell, N. (1993). Identification and measurement of productive behaviors in senile dementia of the Alzheimer type. *The Gerontologist, 33*(3), 403–408. Reprinted by permission.

stage, when placed in the appropriate therapeutic milieu and retested, can actually improve their scores and be considered more accurately to be in the late midstage of the disease.

Accepting people who have an advanced directive of no CPR should help ensure that the family believes the best goal for the resident at this point is palliative care. Family members need to be fully informed of care options available and make informed decisions about treatments. There are many thorny issues related to advanced directives and care of people with late-stage dementia. These include feeding and hydration options, whether hospitalization should be initi-ated under certain circumstances, and optimum treatments for conditions such as acute infection. Difficulty can arise when what one person interprets to mean pal-liative care is different from another person's interpretation. These issues point out the need for continuous dialogue between health care workers and family members. Palliative care does not mean little or no care, and no person with dementia should be left in pain when treatment options are available.

Discharge criteria should not be needed because the goal of these households is to care for the person until death. Short-term transfers may be needed in rare circumstances for acute care (e.g., to alleviate pain from an intestinal obstruction or for more comprehensive geropsychiatric evaluation).

STAFF EDUCATION

Educating staff is an essential component of delivering quality care to people with late-stage dementia. Often, staff have been working on long-term care units in which the focus includes custodial care, comfort care, cure, and rehabilitation. Within this mixture of foci, it is often unclear to staff what the identity and rightful focus of care should be or could be for the person with late-stage dementia. There is a lack of understanding of the differences between early, mid-stage, and late-stage dementia care. Many staff are unaware that people in the late stages of dementia can experience comfort and pleasure. Staff may be uncertain of their role in enhancing quality of life and in providing care related to the death experience.

Chapter 14 presents comprehensive strategies for facilitating change in long-term care settings. Education is one important component of any change process. There should be three parts to the education program: orientation, continuing education, and supportive team building. There is not one right way to implement these types of educational programs. The guidelines that follow are meant to serve as suggestions for curriculum and format but should be adapted as needed. Staff involved in housekeeping, maintenance, and dietary programs should receive an abbreviated education program.

Goals

The goals of the education program for enhanced care of people with late stages of dementia are as follows:

- to make a paradigm shift from task-oriented, institutional, and illness-oriented care to a more holistic, flexible, and life-affirming model of care;
- to apply current knowledge of therapies that maintain personhood and provide comfort, quality of life, and dignity for persons with late-stage dementia;
- to prevent physical iatrogenic problems;
- to care for and support oneself, other staff, residents, and family on the personal and shared journey with the human condition of living and dying.

The most important goal of the educational program is to assist staff in mak-ing a paradigm shift from task-oriented, institutional, and illness-oriented care to a more holistic, flexible, and life-affirming model of care. Staff need to be taught interventions that will assist the low-functioning resident to engage in personally meaningful life activities. There is also a need for administrators and staff to believe that supporting and nurturing the dying and the grieving are meaningful and enriching experiences.

Orientation for New Staff

Not everyone will enjoy working in a late-stage dementia program, and staff who have a need for a task-oriented, routinized day or who are not comfortable making personal, nurturing connections with persons who are severely cognitively impaired should not participate in the program. Experience with several programs has demonstrated that the orientation program can be a powerful and transforming experience. Staff who are at first hesitant about leaving the comfort of a task-oriented focus may become leaders for change following the education program.

A suggested curriculum guide is provided in Table 3.3. Information on these topics is found throughout this book. Training sessions should begin by having staff divide into groups and talk with one another about the daily experiences of residents they know with late-stage dementia. The groups should be asked to provide a written description that expresses (a) the daily events, (b) the possible feelings of the resident, and (c) personal reflections on the meaningfulness of having people suffer from a dementing illness. Placing a strong emphasis on the idea that a late-stage dementia program involves doing something that is truly meaningful with one's life helps staff to see that participation in the program contributes to personal goal attainment as well as professional goal attainment.

Table 3.3 Orientation training for new staff: Suggested curriculum guide

I. Introduction to Concepts of Palliation and Maintaining Personhood
    A. Maintaining personhood
       1. Primary self-needs
       2. Inner self-needs
       3. Social self-needs
    B. Overview and background of hospice movement for end-stage cancer care
       1. Grass roots response to need
       2. Brief history of hospice
    C. Comfort: palliative does not mean decreased care
       1. Comfort needs of people with later stage dementia
       2. Operationalizing palliation in day-to-day situations
    D. Perspectives on quality of life and human dignity
       1. Importance of meaningful human interaction
       2. Encourage range of emotions and experiences to support personhood
       3. Acceptance of person
II. Progression of Dementia
    A. Demographics
       1. Alzheimer's disease, vascular dementia, and others
       2. Differences in demographics at each stage, including living arrangements

Table 3.3   Orientation training for new staff: Suggested curriculum guide   (*continued*)

  B. Pathophysiology
    1. Changes in the brain
    2. Theories of etiology
  C. Stages
    1. Early: anomia, judgment impaired, personality change, difficulty with numbers, forgetfulness
    2. Mid-stage, moderate functional level: anomia, apraxia, agnosia, constructional difficulty, loss of impulse control, confabulation, behavior challenges, progressively lowered stress threshold
    3. Mid-stage, low functional level: mid-stage symptoms more severe; self-care abilities more impaired; nutritional, mobility, and other physical needs increase
    4. Advanced: behavior problems may be less severe, physical needs increase, risk of physical iatrogenic problems, depressed immune function, need for more stimulation
III.   Understanding and Managing Behavioral Expressions
  A. Preventing behavior problems
    1. Environmental considerations
    2. Primary self-needs
    3. Inner self-needs
    4. Social self-needs
  B. Specific behaviors
    1. Alterations in activity: perseverance, wandering and need for movement, rummaging and active hands, null and somnolent behavior, sundown syndrome
    2. Alterations in perception: delusions and hallucinations
    3. Aggressive behavior
IV.   Therapeutic Activity Programming
  A. Therapeutic care vs. custodial care
  B. Characteristics of low and lowest functioning level
  C. Organizing, initiating, and guiding people through individual and group activities
  D. Programming for individual needs and strengths
  E. The role of all health care providers in therapeutic activity programs
V.   Physical Care Interventions
  A. Dysphagia and mealtime interventions
  B. Making bath time pleasant
  C. Basics of skin and incontinence care
  D. Mobility, exercise, and fall prevention
VI.   Physical Assessment
  A. Recognizing changes in condition
    1. Head to toe screening
    2. Recognizing signs and symptoms of infection
    3. Recognizing discomfort
VII.   The Family–Resident Dyad
  A. Family education and support
  B. Family involvement
VIII. Grief and Caring for One Another
  A. The experience of bereavement
  B. Helping family members, self, and peers
  C. Preventing burnout: stress and coping strategies

Orientation classes should involve plenty of time for group discussion. Time should be available for staff to discuss their personal experiences and their views about what they feel are realistic and positive interventions. Sandra Stearns, Director of Nursing at St. Camillus Health Center in Milwaukee, Wisconsin, shared these thoughts regarding their education program for people who will work on the Late-Stage Care Unit (LSCU):

> *Adequate learning of the topics should be assessed by pretesting and posttesting the participants. Based on established standards, successful participants in our program then receive institutional certification. In each facility, this certification should result in some form of recognition such as a pin, diploma, change in job title, or a financial reward. Certification in our facility is maintained through quarterly educational programs which focus on specific aspects of dementia care. Also, our initial certification classes are repeated quarterly to accommodate new employees.*

At the end of the training session, participants are given a pin to wear that is in the shape of a dove. The pin serves as an important symbol of specialized skill and training. A certificate of completion or other external symbol could also be used.

Orientation of new staff should involve having the new employee work with an employee who has experience with the program and with dementia care. A checklist of experiences (such as those in Table 3.4 for a nursing assistant) will help ensure consistent education. Staff experts should demonstrate proper care in situations such as calming an aggressive resident or giving a bath that is comforting. New employees should be taught specific techniques for providing therapeutic activities, such as music, rummaging, massage, and meaningful human interaction. Daily team meetings that involve report from CNAs will help to ensure consistent care and attention to the details of physical, psychosocial, and spiritual care. New employees should be gently guided through care that is provided when death is imminent, as well as care provided to the family, and to the body, after death. Team meetings should involve staff support and dialogue about the person and the feelings of loss.

Continuing Education

Mandatory monthly continuing education programs should be offered. Each topic in the orientation program can be covered in more depth, as well as a host of new topics. Education can occur in many formats: formal lectures, videotape, programmed self-study, loosely structured discussions around a topic, guest speakers, case presentations, journal clubs, or bulletin board inservices. Regardless of format, it is essential that continuing education become a routine, normal part of staff behavior. Administration must support continuing education efforts, and tangible positive reinforcement for involvement in continuing education such as merit raises or promotions are important. If continuing education is not implemented, it is easy for the goals of the program to become lost or diluted and for units to slip back into previous task-oriented routines.

Table 3.4   Orientation experience checklist for certified nursing assistants (CNAs)

_____	Decreased stimuli bath
_____	Comfort dressing techniques
_____	Comfort transfer techniques
_____	Comfort bedding
_____	Comfort positioning
_____	Feeding techniques
_____	Dining environment interventions
_____	Meaningful human interaction techniques
_____	Massage
_____	Sensory stimulating activities (location of equipment, how to's, resident preferences book)
_____	Sensory calming activities (location of equipment, how to's, resident preferences book)
_____	Experience with calm perseverance
_____	Experience with tense perseverance
_____	Experience with aggression
_____	Experience with null behavior
_____	Experience with excessive somnolence
_____	Experience with group process difficulties
_____	Experience with delusions and hallucinations
_____	Experience with family support
_____	Experience with death and body preparation
_____	Experience with spiritual care
_____	Wander guard system
_____	Daily activity schedules
_____	Daily assessment
_____	Charting
_____	Team meeting: contents and flow of CNA report

Because many staff have limited experience with didactic instruction, loosely structured educational programs that are held on the unit are often quite effective. Small group discussions on the unit offer an opportunity for informal presentation of content, venting of concerns, and problem solving.

Journal clubs are also effective for staff who are comfortable reviewing the literature. The purposes of the journal club are threefold: (a) to maintain current knowledge of dementia and other relevant topics, (b) to engage in group discussion and problem solving, and (c) to develop group cohesiveness. A rotating group leader selects an article or section of a book for group members to read. A unit manager or director of education can maintain a folder of articles for this purpose if a library is not available. The group leader makes the articles available on the unit 1 week before the journal club meeting. Journal club meetings usually last 30 min or less. During this time, the leader can present a brief overview of the article or highlight a few key points and lead a discussion.

Supportive Team Building

Too often, when change or innovation is started, the human element involved is forgotten. Inevitably, the program suffers. If staff, who are expected to care for and nurture others all day long in their job, don't themselves have a sense of being cared for, nurtured, and supported in their role, they will burn out. Administrators need to know that time, energy, and money used in support of positive group dynamics are resources well spent. Again, there is not one formula for how best to attend to this need. Meetings that focus on work-related issues are needed as well as some fun and stress-relieving group activities. New employees should have a monthly individual meeting with their supervisor for 4–6 months. Monthly staff meetings should be sure to focus first and foremost on the positive work being done and then on constructive problem solving. Daily report meetings reinforce the goals for each resident but are also excellent times to educate and provide honest, appropriate feedback. Some successful fun and stress-relieving activities are a pizza party, an exercise class held after work at the facility, a bowling or softball league, a drawing for weekly staff appreciation gifts, talent shows, and fashion shows.

In summary, staff education that involves orientation, continuing education, and team building is essential for change to be successful. Caring for people with late-stage dementia is difficult work with unique components. If staff are not educated and supported, staff burnout and movement away from program goals will likely occur. A comprehensive education program will help staff do their job, value their job, and value the facility in which they are employed.

CONCLUSION

Every dementia program will develop its own unique personality. These unique facets of the program help staff to feel a sense of commitment and ownership of the program and often reflect the social mores of a particular cultural, social, or religious group being served by the program. The one essential component of any program is staff who are committed to the project. If several staff members from different disciplines work with enthusiasm to plan the program—and have administrative support—the program will likely succeed. Late-stage dementia care is based on a belief that people in the late stages of a dementing illness can be helped and deserve caring and competent treatment until the time of natural death.

BIBLIOGRAPHY

Atchley, R. C. (1989). A continuity theory of normal aging. *The Gerontologist, 29*(2), 183–190.
Baum, C., Edwards, D. F., & Morrow-Howell, N. (1993). Identification and measurement of productive behaviors in senile dementia of the Alzheimer type. *The Gerontologist, 33*(3), 403–408.
Bleathman, C., & Morton, I. (1988). Validation therapy with the demented elderly. *Journal of Advanced Nursing, 13*, 511–514.

Folstein, M. F., Folstein, S. E., & McHugh, P. R. (1975). Mini Mental State: A practical method for grading the cognitive state of patients for the clinician. *Journal of Psychiatric Research, 12,* 189–198.

Kitwood, T., & Bredin, K. (1992). Towards a theory of dementia care: Personhood and well-being. *Aging and Society, 12,* 269–287.

Kovach, C. R., & Meyer-Arnold, E. A. (1996). Coping with conflicting agendas: The bathing experience of cognitively impaired older adults. *Scholarly Inquiry for Nursing Practice, 10*(1), 23–26.

Kovach, C. R., Wilson, S. A., & Noonan, P. E. (1996). Effects of hospice interventions on behaviors, discomfort, and physical complications of end-stage dementia nursing home residents. *The American Journal of Alzheimer's Disease, 11*(4), 7–15.

Reisberg, B. (1983). Clinical presentation, diagnosis, and symptomatology of age-associated cognitive decline and Alzheimer's disease. In B. Reisberg (Ed.), Alzheimer's disease. New York: Free Press.

Sabat, S. R., & Harre, R. (1992). The construction and deconstruction of self in Alzheimer's disease. *Aging and Society, 12,* 443–461.

Volicer, B. J., Hurley, A., Fabiszewski, K. J., Montgomery, P., & Volicer, L. (1993). Predicting short-term survival for patients with advanced Alzheimer's disease. *Journal of the American Geriatrics Society, 41,* 535–540.

Volicer, L., Hurley, A. C., Lathi, D. C., & Kowall, N. W. (1994). Measurement of severity in advanced Alzheimer's disease. *Journal of Gerontology, 49*(5), M223–M226.

Wilson, S. A., Kovach, C. R., & Stearns, S. A. (1996). Hospice concepts in the care for end-stage dementia. *Geriatric Nursing, 17*(1), 6–10.

Chapter 4

Administration of a Late-Stage Dementia Program in the Nursing Home Setting

Patricia E. Noonan and Sandra A. Stearns

The purpose of this chapter is to provide practical and useful guidance in setting up and managing a late-stage dementia program. The major concepts of administrative structures and committees, operating policies, staffing, budgeting, sources of funding, and volunteers and students are addressed. This guideline is designed for general use and is not directed toward any specific state or other regulatory agency's requirements.

In recent years there has been a proliferation of special care units (SCUs; McConnell, 1994). Recognized SCUs usually have a mission statement, specific admission criteria, staff training, care planning, and programming to meet the needs of the residents (Alzheimer's Association Patient and Family Services, 1992). These units are developed to serve residents with severe cognitive and behavioral impairments (Holmes, Teresi, & Monoco, 1992). As the disease progresses and residents' needs change, residents are either discharged back into the general long-term care facility (LTCF) or retained on the SCU until death. Both alternatives have their pros and cons.

Those preferring retention on the unit cite the emotional ties residents and families of an SCU may develop to each other and the staff. These strong attachments favor having a resident remain on the SCU, even when the resident is no longer benefitting from the programming. Transferring the resident off the SCU into the LTCF may be seen by the family as a failure of staff to meet the residents' needs or as abandonment by SCU personnel. Staff too may view a transfer negatively, especially if there is no special programming for late-stage dementia in the LTCF.

Having residents remain on the SCU ultimately results in a wide range of programming needs. Because of this, the SCU will continually be reevaluating and redefining its mission. Berg et al. (1991) advocated having two levels of SCUs, one for mid-stage dementia and one for late-stage dementia. The mid-stage SCU should have discharge criteria in addition to admission criteria to maintain its mission and effectiveness.

CASE EXAMPLE

A beautiful new state-of-the-art health center was built. Residents' rooms lined two long intersecting corridors, and at the center was the nurses' station, lounge areas, and dining areas. In the facility, both frail nondemented elderly and those with a dementing illness resided.

Soon after residents moved into the facility, chaos ensued. Residents with dementia frequently wandered the four wings of the center. Because the wings looked exactly alike, residents would become agitated as they searched for the familiar. The frail but cognitively intact residents resented intrusions by the wanderers, who often rummaged through their belongings. The central nurses' station became a focal point of noise and activity and seemed to spark physical and verbal outbursts by residents with dementia.

A new director of nursing was hired who had started an Alzheimer's and related dementia SCU in a previous LTCF. Because of the success of that unit, and the chaos in the present facility, an expert in dementia care was retained to facilitate the development of a state-of-the-art SCU, with its own philosophy, activities, and admission and discharge criteria.

Once implemented, the SCU was successful. Residents on the unit seemed less confused, had fewer behavior problems, and began building a sense of community with each other, the staff, and with families (Kovach & Stearns, 1994). The residents and staff remaining on the regular unit immediately noticed that the environment had become more calm and tranquil.

Within months, however, another challenge surfaced. Residents with progressing dementing disease began to decline and no longer met the criteria for residency on the SCU. Most frequently, they came off of the unit because they no longer were capable of engaging in group activities and therefore could not benefit from group programming. They were transferred back to the regular unit, which had been too stimulating for them in earlier stages of the illness.

A commonly held view is that care of residents with late-stage dementia is often custodial, consisting of feeding, diapering, restraining, and medicating. However, it soon became clear that they had other unique needs requiring special interventions, programming, and care.

At that time, the facility's administration was asked to participate in a study utilizing a hospice approach to residents with late-stage dementia. The administrator and the director of nursing strongly supported the study and agreed to continue to use the hospice approach when the research protocol was completed if the study demonstrated that the new program was beneficial to residents with late-stage dementia.

A clinical nurse specialist at the facility was selected as the case manager for the study. Monthly meetings were held with the researchers to prepare for the study, and weekly interdisciplinary meetings were held with key management people to assure smooth implementation. Staff were also involved from the onset and later received a full education day at a local university focusing on dementia care, the hospice approach, activity programming, spiritual care, and care of the family.

When the program was implemented, the staff were generally excited about and supportive of the study. The residents selected for inclusion in the hospice program were scattered on three general care nursing units. Constant monitoring, modeling, and management of the study was required to prevent staff from slipping into old habits of caregiving. Soon the staff became excited and convinced the program was worthwhile as they saw some of the residents in the study group become more interactive, described by some staff as "waking up." They also expressed satisfaction with their jobs because they felt that they had helped make a difference.

After the study was completed, care continued to be based on the hospice concepts that had been implemented. Even though several of the residents died, there was still a feeling of satisfaction in knowing that their quality of life had been improved and that they had been treated as unique individuals deserving of respect and dignity.

ADMINISTRATIVE SUPPORT

Before beginning a late-stage dementia care unit (LSCU), it is imperative to evaluate several issues. Most facilities were not built with a dementia unit in mind, much less two. A brand new dementia unit with beds waiting to be filled is a luxury. Most facilities contemplating an LSCU will need to make some structural changes, which will affect various departments as well as the residents. Renovations may need to be made with residents living in the area. In addition, when the area is ready, appropriate residents will need to be moved onto the unit and inappropriate residents moved off. The administrator and the director of nursing must fully buy into this project. They must be able to have the vision and articulate the advantage of an LSCU for all residents of the facility, not just those with dementia. It is recommended that letters be sent to the residents and family members. The administrator and the director of nursing may also want to host family meetings to explain the project and its advantages, as well as answer questions. It is extremely important that administrators be visible and supportive of the staff and residents throughout the renovations and transition.

MEDICAL SUPPORT

It is also imperative that concepts of late-stage palliative care be embraced by the medical director of the facility. The emphasis is on more holistic care that includes interventions addressing palliative system control; psychosocial needs of the patient and family; amelioration of the negative effects of the disease process that impair the patient's quality of life, dignity, and safety; respect for personhood; emphasis of intact patient abilities; and manipulation of the environment (Kovach, Wilson, & Noonan, 1996). Volicer, Rheaume, Brown, Fabiszewski, and Brady (1986) defined a hospice approach as one providing maximal comfort without striving for maximal survival time of the patient. The medical director needs to understand, support, and implement the aims of the late-stage dementia program before a patient's condition deteriorates and decisions regarding tube feeding, hospitalizations, and antibiotic therapy are discussed with the family.

STEERING COMMITTEE

In the case study, a steering committee was developed as soon as the administrator and director of nursing agreed to study hospice care approaches for residents with late-stage dementia. It is recommended that such a steering committee be developed in any facility that has an SCU for residents with early to mid-stage dementia or that does not segregate residents with dementia from frail residents without dementing illness. The steering committee should discuss the challenges inherent in providing care for the residents with late-stage dementia under the current system used at the facility. For example, what problems are identified when people with late-stage dementia are on an SCU for people with mid-stage dementia? What are the problems when people with late-stage dementia are on a general unit where the goals are a mix of curative, rehabilitative, and palliative? Are there advantages to the current system? Is a late-stage dementia program feasible from the perspective of the admissions coordinator? What problems would an LSCU solve and what problems might it create? How might care improve in the facility under this system? What impact might the LSCU have on staff and staffing? Is the time right for initiating this type of change? Suggested members of the steering committee include the administrator, director of nursing, activities director, music therapist, dietary director, housekeeping director, pastoral care minister, nurse managers, certified nursing assistants, family members, and social workers.

LEADERSHIP OF THE UNIT

An extremely important consideration is leadership of the unit. To plan and implement care that is flexible and unique to the resident and supportive of the family, an interdisciplinary approach is imperative. Within an environment of administrative and medical support, the rest of the team is empowered to care for those in the final stages of dementia. The support team consists of housekeeping, dietary care, maintenance, pastoral care, therapies, central service, laundry, and volunteers. This large team creates a supportive environment for the direct caregivers. Three major disciplines compose the central core of most units. Those disciplines are social work, nursing, and activities. When all three of these professions are united in goals, purpose, and vision, a comprehensive and coordinated program unfolds. Without strong commitment and support from each of these essential areas, the residents' and families' needs cannot be met at the level necessary to achieve success of the program.

Because the roles of the disciplines of social work, nursing, and activities overlap in many areas, confusional leadership may ensue. However, the overlap can serve as a strength rather than a weakness when all three disciplines are united in vision and purpose.

In the case study presented, the administrator, director of nursing, nurse manager, social worker for the dementia units, activities director (dementia care coordinator), and clinical nurse specialist meet weekly to discuss current needs, make future plans, coordinate efforts, and discuss outcomes on the unit. Consequently, there was a strong multidisciplinary cohesive core that guided and oversaw the care delivered.

The social work staff provided family support, guidance concerning advance directives, and assurance of resident rights and assisted families with financial concerns. Activity therapy staff completed a detailed assessment of each resident's past skills, roles, occupations, interests, hobbies, and accomplishments and formulated individualized daily activity plans that provided both sensory stimulating and sensory calming activities. Nurses typically focused on health and functional needs, physical care, and resident comfort. There were, however, many areas in which the interests of the disciplines merged.

Some areas of joint interest and concern are environmental needs and concerns, resident selection, the psychosocial and emotional needs of residents, quality of life and dignity, care planning, working to maintain personhood, and problem solving when dealing with difficult behaviors. Activity therapists and social workers together can plan activities and celebrations that include both residents and families. For example, the residents may make invitations that are sent to families before each annual celebration of the unit's opening. Social workers and nursing staff share responsibilities in keeping families involved and informed when the resident has a change in condition. An example of joint effort by nursing and activity therapy staff is prevention of excess disability by focusing on life skills such as dressing, bathing, or eating. These may be the last skills retained in late-stage dementia. Therefore, rather than rushing through bathing, dressing, and eating so that the resident arrives at activities exhausted and overstimulated, the life skills themselves may be designed into meaningful activities.

START-UP COSTS

Start-up costs will vary depending on the location of the LSCU. Ideally, the LSCU should be located adjacent to or near the mid-stage SCU. This arrangement facilitates sharing of supplies and staff if needed. It also helps the families of the SCU residents to gain familiarity with the LSCU staff and program, thereby easing some of the anxiety of a future transfer onto the unit. The two units (SCU and LSCU) together can be viewed as the dementia area or program, again reinforcing the continuum and assisting with future transition.

Four key structural issues should be considered: egress control devices, a private dining room for the unit, a quiet room, and a nurses' station located on the unit. The LSCU should be self-contained to prevent wandering off or onto the unit. Wandering off the unit may not be as big a problem as residents wandering onto the LSCU because residents with late-stage dementia may no longer be capable of wandering. However, uncontrolled extraneous stimuli can be very unsettling to the residents and increase acting out behavior. The goal of the LSCU should be to control stimuli and maintain a quiet, peaceful environment. Therefore, closed doors with egress-control devices are needed. The cost of these devices may range from $1,200 to $1,800 per door. Devices should be used that lock when exits are attempted. Alarms alone will not stop exit attempts. In fact, wandering will continue, and extraneous stimuli will increase by having the alarms triggered frequently.

The LSCU should have its own dining room and recreational area. Smaller dining areas have been shown to reduce noise and escalating behaviors (Weisman, Cohen, Ray, & Day, 1991). In addition, another room is needed as a quiet room for the residents experiencing loud behaviors, especially during meals. Taking an agitated resident to another room helps quiet him or her and prevents other residents from reacting. If the designated new LSCU has available rooms, costs will be minimal. If not, structural changes may be needed or a resident room may be converted into a common area. Using a resident room as a common area is costly because of the loss of revenue from the room. Even if a private room can be converted into a semi-private room to make up for the loss, private room charges are higher. Consequently, there will still be a revenue loss.

The LSCU should have its own nurses' station on the unit. This desk area should be small and should not be the focal point of the unit. The nurses' area should be constructed so that it does not detract from the homelike ambiance. Developing a new nurses' station will also have varying costs, depending on what is currently available. A new chart rack, desk, phones, and so forth will be needed.

It is worth the cost to have an architect or architectural firm with expertise in dementia projects consult during the early planning phase of the project. An expert from outside the facility can be objective in evaluating available space and can make suggestions for the best utilization of resources. It is imperative to set the consultant fees up front and communicate budgeting constraints to the architect. Compromises may need to be made, again stressing the importance of interdisciplinary involvement throughout the entire process.

STAFFING

Environmental design is important. However, less than ideal environments can be compensated for by quality staff and programming. The importance of adequate numbers and appropriate expertise of staff cannot be underestimated. Likewise, high staffing levels alone do not guarantee quality care. There needs to be a mix of nurses, certified nursing assistants (CNAs), activity therapists, and social workers. A daytime ratio of 1 to 5 (direct caregivers to residents) and a nightime ratio of 1 to 6 is needed. All disciplines should be included in the ratio, but the time spent with preparation or paperwork should not be counted (Mace, 1991).

The LSCU in the case example had 24 residents with late-stage dementia. Staffing was as follows:

Days: 1 registered nurse (RN) or licensed practical nurse (LPN) and 3.5 CNAs or 2 RNs or LPNs and 2.5 CNAs
Evenings: 1 RN and 3 CNAs or 1 RN and 1 LPN and 2 CNAs
Nights: 0.5 LPN (shared position between the SCU and LSCU) and 1 CNA

Positions shared with the SCU were 1 full-time activity CNA, 1 part-time activity coordinator, 1 full-time social worker, and 1 unit clerk. Also available for the LSCU but not solely designated for the area were a clinical nurse specialist, nurse manager, music therapist, pastoral care, and a shift supervisor.

On the LSCU described in the case example, all staff are cross-trained in activities. An important position that evolved over time is the activity CNA. A CNA is hired into this position and trained for activities. It has been extremely valuable for residents with late-stage dementia. The philosophy of both the SCU and LSCU is that everything is an activity. Therefore, staff are not encouraged to rush through physical care and grooming so that the resident can attend an activity. Rather, bathing, applying lotion, eating, and so forth are considered as important as other activities (i.e., music, art, etc.). Thus, an activity aide who is also a CNA can assist with these direct care activities. This activity CNA is never given a CNA assignment.

PERSONNEL ISSUES

As discussed in chapter 3, staff burnout and turnover are a major concern, with national turnover rates of CNAs running 100% per year (Gold, 1995). Working with residents with late-stage dementia can be very taxing and lead to burnout. However, several factors can help reduce turnover in the nursing department. Of utmost importance is maintaining fair and equitable assignments. This means replacing all call-ins, even if it means having to use outside agency help. In the case study, double-time pay was first offered to facility staff before an agency was called. The cost is comparable, but there is a considerable advantage in having staff that know the residents, policies, procedures, and so forth. Additional advantages are improved morale, quality care, and reduced turnover, all of which have a cost. A consistent positive staff and quality care are the best marketing for future admissions.

Another factor that can help with turnover is self-scheduling and monthly staff meetings. All staff should have input on unit activities and resident care planning. Decision making at the lowest level possible should be encouraged and supported. Although each staff member is valued, the nurse manager of the area is a critical role. Research has demonstrated that effective middle managers who work with the staff yield positive outcomes (Robinson & Spencer, 1991).

There are varying opinions regarding permanent resident assignments within a unit. Some staff prefer a permanent assignment, whereas others prefer to rotate which residents they will care for within the unit. Regardless, it is important that there are permanent staff assigned to the SCU and LSCU (Robinson & Spencer, 1991). Staff should not be expected to float off the unit unless there is over-staffing on the unit. If this occurs, it is advisable to encourage floating only within the dementia areas.

Finally, some personalities do not work well with residents with dementia. New staff should be interviewed specifically for the unit, not just assigned there. Patience, creativity, and an easygoing demeanor are needed (Peppard, 1985). Rigid schedules do not work well with dementia residents. If a staff member ver-balizes a dislike or inability to work with residents with dementia, believe them and do not force the issue. Transferring the staff person to another area may save an otherwise good employee (Astrom, Nilsson, Norberg, & Winblad, 1990).

Staff orientation, education, and ongoing inservices are imperative. When staff members are experts in dementia care, they are better able to intervene and control negative resident behaviors without increased use of chemical or physical restraints. This in turn has the additional benefit of decreasing staff burnout and turnover (Everitt, Fields, Soumerai, & Ovarn, 1991; Swanson, Mass, & Buck-walter, 1994). Therefore, money spent on staff preparation and education is recaptured in reduced turnover and improved quality care.

FUNDING

Frequently, the funding source for residents with late-stage dementia is Medicaid. Because of the length of the illness, the resident usually has spent any personal funds he or she had accumulated. In addition, there are only a few long-term care insurance plans, and those that do exist may not pay for what they consider cus-todial care. Residents with late-stage dementia are often considered in need of custodial care by insurance companies because they usually do not require IVs, tube feedings, pain management, wound care, and so forth.

As noted in chapter 2, some residents may qualify for the Medicare hospice benefit if their condition is terminal (i.e., expected survival of 6 months or less). This benefit is administered under home hospice. The long-term care facility is designated as the resident's home, and Medicare pays all monies to the home hospice, including 95% of the Medicaid rate. The home hospice in turn reim-burses the long-term care facility 100% of their Medicaid rate. The facility is required to provide all direct and professional cares. The home hospice is in charge of the resident's care. Consequently, the care plan of both the facility and the hospice must be congruent. The advantage to the resident is more individualized care and increased resource availability. The hospice provides volunteers, pastoral care, and CNAs to meet additional one-on-one care needs, which the typical long-term care facility cannot provide. Together, there is increased quality of care for both the resident and the family.

Consider obtaining some start-up funds for the project from individual donors or foundations. The program is a valuable cause, and donors can be easily assured that their contribution will be used to improve quality of life for a very special group of residents. Members of the boards of directors and administrators of religion-affiliated homes can often readily identify names of potential donors.

Many foundations are interested in the needs of older adults. In most areas a book is available that lists local and some national foundations. Included in the listing is the funding interests of each foundation and the average amount of each grant awarded. For example, in the state of Wisconsin, Marquette University compiles the book and updates it regularly. Most foundations require that a brief proposal be submitted that outlines the goals and activities of the project, provides a timeline for completion of the project, and provides a detailed budget and budget justification. It is acceptable to apply to several foundations for partial funding, thus increasing the chances of receiving some funds and possibly receiving the total amount needed to begin a new program.

VOLUNTEERS AND STUDENTS

The concept of volunteerism is central to the hospice approach, and judicious use of volunteers and students to augment the staff can be a benefit to the residents, staff, and individual volunteer or student. Because residents with late-stage dementia require a daily routine with consistent caregivers, student groups are not recommended. Furthermore, the increased noise, stimulation, and bustle created by a group of seven to eight students would reverse the calm and soothing environment that is central to dementia care. However, individual students in art therapy, recreational therapy, occupational therapy, or nursing could immerse themselves in dementia care and make a strong contribution to meeting the resident's needs.

Volunteers of all ages also have a lot to contribute to those with late-stage dementia. Children seem to have a special relationship with the elderly, and visits by youth groups can evoke emotions and trigger memories. Teens can participate in simple activities or crafts. Mature volunteers can perform very successful one-to-one activities such as reading, reminiscing with a picture book or flash cards, or just spontaneous conversation.

The single most important requisite to a successful volunteer program is education. The volunteers need to know what to expect of the residents, tour the unit, spend time shadowing unit personnel when appropriate, know where necessary supplies are, and learn to be supportive of the residents' responses when they make a connection with them.

Consistent, mature volunteers can build strong bonds with the residents and play a very important role. However, recruitment and retention of adult volunteers is difficult. Many find working with the demented very difficult to handle because it either reminds them of a loved one with Alzheimer's disease or makes them realize how vulnerable they are to the same disease. Recruitment of volunteers with experience in the health care field seems to improve their satisfaction and promote retention.

The judicious use of volunteers can enrich the program and provide another avenue to connect with the individual with late-stage dementia. Using a simple, nonthreatening, social approach can create a powerful experience for both the volunteer and the resident.

CONCLUSION

The concept of creating SCUs exclusively for those with late-stage dementia is in its infancy. There is a great need for careful study of LSCUs so that practice can be guided by research rather than by anecdotal reporting of experiences. The purpose of this chapter was to guide health care professionals in developing SCUs. The hope, however, is that LSCUs will be developed and then studied to evaluate their impact on quality of life.

BIBLIOGRAPHY

Alzheimer's Association Patient and Family Services. (1992). *Guidelines for dignity: Goals of specialized Alzheimer/dementia care in residential settings.* Chicago: Author.

Astrom, S., Nilsson, M., Norberg, A., & Winblad, B. (1990). Empathy, experience of burnout and attitudes towards demented patients among nursing staff in geriatric care. *Journal of Advanced Nursing, 15*, 1236–1244.

Benson, D. M., Cameron, D., Humbach, E., Servino, L., & Gambert, S. R. (1987). Establishment and impact of a dementia unit within the nursing home. *Journal of the American Geriatrics Society, 35*, 319–323.

Berg, L., Buckwalter, K. C., Chafetz, P. K., Gwyther, L. P., Holmes, D., Koepke, K. M., Lawton, M. P., Lindeman, D. A., Magaziner, J., Maslow, K., Sloane, P. D., & Teresi, J. (1991). Special care units for persons with dementia. *Journal of the American Geriatrics Society, 39*, 1229–1236.

Everitt, D., Fields, D., Soumerai, S., & Ovarn, J. (1991). Resident behavior and staff distress in the nursing home. *Journal of the American Geriatrics Society, 39*, 792–797.

Gold, M. F. (1995). Bridging the salary gap in long-term care. *Provider, 21*(4), 43–48.

Holmes, D., Teresi, J., & Monoco, C. (1992). Special care units in nursing homes: Prevalence in five states. *The Gerontologist, 32*(2), 191–196.

Kovach, C. R., & Stearns, S. (1994). DSCUs: A study of behavior before and after residence. *Journal of Gerontological Nursing, 20*(12), 33–39.

Kovach, C. R., Wilson, S. A., & Noonan, P. E. (1996). Effects of hospice interventions on behaviors, discomfort, and physical complications of end-stage dementia nursing home residents. *Journal of Alzheimer's Disease, 11*(4), 7–15.

Mace, N. L. (1991). Dementia care units in nursing homes. In D. H. Coons (Ed.), *Specialized dementia care units* (pp. 55–82). Baltimore, MD: Johns Hopkins University Press.

McConnell, S. (1994). Policy issues surrounding special care units. *Caring Magazine, 13*(8), 30–33.

Peppard, N. (1985). Alzheimer special-care nursing home units. *Nursing Homes, 34*(5), 25–28.

Robinson, A., & Spencer, B. (1991). Reducing staff burnout in the dementia care unit. In D. H. Coons (Ed.), *Specialized dementia care units* (pp. 144–160). Baltimore, MD: Johns Hopkins University Press.

Swanson, E., Mass, M., & Buckwalter, K. (1994). Alzheimer's residents' cognitive and functional measures. *Clinical Nursing Research, 3*(1), 27–41.

Volicer, L., Rheaume, Y., Brown, J., Fabiszewski, K., & Brady, R. (1986). Hospice approach to the treatment of patients with advanced dementia of the Alzheimer type. *Journal of the American Medical Association, 256*(16), 2210–2213.

Weisman, G. D., Cohen, U., Ray, K., & Day, K. (1991). Architectural planning and design for dementia care units. In D. H. Coons (Ed.), *Specialized dementia care units* (pp. 83–106). Baltimore, MD: Johns Hopkins University Press.

Part Two

Treatment Approaches for Common Needs

Chapter 5

Medical Care During Late-Stage Dementia

Edmund H. Duthie, Jr.

Goals for the medical care of patients with dementia vary with the stage of the patient's illness. In early stages, medical care is generally directed at making the diagnosis of dementia and finding the etiology for the problem (i.e., degenerative neurologic disorder, vascular dementia, alcohol induced, etc.). Medical conditions and drugs that can masquerade as dementia or aggravate dementia need to be aggressively pursued and managed. The patient and family gradually are oriented to the diagnosis and begin to adjust to the implications of the disease and plan for the future.

As dementia progresses through the moderate stages, the goal of medical care is still to optimize the patient's general health to promote maximal cerebral function. Drugs that affect the central nervous system should be avoided unless required for the management of behavioral disturbances (e.g., paranoia, hallucinations, depression, agitation, aggressiveness, insomnia). Sensory function should be optimized so that eyesight and hearing impediments do not further aggravate impairments in thinking. Good nutrition may need to be reemphasized to prevent nutritional deterioration, which might accelerate cerebral decline. The following list summarizes medical management for patients in the early and middle stages of dementia (modified from *Losing a Million Minds: Confronting the Tragedy of Alzheimer's Disease and Other Dementias,* U.S. Congress, Office of Technology Assessment, 1987):

- Diagnosis of the disease causing dementia.
- Search for diseases of other organ systems that can be treated, which might improve the patient's mental function.

• Assessment of the type and severity of the disease or diseases causing the dementia.

• Management of those aspects of the disorder than can be treated (e.g., behavioral problems amenable to treatment by medication or to family education on avoidance or management).

• Referral for clinical trials of agents that might manage the underlying disease causing the dementia.

• Trial of approved drugs that have been shown to slow disease progression.

• Treatment of conditions leading to the dementia (e.g., rehabilitation of the alcoholic with alcohol-induced dementia; risk-factor modification for individuals with hypertension or lipid disorders; and encouraging smoking cessation in patients with atherosclerotic vascular dementia).

• Education of patient and family about the disease (e.g., what to expect, genetic risks, drugs and foods to avoid).

• Referral to social and legal supports (e.g., family support groups, legal services, government programs).

As with most illnesses, the end stages of dementia present new challenges and may require a redirection of goals and objectives. This chapter focuses on medical management in the patient with advanced dementia. A case study is described to give the reader a flavor of the types of medical issues presented by patients with late-stage dementia.

CASE EXAMPLE

Mrs. Rodriguez is an 85-year-old woman who came to a hospital emergency room 6 years ago with acute confusion and some left-sided weakness. She was single and lived with her sister. The sister noted that Mrs. Rodriguez has been diagnosed as having high blood pressure for many years and that for the last year or two she had been "failing" mentally. Her physician believed that she had had strokes causing mild dementia. With modest oversight, Mrs. Rodriguez had done well living with her sister.

In the emergency room, Mrs. Rodriguez was alert and cooperative. She had prominent weakness in her left arm and leg. A computed tomography scan showed a right hemispheric stroke, and she was admitted to the hospital. Her hospital course was complicated. Attempts at rehabilitation were foiled by a number of problems.

On Hospital Day 19, Mrs. Rodriguez developed a serious upper gastrointestinal bleed that resulted in low blood pressure and the need for transfusions. Evaluation showed esophageal ulcers. Despite aggressive medical management, she re-bled on Day 29 and again required blood transfusions.

On Day 40, she became acutely unresponsive and could no longer eat. She became comatose. Her evaluation showed a new cardiac arrhythmia (atrial fibrillation) and in association with this she had multiple pulmonary emboli (blood clots in the lungs). She was also found to have blood clots in her leg veins. Because of her gastrointestinal hemorrhage, standard therapy with anticoagu-

lants was impossible. After agonizing over what to do, Mrs. Rodriguez's sister agreed to a procedure that would prevent further clots from the legs embolizing to the lungs.

Subsequently Mrs. Rodriguez was not alert or responsive. Her sister agreed to intravenous fluids and nasogastric feedings. Mrs. Rodriguez gradually resolved her comatose state. She was no longer judged to be a rehabilitation candidate, and 2 months after admission was transferred to a skilled nursing facility. Just prior to transfer, a gastrostomy tube was placed.

At the time of this writing (6 years after her initial emergency room presentation), Mrs. Rodriguez remains alive in the nursing home. Her sister could not bear the emotional burden of serving as a surrogate decision maker, and therefore a court-appointed guardian serves this role. The guardian and Mrs. Rodriguez's sister do confer about her and visit on occasion. Mrs. Rodriguez has been designated as "no code" since her nursing home transfer.

Mrs. Rodriguez has been clinically unchanged during her 6-year nursing home stay. She is completely bedridden. She opens her eyes and will blink when startled or threatened. She does not follow commands. Her gaze is conjugate, but she does not seem to track with her vision. All four extremities are flexed, and she has developed flexion contractures about most of her major joints. She has very coarse movement of her limbs, primarily the right arm. She has no speech and only occasionally will utter a groan. She cannot assist with transfers and must be lifted in and out of bed. She is incontinent of urine and feces. She has a gastrostomy tube, and all food, fluids, and medicine are administered through the tube.

She has been hospitalized three times over the past 6 years. Most recently, she developed a severe facial skin infection. Antibiotic therapy in the nursing home was ineffective, and a bright red weeping facial rash required hospitalization, aggressive intravenous antibiotics, and local care to manage.

Three years after her nursing home admission, Mrs. Rodriguez developed a sudden onset of bleeding from her gastrostomy tube. On examination at that time she also had cellulitis (infection) of the skin around a decubitus ulcer of her right hip. She was hospitalized for treatment of the skin infection and her gastric bleeding. She received antibiotics. No transfusions were needed, and her guardian declined to have the source of the bleeding identified. Intravenous medication to control gastric acidity was given.

Her other hospitalization occurred 1 year after admission to the nursing home. She developed such a severe flexion contracture of her right hand that the nails were penetrating the skin of the palm of the hand. Nursing staff could not open the fist or cleanse the area. A plastic surgeon agreed to hospitalize her and perform a tendon release. The result was excellent, and there have been no further problems with management of this contracture.

In addition to the hospitalizations described above, Mrs. Rodriguez has had a number of medical problems. She developed a decubitus ulcer over her right hip. This was difficult to heal, and x-rays and scans to exclude osteomyelitis (bone infection) were performed. No bone involvement was found. The plastic surgeons were reluctant to cover the wound with a skin graft. With aggressive nursing care, the wound eventually healed after 4 years. Mrs.

Rodriguez has had a number of other skin problems, including recurrent facial skin cancer that has been treated by a dermatologist. On occasion, skin tears have occurred as well as some trauma to the legs, including avulsion of the great toenail. Episodic fungal skin infections have occurred.

Mrs. Rodriguez has maintained her weight with the tube feeding. She was 124 lbs on admission, and her weight increased to to 150 lbs after 2 years. The gastrostomy tube periodically needs replacement. Measures of nutritional status have shown a mildly depleted albumin, but otherwise she seems well nourished. Her serum sodium has been mildly depleted, and no readily recognizable cause for this has been identified. This minor metabolic disturbance has not seemed to cause her difficulty.

Mrs. Rodriguez's blood pressure was elevated during her initial nursing home stay. Antihypertensive therapy has been administered through her gastrostomy tube, and her blood pressure has normalized on two agents (an angiotensin converting enzyme and a calcium channel blocker). She was iron deficient after her intestinal bleeds and received iron tablets as supplements until she was iron replete. This medication is no longer necessary. She is maintained on a histamine-2 blocker to reduce gastric acidity and hopefully prevent further intestinal bleeds.

Over time, Mrs. Rodriguez's sister has accepted that she will not improve. Her sister and her guardian visit on occasion. They have agreed to a do-not-resuscitate (DNR) order and have requested that Mrs. Rodriguez's care be managed in the nursing home without hospitalization, if possible. No advance directives were ever prepared by Mrs. Rodriguez. Specific discussions about her wishes in case she ever developed her current condition were not recalled. Her sister and her guardian have emphasized that comfort is the primary goal. They expect that she will die soon and are surprised she has lived so long. They desire no measures that will prolong life unless they are used primarily for comfort.

Episodically, her sister and her guardian have inquired about cessation of the tube feeding. The treatment team has suggested review by the ethics committee about this matter. Her sister and guardian are reluctant to meet with the ethics committee or to bring the matter forward, however. They are ambivalent about the tube feeding and have decided to continue the present course for the time being.

CASE DISCUSSION

This case is illustrative of some of the scenarios that occur in the care of patients with late-stage dementia. Late-stage dementia is often associated with lost verbal abilities, total incontinence, complete lack of ability for self-care, and loss of basic psychomotor skills including the ability to walk (Reisberg, 1983). Reisberg succinctly stated that in the end stages of dementia "the brain appears to no longer be able to tell the body what to do" (1983, p. 175). In a situation such as this, it is appropriate to confer with the family about the goals of treatment. As emphasized throughout this text, palliative care becomes the primary medical intervention. The principles of palliative care (Doyle, Hanks, & MacDonald, 1993) are outlined below:

- Affirm life.
- Regard dying as a normal process.
- Never hasten or postpone death.
- Provide relief from pain and other distressing symptoms.
- Prevent injury.
- Integrate the psychological and the spiritual aspects of care. Offer a support system to help the patient live as actively as possible until death.
- Offer a support system to help the family cope during the patient's illness and their own bereavement.

Some of these principles have been highlighted in the case of Mrs. Rodriguez. The treatment team and her sister were unified in their desire to promote comfort. Injury prevention was key. Although it may seem overly aggressive, the tendon release surgery was required to prevent injury to the hand and promote proper hygiene. Ongoing vigilance also was necessary to prevent other trauma, particularly the skin tears, abrasions, and nail trauma that Mrs. Rodriguez experienced. For all late-stage dementia patients, falls are an important consideration and another form of trauma. Caregivers require the proper equipment (beds, lifts, specialized chairs, bathing facilities, etc.) to safely manage these patients. Nothing replaces care and attention to the task at hand when handling these patients. Staff cannot be distracted by conversation, radios, or television.

Tresch, Sims, Duthie, and Goldstein (1991) studied patients with severe neurologic dysfunction (persistent vegetative state), many of whom had end-stage dementia. In interviews with family members, it became clear that although families were frequently realistic about the patients' abilities and prognosis, they remained involved and committed. Families were particularly needy of psychological support and education. Interdisciplinary teams must make this a priority in order to agree to mutual goals and promote optimal care. This aspect of care is frequently overlooked, resulting in frustration for the family and for the care team.

Families should be approached about the range of options for medical care available to patients. Table 5.1 lists a variety of levels of medical care for patients with dementia (Volicer, Rheaume, Brown, Fabiszewski, & Brady, 1986). The treatment team needs to present the range of options available to gain informed consent from surrogate decision makers. Once this is done, the surrogates should be queried about any advance directive (written or oral) prepared by the patient that can provide direction to the treatment team so that the patient's wishes might be followed. In many cases, the patient's wishes are unknown. In this event, the surrogates will need to provide their best guess as to what the patient would choose if she or he were cognizant and aware of the current clinical circumstances (i.e., late-stage dementia). The treatment team should also offer recommendations about the level of care on the basis of their knowledge of the patient's clinical circumstances and clinical studies detailing the management of patients with late-stage dementia.

Table 5.1   Levels of medical care for patients with dementia

Level	Description
Level 1	The patient receives aggressive diagnostic workup, treatment of coexisting medical conditions and transfer to acute unit if necessary. In the event of a cardiac arrest, resuscitation is attempted. Tube feeding is used if normal food intake is not possible.
Level 2	The patient receives complete care as defined above, but under the condition of a do-not-rescuscitate (DNR) directive. Resuscitation is not attempted in the event of cardiac or respiratory arrest.
Level 3	This level involves DNR and no transfer to an acute care unit for medical management of intercurrent life threatening illnesses. This eliminates use of respirators, cardiovascular support, and other treatment options that are available only in an acute medical setting.
Level 4	This level includes DNR, no transfer to an acute care unit, and no workup and antibiotic treatment of life-threatening infections such as pneumonia or urinary tract infections (UTIs). Only antipyretics and analgesics are used to ensure patient comfort. Partial isolation techniques are used for staff protection.
Level 5	Supportive care is given as defined above but eliminating tube feeding by a nasogastric tube or gastrostomy when normal food intake is not possible. Fluids necessary for hydration are provided orally only if the patient is not comatose.

Source: Volicer et al., 1986.

It is essential that the treatment team work together on developing a plan of care and be consistent in their communication with caregivers. Physicians who work independently of the care team (nurses, social workers, chaplains, psychologists, therapists, and nutritionists) will find themselves frustrated and perhaps angry about caring for these patients. Families receiving disparate information and advice can become confused, angry, and recalcitrant. A priority when caring for people with late-stage dementia is the development of excellent communication among members of the interdisciplinary team and then between the team and patient–family unit.

Professional caregivers must recognize that they have to be flexible in caring for patients with late-stage dementia. The options listed in Table 5.1 are presented for clarity of thinking, but in practice there may be some overlap of the groups or fluctuation among the groups. Families and surrogates have the right to change their minds depending on the patient's clinical situation or the circumstances of the surrogate. For example, when adjusting to the finality that the patient has late-stage dementia, a family may initially state they desire Level 1 care (Table 5.1). Over time, as they adjust to the patient's condition and come to trust the treatment team, they may choose to alter the level of care. Treatment teams and institutions need to respect the evolution that patients and surrogate decision makers go through. An approach that seeks to help patients and families grow through the course of the illness is preferable to forcing them to accept policies and procedures that agencies or institutions view as preferable. For example, some agencies or institutions may insist that patients with end-stage dementia accept a DNR order. If the patient or surrogate will not abide by this, the agency or institution may refuse care or admission. Up-front barriers such as this may serve professional staff or their institutions, but they border on coercion and do not permit development of the proper therapeutic alliance between patients, families. and the treatment team. Setting goals for medical care requires time for the treatment team and patient or family to get to know one another and to work together.

Barriers to goal setting include (a) lack of an interested family member or surrogate decision maker; (b) transition of the patient to new care providers (e.g., many physicians will not provide care in long-term care facilities and therefore patients with late-stage dementia who enter a facility gain a new physician and lose the care of a provider who may have known them for years); (c) a dysfunctional treatment team—professionals who work independently and do not formally meet to discuss cases, develop treatment plans, and build teams (the nonparticipation of physicians on these teams is a common problem); (d) a dysfunctional family or problems among family members and maladaptive psychodynamics between the patient and the family or among family members; and (e) lack of flexibility by the agency or institution, professional staff, the patient, or the family.

To return to the case study, Mrs. Rodriguez and her sister did have to cope with transitions in medical care and treatment team providers. Mrs. Rodriguez had a number of physicians (internists, neurologists, gastroenterologists, interventional radiologists, intensive care specialists) who provided care during her acute illness. When she entered the nursing home, she had a new primary care physician (an internist and geriatrician) assigned. This physician worked with a nurse practitioner. The physician worked as a member of an interdisciplinary treatment team (dentistry, nursing, nutrition, occupational therapy, pharmacy, physical therapy, psychology, recreation, social work, and speech-audiology). The team met 2 weeks after Mrs. Rodriguez's admission to the nursing home to establish a plan of care and then reviewed the plan quarterly. Her sister was advised about the team's recommendations and her input was solicited. Her sister's reluctance to serve as a decision maker was an initial problem the team had to solve. The appointment of a guardian by the court facilitated medical care and comforted the sister.

The sister and guardian opted for Level 3 care (see Table 5.1). However, some clinical circumstances have modified this. For example, Mrs. Rodriguez was transferred to the hospital for the tendon release surgery on her hand. The treatment team and guardian were flexible enough to recognize that the clinical condition warranted hospitalization and surgery to meet the goals of palliative care. In the case of the facial skin infection, the violation of skin integrity, the lack of response to conservative measures, and patient discomfort also required a modification of the plan of care to permit hospitalization so that skin integrity and patient's comfort could be restored. In the case of Mrs. Rodriguez's recurrent gastrointestinal bleed and skin cellulitis, hospitalization resulted because of a breakdown in communication. Weekend nursing staff were not familiar with the medical care plan; an on-call physician was similarly unaware of the medical plan for care; and neither the guardian nor sister could be reached to be notified of the change in Mrs. Rodriguez's condition. As a result, a hospitalization occurred, with ensuing therapy that was not originally planned by the treatment team or family. Scenarios such as this are not infrequent in the care of patients with late-stage dementia. Thoughtful attention to systems of care provision may help to avoid such breakdowns.

MEDICAL CONDITIONS IN LATE-STAGE DEMENTIA

A number of medical conditions are likely to be present in patients with late-stage dementia. To begin with, the vast majority of these patients are elderly. Eighty-five percent of persons age 65 and over have at least one chronic illness. The six most common chronic problems seen in older adults are arthritis, hypertension, hearing loss, heart condition, chronic sinusitis, and vision loss.

In the case study presented, Mrs. Rodriguez suffered from vascular dementia. Patients such as this are prone to high blood pressure (hypertension), cardiac disease (heart failure, angina pectoris, atrial fibrillation), renal insufficiency, and peripheral vascular insufficiency. Patients with alcohol dementia can have other complications of alcohol use such as anemia, neuropathy, cerebellar degeneration, osteoporosis, nutritional deficiency, or liver disease. These comorbidities can require medical management and drug therapy. Assessment and management of sensory dysfunction in late-stage dementia is impaired by the patient's inability to cooperate with testing.

PHARMACOLOGY

The medical regimens of patients with late-stage dementia require careful review. The principles of palliative care should be reviewed and medicine adjusted accordingly. In the case study, antihypertensives were used to try to prevent further neurologic damage. A case could be made, however, that the extent of Mrs. Rodriguez's nervous system damage was so severe that not much preservation of neural function could be gained by blood pressure control. On the other hand, uncontrolled hypertension could also lead to eventual cardiac dysfunction, with heart failure and patient discomfort as a result.

Another medical condition present in this case study included gastrointestinal bleeding. Although it is not clear that the bleeding and esophagitis caused any patient discomfort, the treatment team assumed that there might be discomfort from the esophagitis and elected therapy with histamine-2 blockers. Similarly, anemia due to iron deficiency after the upper gastrointestinal bleed was managed with iron replacement. Because of Mrs. Rodriguez's advanced dementia, it is only speculation whether she benefited from having her blood count and iron status restored. It is unlikely that any objective measures of function improved because of either of the just-mentioned therapies.

When using drugs with geriatric patients, principles of geriatric pharmacotherapy should be followed. These are briefly summarized below, and texts of geriatric medicine should be consulted for details.

- Carefully review the need for drugs and eliminate agents that are not achieving any patient benefit.
- Be alert for drug-induced symptoms or adverse drug reactions.
- Consider pharmacokinetic and pharmacodynamic changes with age when prescribing, for example, the lower ratio of body water to lean body mass and the gain in body fat, which will affect the volume of distribution of drugs; the changes in hepatic metabolism and decline in renal function, which affect the elimination of certain drugs; and the greater sensitivity elderly patients have to certain drugs.
- Minimize the number of agents to avoid adverse drug reactions and drug interactions.
- Consider diseases that influence drug absorption, distribution, clearance, and effect.

PREVENTION

Prevention is another important issue in the management of any patient. Immunization with influenza vaccine yearly, pneumococcal vaccine once, and tetanus vaccine every 10 years is reasonable. Most skilled nursing facilities will test tuberculosis skin test status to help identify active cases of tuberculosis and assist with case finding and patient management in case of a tuberculosis outbreak in a facility.

Measures for early detection of cancer are controversial. The surrogate decision maker or the family need to confer about whether they would pursue the result of a positive screening test. For example, would a mammographic finding of a breast mass lead to a biopsy and treatment? Would the discovery of occult blood in the stool be pursued with proctosigmoidoscopy, barium x-ray studies, or colonoscopy? Would a positive Pap smear result in further evaluation or treatment for cervical cancer? In general, late-stage dementia is a serious enough impairment with limited longevity that the usual preventive measures employed to detect cancer early would not be recommended. In the case study, skin cancer was discovered by the team during the course of regular care. Because this is easily treated and, if allowed to progress, can significantly impair skin integrity, the guardian agreed to therapy.

Other preventive measures that may be used in the medical management of patients with late-stage dementia are the periodic evaluation of thyroid function tests to exclude a derangement of thyroid function that might affect the patient's health. In the case study, the occurrence of atrial fibrillation prompted the search for excessive thyroid hormone levels. Oral care is very important because patients with late-stage dementia are incapable of self-care. Staff must regularly inspect the mouth and assist with flossing, brushing, and tongue and mucous membrane hygiene. Dentures need to be cleaned and properly inserted and removed in patients who can benefit from their use.

Prevention of skin breakdown is another area of medical management. A majority of patients with late-stage dementia are significantly limited in their mobility. In a multivariate analysis of patients with limited mobility, Allman, Goode, Patrick, Burst, and Bartolucci (1995) found a number of factors associated with increased risk for developing pressure ulcers, including nonblanchable erythema of intact sacral skin, lymphopenia ($\leq 1.5 \times 10^9$/L), immobility, dry sacral skin, and decreased body weight.

The implications of these factors for patient management is that potential pressure sites must be inspected frequently. The presence of nonblanchable erythema or dry skin require aggressive measures to relieve pressure and improve skin moisture. Patients who do not assist in any way with position changes or who cannot change position without assistance are at high risk for pressure ulcer formation. The treatment team needs to use a program of frequent turning to avoid excessive pressure in these patients. Data are not conclusive regarding the use of specialized beds, mattresses, or devices as aides to prevent pressure ulcers in these high-risk patients.

In the case study, Mrs. Rodriguez was immobile and did develop a large decubitus ulcer that took years to heal. The possibility of osteomyelitis resulted in further testing and consultation. The open skin was associated with at least one episode of surrounding skin cellulitis. Prevention of these ulcers can decrease patient morbidity and cost of care.

Pressure ulcers are also associated with decreased body weight and depressed blood lymphocyte count. These measures likely reflect the nutritional status of the patient. Patients with late-stage dementia merit nutritional assessment by a dietitian. Follow-up is required on a regular basis, generally quarterly, in a skilled nursing facility. Weight should be assessed monthly at least. Other measures of nutrition such as albumin, prealbumin, cholesterol, lymphocyte count, hemoglobin, and blood urea may assist with assessment and management. Although medical indicators of nutrition can be used to predict the need for nutritional intervention, the decision to initiate feeding assistance with nasogastric tubes, a gastrostomy tube, or jejunostomy tubes is primarily an ethical issue.

There is little doubt that assisted feeding should be provided. Regulating bodies (e.g., state inspection teams) often view malnutrition and the occurrence of dehydration to be indicators of poor care. This places pressure on agencies and institutions to aggressively manage nutrition and fluid status with artificial means. Debate exists whether malnutrition or dehydration result in suffering in the case of advanced degenerative neurologic illness such as end-stage dementia. This is a key point because it does appear that the natural history of degenerative dementia includes a gradual lessening of food and fluid intake. Whether the provision of calories and fluids through tube or intravenous route meets the goals of palliative care is debatable. Treatment teams must educate patients and surrogate decision makers about the issue and develop a plan of care. It is possible that patients in similar clinical circumstances will be managed differently. Flexibility is again required by staff. Institutional ethics committees are an important resource in these cases. Legal advice is often needed to advise agencies and institutions about case law affecting the provision of nutrition and about patients' and families' right to refuse treatment.

In the case study, the surrogate decision makers opted to have a gastrostomy tube inserted. Over time, the sister has had some misgiving about the tube feeding, which she views as postponing death. Although an institutional ethics panel is available to confer with the sister and guardian, they have been reluctant to bring the matter forward. With tube feeding, Mrs. Rodriguez's nutritional status has been well maintained

MEDICAL CONDITIONS POTENTIALLY SEEN AS A RESULT OF LATE-STAGE DEMENTIA

Late-stage dementia can result in a predisposition to a number of medical conditions. Some of these have already been mentioned (e.g., poor oral hygiene, decubitus ulcers, and malnutrition). Other medical conditions that may occur as the result of late-stage dementia include behavioral or psychiatric disturbances, constipation, delirium, dental or oral disease (plaque, gingivitis, caries, fungal infection), falls, infections (urinary tract, pneumonia, skin, conjunctivitis), joint contractures, seizures, urinary or fecal incontinence, and venous thromboembolism.

Seizures can occur as the result of degenerative, vascular, or other dementia. Anticonvulsants can be used to control these. A search for structural central nervous system abnormalities or metabolic conditions (e.g., hypoglycemia, electrolyte disturbance, drug reaction) that may contribute to seizure occurrence should be made. Patients with late-stage dementia are often immobile and predisposed to venous thromboembolism. Trials examining the long-term use of anticoagulants, sequential compressive devices, or compressive stockings in this population are lacking. In the case study, Mrs. Rodriguez did develop venous thrombosis with subsequent pulmonary embolus. This occurred early in her course of illness. The placement of a filter in the vena cava has resulted in no recurrence of the problem over many years.

Infections are an important medical consideration for patients with late-stage dementia. Although precise data are lacking, clinical experience with patients with end-stage dementia suggests that death in these patients is the result of a lack of nutrition or hydration and infection. Common infections include urinary tract infections, respiratory tract infections (especially pneumonia), skin infections (cellulitis or infected decubitus ulcers), diarrheal illnesses, and conjunctivitis. Infections are the leading cause for hospitalization among nursing home patients. They are costly and can cause suffering (e.g., fever, shortness of breath, painful urination, abdominal discomfort, etc.).

Some measures can be used to prevent infections. Urinary catheters should be avoided unless absolutely necessary (e.g., inability to void or presence of an open wound that cannot be contaminated with urine). There is evidence that cranberry juice (300 ml daily) can reduce white cells and bacteria in the urine of elderly women (Avorn et al., 1994). Whether this strategy is effective in patients with late-stage dementia requires further study. Urinary tract infections should be treated with antibiotics only when symptomatic. No clear benefit has been shown for treating asymptomatic urinary tract infections.

Prevention of pneumonia is primarily accomplished with influenza vaccination and pneumococcal vaccine administration. Benefits of deep breathing or physical therapy modalities to prevent pneumonia are not well proven. During influenza outbreaks, cohorting patients, restricting visitors, and using amantadine may help to prevent the spread of influenza. Caregivers who attend patients with late-stage dementia should be immunized against influenza.

Swallowing problems have been reported to increase the risk of pneumonia. Consultation with a speech therapist may be helpful in suggesting ways of assisting patients with feeding that might lessen the amount of aspiration. Oral hygiene is also key in this regard because debris in the oral cavity, plaque, and gingivitis may be a source for bacterial colonization and eventual aspiration with pneumonia. Grossly decaying teeth should be properly treated to lessen the ability of bacteria to reside in the oral cavity and be aspirated into the lungs. Recurrent pneumonia suspected to be the result of uncoordinated swallowing may require placement of a feeding tube. The risk of tube placement versus oral feeding must be weighed against potential benefits. Prevention of aspiration through tube placement may prolong life.

Skin infections should be lessened by protecting skin integrity and avoiding trauma to the skin. Diarrheal illness can be minimized through careful handwashing by caregivers. This is especially important for staff who attend multiple patients in community or institutional settings. In fact, the single most important measure that caregivers can use to prevent infection in debilitated patients is handwashing. Because the use of disposable gloves is so common in patient care, caregivers must also remember to change gloves before moving to another patient.

Another factor contributing to diarrheal illness is widespread antibiotic use. Antibiotics can result in the proliferation of an intestinal pathogen, *Clostridium difficile (C. difficile)*. This bacteria can produce a toxin that causes severe diarrhea. During the past decade, diarrhea due to *C. difficile* has become commonplace in hospital and nursing home patients.

Conjunctivitis should be minimized by following appropriate techniques for the storage and administration of eye medications. Handwashing is also key in preventing the transmission of conjunctivitis between patients.

In the case study, Mrs. Rodriguez was free of symptomatic urinary tract infections. No catheter was used. She has not had pneumonia. She has received pneumococcal vaccine and an annual influenza vaccine. She does have a gastrostomy tube in place. She has not had diarrheal illnesses. Although not mentioned specifically in the case discussion, she did have a few episodes of conjunctivitis. These were managed with local antibiotic ointments. Prevention with lid scrub (1/2 strength solution of water and baby shampoo at bedtime) was also utilized.

Skin infections were a major problem for Mrs. Rodriguez. These were due in part to interruptions in skin integrity from facial skin cancer, decubitus ulcer, and skin tears or trauma that occurred in the course of caring for her. Although antibiotic use was attempted in the nursing home setting, hospitalization was required in a couple of instances to control the skin infections.

Beyond the issue of infection occurrence and prevention is the management of infections in patients with late-stage dementia. Studies show that untreated fever or infection among nursing home residents results in high mortality. Table 5.1 notes that Level 4 or 5 care precludes the use of antibiotics. The treatment team and surrogate decision makers need to discuss what action should be taken in the event of an infection, and this decision probably merits review on a quarterly basis and whenever infection is suspected. Surrogates should be aware that rational infection therapy requires assessing the source of the infection, monitoring parameters of infection (e.g., white blood cell count), and obtaining specimens (e.g., blood, urine, stool, fluid, or sputum) so that appropriate specific therapy can be given.

Randomized controlled trials of end-stage dementia patients with infection examining the outcome with and without antibiotics are not feasible or ethical. It is notable, however, that there are data comparing outcomes between infected patients with dementia who opted for antibiotic therapy and those who declined therapy. In a small number of patients, those with more severe dementia did not have a greater probability of survival over a 34-month period when fever was aggressively diagnosed and infection treated compared with comparably severely demented patients who received palliative treatment with antipyretics, analgesics, and comfort measures. In patients with less advanced dementia, antibiotic use was associated with higher survival than was palliative treatment. In other words, for patients with advanced end-stage dementia there are data suggesting that antibiotic use in the case of infection does not affect 3-year survival. (Fabiszewski, Volicer, & Volicer, 1990).

CONCLUSION

Persons with late-stage dementia are frequently elderly. They will often have the common chronic conditions seen in late life as well as complications related to their abnormal neural dysfunction. Complications from prolonged immobility and neural damage (e.g., swallowing problems and urinary or fecal incontinence) should be anticipated. Management requires an interdisciplinary team approach utilizing the principles of palliative care. The team must spend time with patients and surrogate decision makers to decide on the goals of care and the level of care to be given. Having agreed to a plan of care, the team must regularly review the plan and make efforts to support the patient and family through the patient's illness.

BIBLIOGRAPHY

Allman, R. M., Goode, P. S., Patrick, M. M., Burst, N., & Bartolucci, A. A. (1995) Pressure ulcer risk factors among hospitalized patients with activity limitations. *Journal of the American Medical Association, 273,* 865–887.

Avorn, J., Monwe, M., Gurwitz, J. A., Glynn, R. J., Choodnovskiy, I., & Lipsitz, L. A. (1994). Reduction of bacteriuria and pyuria after ingestion of cranberry juice. *Journal of the American Medical Association, 271,* 751–754.

Cummings, J. L., & Benson, D. F. (1992). *Dementia: A clinical approach* (2nd ed.). Boston, MA: Butterworth-Heinemann.

Doyle, D., Hanks, G. W. C., & MacDonald, N. (1993). *Oxford textbook of palliative medicine.* Oxford, England: Oxford University Press.

Fabiszewski, K., Volicer, V., & Volicer, L. (1990). Effect of antibiotic treatment on outcome of fever in institutionalized Alzheimer patients. *Journal of the American Medical Association, 263,* 3168–3172.

Reisberg, B. (1983). Clinical prevention, diagnosis, and symptomatology of age-associated cognitive decline and Alzheimer's disease. In B. Reisberg (Ed.), *Alzheimer's disease: The standard reference* (pp. 173–187). New York: Free Press.

Tresch, D. D., Sims, F. H., Duthie, E. H., & Goldstein, M. D. (1991). Patients in a persistent vegetative state: Attitudes and reactions of family members. *Journal of the American Gerontological Society, 39,* 17–21.

U.S. Congress, Office of Technology Assessment. (1987). *Losing a million minds: Confronting the tragedy of Alzheimer's disease and other dementias* (Publication No. OTA-BA-323). Washington, DC: U.S. Government Printing Office.

Volicer, L., Rheaume, Y., Brown, J., Fabiszewski, K., & Brady, R. (1986). Hospice approach to the treatment of patients with advanced dementia of the Alzheimer's type. *Journal of the American Medical Association, 256,* 2210–2213.

Chapter 6

Treatment Approaches to Common Physical Care Needs

Thelma J. Wells

The increasing physical dependency common to late-stage dementia creates numerous physical problems. This chapter reviews key assessment points, discusses bladder problems, and highlights aspects of bowel problems, pressure ulcers, contractures, and falls. The emphasis is on prevention.

Good physical care starts with establishing a good baseline assessment and regularly monitoring physical status over time. Dependent patients with communication difficulty may express physical pain and discomfort through agitated or withdrawn behavior. Thus, it is essential that caregivers regularly examine the patient's total body. There are excellent textbooks that provide detailed physical examination procedures. Advanced practice nurses learn these skills as part of their education. However, any nurse can learn to look more closely, touch more knowingly, and generally attend to critical physical areas. The following section briefly reviews key assessment points.

ASSESSMENT OF PHYSICAL STATUS

Patient cooperation to some degree is essential, but creative planning can avoid many difficulties. Usually a full assessment done in one time period is more stressful than short regional examinations. Combining evaluation with bathing or other related care functions and modifying techniques are helpful. The assistance of another to divert attention or provide support may be required.

Head and Neck

Ears, eyes, and mouth are the major items for head and neck examination, but attention to skin, soft tissue, and neck mobility are important too. Impacted ear wax acts as an effective ear plug to isolate an individual and impede communication. Mahoney (1993) assessed ear wax impaction in 104 residents chosen randomly from eight nursing homes and found a prevalence rate of 25% for total impaction and an additional 23% for partial impaction (two thirds of the canal blocked). The ear canal must be examined with an otoscope to determine ear wax status. If the ear drum cannot be visualized because of ear wax accumulation, ear wax softening agents are recommended. These agents alone or with ear irrigation can clear the ear canal.

The eyes should be examined for any signs of infection in surrounding tissue or evidence of conjunctival irritation; sties and eyelash irritation are not uncommon. The mouth should be examined with dentures and bridges removed so that one can look for irritation. More information on care of the mouth is presented in chapters 7 and 9.

Trunk

Examine the back and sides for signs of pressure areas over bony prominences and any evidence of tenderness. The abdomen should be soft to touch; listening with a stethoscope should yield normal bowel sounds. It is important to examine the perineum for signs of irritation or infection. Men who have penile foreskin should have the foreskin retracted during the examination of the head of the penis. This area may need special attention during bathing. Women should have at minimum a simple digital examination of the vagina to check for tenderness and discharge. Atrophic vaginitis is common and often severe in women with late-stage dementia. It is likely to cause discomfort and can be easily treated with small applications of estrogen topical creams. Incontinent women may also have significant vulval and vaginal tissue irritation from urine. Careful cleaning, anti-inflammatory agents, and an indwelling catheter may be necessary to resolve severe irritation. The rectum should be checked for stool consistency.

Because pneumonia and congestive heart failure are common problems of frail older adults, nursing staff should be skilled in listening to breath sounds. Books and courses on assessment techniques are available to provide nurses with skill in the following auscultatory techniques and findings: bronchophony, egophony, hearing bronchial or bronchovesicular sounds where only vesicular sounds should be heard, and identification of crackles, wheezes, and rhonchi. Skill in these specific auscultatory methods as well as inspection techniques can be helpful in identifying changes in health status early in the course of illness. Decisions regarding treatment options are facilitated when choices are discussed before there is a crisis. Also, early conservative treatment is often more desirable than aggressive treatment when the illness is advanced.

Extremities

Skin, nails, and range of motion are the major foci of the extremities check. Look for bruises and skin tears; be sure to feel the heels for tissue firmness, a change in which may herald a heel pressure sore. Consider skin coolness or warmth in terms of patient comfort. Keep patients' nails cut short. Move small and large joints in their normal ranges, judging ease of movement and signs of tenderness. Look between the toes for skin care and signs of fungal infection.

Bladder Problems

Bladder problems can be thought of as having simple or complex causes. Simple causes are fairly easy to assess and treat, but complex causes may require more evaluation and various treatment trials. Bladder problems of people with late-stage dementia need to be carefully evaluated because simple causes can make incontinence worse and, more important, cause significant patient discomfort. Complex causes may be improved with specific treatment. Further, a thorough evaluation is required before using behavioral treatment or wetting management products.

Common simple causes of urinary incontinence include drugs, fluid amount and type, constipation and impaction, urinary tract infections, and the broad domain of environment. Diuretics are drugs given to increase urine output and may be necessary in the treatment of cardiovascular disease. However, consideration should be given to individualized dosage, with the smallest amount given to achieve satisfactory results. Three types of drugs may be given for behavior problems: antidepressants, neuroleptics, and psychotropics. These all can cause drug-induced urinary incontinence (Agency for Health Care Policy and Research [AHCPR], 1992a). Thus, a first step in evaluating urinary incontinence is to examine the patient's drug orders, discontinue all unnecessary medication, and reduce dosage of essential medication to the minimum needed.

Adequate fluid intake may be a problem in patients with late-stage dementia who may have difficulty swallowing or refuse fluids. Fluid intake needs per 24 hr can be calculated from a formula based on body weight in kilograms. For the first 10 kg of body weight, the fluid need is 100 ml/kg, or 1,000 ml. For the second 10 kg of body weight, the fluid need is 50 ml/kg, or 500 ml. For weight over these 20 kg, the fluid need is 20 ml/kg (Herfindal, Gourley, & Hart, 1992). So, a 120-lb person (54.5 kg) would need 1,000 ml for the first 10 kg, plus 500 ml for the next 10 kg, plus 690 ml (20 ml $\times$ 34.5 kg) for a total of 2,190 ml of fluid per day. However, in frail, inactive individuals adequate fluid intake could be substantially less. Checking mucous membrane status and monitoring urine concentration and stool consistency are useful nursing observations in evaluating body hydration. Inadequate fluid intake is associated with constipation, impaction, urinary tract infection, and discomfort. In general one should avoid caffeine-containing fluids when dealing with problems of urine control. Caffeine is a natural diuretic and is found in coffee, tea, and sodas, especially colas. Decaffeinated coffee and soda as well as herbal teas are better for patients who like these beverages.

Constipation is defined as stool frequency less than 3 times per week (Brocklehurst, 1994). In frail, inactive individuals with low food and fluid intakes, constipation can be expected and is best monitored by a combination of stool frequency and consistency records. Infrequent but soft stool may be acceptable, but infrequent and hard stool is not.

It is very important to recognize fecal impaction, that is, a hard mass of stool in the rectum or lower colon. Overflow fecal incontinence is a common sign, which can be misinterpreted as normal stool or diarrhea. Other physical signs include abdominal tenderness, marked abdominal distention, and a mass in the lower left quadrant of the abdomen. Individuals with fecal impaction are usually very uncomfortable and experience abdominal pain.

Constipation and impaction cause an overflow type of urinary incontinence because the mass of feces exerts pressure through the perineal soft tissue to obstruct the bladder outflow. One can usually palpate the distended bladder, which will be sensitive to touch. Removing the stool mass results in bladder emptying.

Preventing constipation can be a major challenge, especially if fluid and food intake are limited. Natural laxatives, such as prunes, can be highly effective. Adding fiber such as bran to the diet of frail individuals must be done cautiously but can have good results. Stool softening agents are a useful therapy. Should a fecal impaction occur, disposable low-volume phosphate enemas are the first choice of treatment. It is unlikely that a single enema will be adequate, even though a large fecal return is obtained. One to two enemas daily for a series of days may be necessary to clear the impaction. Occasionally the hard fecal mass in the rectum needs to be broken up with digital manipulation. Care must be taken in removing impactions to avoid damage to the anal sphincter and pain or discomfort to the patient. Lidocaine 5% applied as a topical cream to the anus 5–10 min before the procedure and gentle dilation of the anal sphincter are helpful approaches.

A basic evaluation for urinary incontinence includes obtaining a urine specimen for analysis. Recent studies have shown the validity of clean catch specimens in women (Ouslander, Schapira, & Schnelle, 1995), external catheter collection in men (Ouslander, Greengold, Silverblatt, & Garcia, 1987), and diaper squeeze samples from women (Belmin, Hervias, Avellano, Oudart, & Durand, 1993) as alternatives to in-and-out catheterization in nursing home populations.

Bacteriuria is common in the elderly and when asymptomatic should generally not be treated (Nicolle, 1993). Symptoms of urinary tract infection may be difficult to detect in patients with late-stage dementia. The classic fever, chills, nausea, vomiting, and hematuria may not be present. Incontinence may worsen; there may be signs of discomfort or lethargy. A trial of antimicrobials is reasonable for bacteriuria with these suspected symptoms. However, the patient should be watched carefully for specific improvement in response to treatment and, if none is observed, then the trial should be discontinued.

Environment is a broad area that refers to adequate equipment, caregiver attitude and skills, and resources in general. Patients should be toileted as long as possible in the course of their dementia. The toilet seat is a learned stimulus to bladder and bowel emptying and an upright seated position facilitates complete emptying. If travel to the toilet is problematic, then a commode is needed. There are a range of commodes available that differ in seat and arm discomfort (padded or not), back height (full or short), as well as seat height, receptacle design, and mobility. Commodes that fit the individual and are comfortable are worth the effort to find and implement. Caregivers need to be committed to normal function as long as possible but sensitive about comfort and quality of life. Toileting includes a need to have patient clothing that facilitates rather than hinders access, such as lapover skirts for women and Velcro fastenings in general. Pant or pad systems encourage toileting with a greater ease than diapers, yet provide precautionary protection.

Patients with late-stage dementia are likely to have complex urological problems common to old people in general. Thus, men likely have prostate enlargement, with the potential for overflow incontinence, and women may have an incompetent urethra with stress urinary incontinence (SUI). Increased age in both sexes is associated with a neurological type of incontinence, urge, which may be made worse by dementia. These common complex causes of urinary incontinence are briefly reviewed in the following paragraphs.

Benign prostate hypertrophy (BPH) is the enlargement of the prostate gland, which is located at the base of the male urethra. The majority of men who reach 80 years of age have prostate tissue changes, and about half display symptoms of urine outflow obstruction (Riehmann & Bruskewitz, 1994). The signs and symptoms include a distended bladder with constant urine dribbling, large residual urine, and urinary tract infection. Surgical transurethral resection of the prostate gland is the common treatment for this problem when kidney function is at risk or symptoms cause considerable discomfort. Such treatment may not be advisable for patients with dementia. Transurethral incision is a newer technique that requires shorter operative time and may be an option. Of interest is the advance in pharmacologic treatment of BPH with a number of medications that may be appropriate for a patient with late-stage dementia (Manyak, 1992). However, it is often the case that neither surgery nor medication is an appropriate treatment. Because an obstructed bladder is painful, relief is provided by either an indwelling catheter or clean intermittent catheterization (Duffy et al., 1995) or by a suprapubic catheter.

SUI is caused by either structural or neurological damage to the female urethra such that it no longer is an effective barrier to sudden increases of bladder pressure. It displays as small urine leakage during times of increased intra-abdominal pressure, such as coughing, sneezing, and rising to a standing position. The common treatment has been surgical, but the AHCPR guidelines advocate pelvic muscle exercise or medication (or both) as an initial approach (AHCPR, 1992a). However, it is unclear if any of these targeted SUI treatments are appropriate for patients with dementia.

Urge incontinence presents as sudden, unpredictable urges to urinate that cannot be controlled and results in large-volume urine leakage. This bladder hyperactivity is due to loss of central nervous system inhibition. Usually idiopathic in the elderly, urge incontinence is common after acute cerebral vascular accident and Parkinson's disease (Geirsson, Fall, & Lindstrom, 1993). It is also associated with dementia. Recommended treatments are bladder training exercise, which requires learning ability, or medication. But a learned exercise is not feasible for patients with late-stage dementia, and Skelly and Flint (1995) reported that medication is largely ineffective for this group and also causes unpleasant side effects, such as dry mouth and constipation. Thus, at this time there is no urge incontinence treatment specific to patients with late-stage dementia.

The term functional incontinence may be applied to urine loss in patients with dementia. This label is appropriate for individuals with normal bladder and sphincter function who have problems with urine control due solely to immobility, communication inabilities, or cognitive impairment (AHCPR, 1992a). True functional incontinence is probably uncommon in patients with dementia because the incontinence is generally also associated with a physical urological problem. This diagnosis should not be used unless a careful assessment has excluded all other causes of incontinence. Treatment for functional incontinence consists of a range of toileting techniques that are managed by caregivers. These techniques are also appropriate for patients with dementia who have known urologic diagnoses for their incontinence but who are unable to be treated with conventional therapies, as just discussed.

The most basic toileting technique is routine toileting, sometimes called timed voiding. It consists of toileting the patient every 2–3 hr on a fixed schedule (usually 8, 10, 12, etc.). The goal is to decrease bladder volume, with a corresponding decrease in stimulus to void between toiletings and lower volume wetting if incontinence does occur. It is a common and old technique that has received little research, perhaps because it is thought to be effective in practice. Indeed, two descriptive studies found an 85–91% improvement in incontinence (Lowenthal, Metz, & Patton, 1958; Soybein & Awad, 1982).

A slightly more complex toileting technique is habit retraining, also known as patterned urge-response toileting. In this technique the patient's bladder-emptying pattern is determined through pant checks or electronic sensor monitoring systems. In this way a toileting schedule can be individualized rather than set to fixed and arbitrary times. The technique has had little research, but one comparative study found an overall 86% improvement in control, with one third of patients improving by 25% or more (Colling, Ouslander, Hadley, Eisch, & Campbell, 1992).

Prompted voiding is a toileting technique that combines routine toileting on a 1–2 hr frequency with patient-directed communication and social reinforcement of bladder cues. This technique has had substantive research, showing an overall 75% improvement, with about one third of patients decreasing incontinence to less than once in 12 hr (Schnelle, 1991; Schnelle et al., 1993).

All three techniques can be used with people with late-stage dementia. The key is staff training and monitoring in implementing the techniques. It is not surprising that such staff-intensive toileting programs have been found to be more costly than usual care, which results in higher rates of incontinence (Schnelle, Sowell, Hut, & Traugher, 1988). Thus, one needs to examine cost–benefit factors on an individual basis. Although toileting in general is a desirable goal, it may be that patient comfort levels during late-stage dementia dictate either a combination of toileting and use of incontinence products (e.g., daytime toileting with a nighttime pad) or no toileting and management with several products (e.g., daytime management with a condom or diaper or brief and nighttime management with a pad). Indwelling catheters or even intermittent catheterization for other than urethral obstruction or other specific bladder or skin problems is not recommended (Skelly & Flint, 1995).

There are a wide range of incontinence products on the market, and caregivers should be familiar with what is available. An excellent resource guide is available for modest cost from a nonprofit organization, Help for Incontinent People (1995). Unfortunately, there have been few comparative trials of these products within the United States, and there are no data on products specific to people with late-stage dementia. However, several authors have provided useful discussions to aid in incontinence product use (Cottenden, 1992; Jeter, 1990). It is helpful to become familiar with product terminology and specific features. Consider exactly how the product will be used (e.g., if it is a pant or diaper to be worn while seated, then size measurements should be made while the patient is seated). Consider storage and disposal or washing instructions. Seek product use information; many companies provide good teaching materials. And provide good skin care, checking for signs of irritation regularly.

Case example   *Mrs. Jackson was an 86-year-old who had had progressive dementia for 3 years. She was bedfast, in a fetal position, and showed little response to stimuli. She required total care, and her urinary incontinence, which had been large volume was now a constant dribble. Recently she had developed diarrhea. On examination Mrs. Jackson was found to have a distended bladder and a mass of hard stool in her rectum.*

With Mrs. Jackson positioned and padded, a disposable low-volume phosphate enema was administered with a poor return. Lidocaine 5% was applied topically to the anus, and in 5–10 min, a digital manipulation to break up the fecal mass was attempted with some success. A second disposable enema was administered with an improved return, and Mrs. Jackson's bladder emptied at the same time. For the next 3 days Mrs. Jackson received a daily disposable enema 30 min after breakfast, which was her best meal of the day. It was discovered that Mrs. Jackson would drink 4–5 oz. of a mixture of prune juice and warm water. She was begun on a daily schedule of this beverage, a stool softening agent, and a fluid goal of at least 1,000 ml per day.

Case discussion   Mrs. Jackson had overflow incontinence caused by a fecal mass pressing through soft tissue to obstruct her bladder outflow. The fecal mass acted as both a block and an irritant to the bowel, preventing stool from passing and causing a thin diarrhea. Treatment was directed at softening and breaking up the fecal mass in her rectum as well as developing a plan to prevent constipation in the future. After treatment, Mrs. Jackson had a soft bowel movement every 2 or 3 days and was more comfortable.

Fecal Incontinence

Fecal incontinence displaying as diarrhea or thin, watery stool may be a sign of fecal impaction, as discussed previously. Three other factors are primary in initial assessment of a diarrhea type of fecal incontinence: overaggressive bowel programs, nutritional consequences, and medication. Bowel programs to prevent constipation need to be individualized to take into account body size and nutritional intake. A daily bowel movement probably is not a realistic goal for frail patients with late-stage dementia. Finding the patient's comfort level and body rhythms may mean that a bowel movement once or twice a week is perfectly satisfactory. Nutritional consequences are many and include the need to adjust hyperosmotic enteral feedings for those so fed, determining whether there is lactose intolerance, and examining for infectious diarrhea. Medication side effects often cause bowel hypermotility, and this may be especially so when there is a need to adjust for decreasing body weight and activity with smaller dosages. Of course, fecal incontinence can be caused by many other different conditions and needs to be evaluated (Barrett, 1992). However, fecal incontinence of formed stool in patients with late-stage dementia is most likely due to patients' failure to recognize and communicate full bowel sensations. It is helpful to know when a patient has typically moved his or her bowels and to target that timeframe. Using the gastrocolic reflex (i.e., food in the stomach causes rectal contractions), would suggest bowel toileting after meals as a useful approach (Ganong, 1985). Further, it is possible to train the bowel to empty at a specific time by using glycerin or bisacodyl suppositories (Goldstein, Brown, Holt, Gallagher, & Winograd, 1989).

Pressure Ulcers

Pressure ulcers, also known as pressure sores or decubiti, are skin lesions caused by pressure to underlying tissue. They are typically over bony areas such as the hip or coccyx. Patients with late-stage dementia may have multiple risks for pressure ulcers: decreased mobility, malnutrition, urinary and fecal incontinence, and fluctuating levels of consciousness (Evans, Andrews, Chutka, Fleming, & Garness, 1995). These ulcers complicate and compromise care to debilitated patients. Thus, care to prevent pressure ulcers is critically important.

Daily skin inspection, especially over vulnerable areas, helps identify potential problems early. Because dry skin is often found in old people, a topical moisturizer is good preventive care if it is applied gently and without massage over bony prominences. This latter precaution, no massage over bony areas, is important to teach caregivers because it may require a change in common practice. Research has not shown that such massage is helpful and, of more concern, it has shown that it may be harmful (AHCPR, 1992b).

Attention should be paid to potential skin friction or sliding damage while moving the patient up or down in bed, turning the patient, or transferring the patient from bed to chair. Use of a draw sheet or special lifting pad can be very helpful. Individuals at risk need to be repositioned at least every 2 hr and may benefit from pressure-reducing devices such as special pads or mattresses (AHCPR, 1992b).

Contractures

Patients with late-stage dementia are at risk for contractures and fixed joints because of immobility in general and specific dementia-related neurological changes. These changes include abnormal muscle tone, joint rigidity, and the inability to relax voluntarily (*paratonia;* Mayeux, Foster, Rossor, & Whitehouse, 1993). From a simple framework, many contractures can be prevented by passive or active range of motion exercise in which joints are moved through a normal activity pattern. However, neurological motor system changes and a patient's inability to cooperate limit the success of prevention programs. Still, it is worthwhile to start such programs early and continue them as long as possible. Helpful considerations include combining range of motion exercise with bathing, precautionary use of analgesic medication, and use of music to move by.

Falls

The simplest way to prevent falls is to prohibit mobility, an action contrary to good care. The risk of a fall is a reasonable risk in an effort to maximize mobility as long as possible. Attention should be paid to patient foot care and foot wear. There may be need for podiatry service for hard nail and callus problems. Sturdy shoes with skid proof soles are best for walking. Examine the environment carefully for nonglare lighting and nonshiny floors. Bed height should permit the patient to sit on the edge with his or her feet flat on the floor. Chair dimensions should fit the patient without the need for pillows or constant adjustment. Thus, chair seat height is determined by the patient's lower leg to foot length, seat depth by thigh length, seat width by hip width, and back height by fit to the patient's back and head. Patients with contractures or particular comfort needs may require special or individualized chairs.

Evaluation of patient ability with adjustment for change is critical. Check for balance, gait, and energy level. Test for postural hypotension and examine current medications carefully for possible side effects that could increase fall risk. Consult with a physical therapist, not only for chair problems, but also for ambulation guidelines and the potential for assistive devices. Keep in mind the essentials such as correct, clean eyeglasses and working hearing aids for patients using these. Analgesic medication may be of great help because of common osteoarthritis or motor system dysfunction specific to dementia. In general, patients with late-stage dementia may be undermedicated for pain and discomfort but overmedicated with behavior-altering drugs.

CONCLUSION

Most of the physical iatrogenic problems in this patient population can be prevented by thorough and frequent assessments, anticipation of needs, and implementation of preventive protocols. Patients with late-stage dementia are usually not candidates for high technology services. They do, however, have complex physical care needs that require attention. Conscientious implementation of assessment and problem prevention protocols will likely save time, money, and staff frustration and will surely promote patient comfort.

BIBLIOGRAPHY

Agency for Health Care Policy and Research. (1992a). *Clinical practice guidelines, urinary incontinence in adults.* Rockville, MD: U.S. Department of Health and Human Services.

Agency for Health Care Policy and Research. (1992b). *Pressure ulcers in adults: Prediction and prevention.* Rockville, MD: U.S. Department of Health and Human Services.

Barrett, J. A. (1992). Fecal incontinence. In B. H. Roe (Ed.), *Clinical nursing practice: The promotion and management of continence* (pp. 196–219). New York: Prentice-Hall.

Belmin, J., Hervias, Y., Avellano, E., Oudart, O., & Durand, I. (1993). Reliability of sampling urine from disposable diapers in elderly incontinent women. *Journal of the American Geriatric Society, 41,* 1182–1186.

Brocklehurst, J. C. (1994). Constipation in the elderly. In M. A. Kamm & J. E. Lennard-Jones (Eds.), *Constipation.* Bristol, PA: Wrightson Biomedical.

Colling, T., Ouslander, T., Hadley, B. J., Eisch, J., & Campbell, E. (1992). The effects of patterned urge–response toileting (PURT) on urinary incontinence among nursing home residents. *Journal of the American Geriatric Society, 40,* 135–141.

Cottenden, A. M. (1992). Aids and appliances for incontinence. In B. H. Roe (Ed.), *Clinical nursing practice: The promotion and management of continence* (pp. 129–156). New York: Prentice-Hall.

Duffy, L. M., Cleary, T., Ahern, S., Kuskowski, M. A., West, M., Wheeler, L., & Mortimer, T. A. (1995). Clean intermittent catheterization: Safe, cost-effective bladder management for male residents of VA nursing homes. *Journal of the American Geriatric Society, 43,* 865–870.

Evans, J. M., Andrews, K. L., Chutka, D. S., Fleming, K. C., & Garness, S. L. (1995). Pressure ulcers: Prevention and management. *Mayo Clinical Proceedings, 70,* 789–799.

Ganong, W. F. (1985). *Review of medical physiology.* Los Altos, CA: Lange Medical Publications.

Geirsson, G., Fall, M., & Lindstrom, S. (1993). Subtypes of overactive bladder in old age. *Age and Aging, 22,* 125–131.

Goldstein, M. K., Brown, E. M., Holt, P., Gallagher, D., & Winograd, C. H. (1989). Fecal incontinence in an elderly man. *Journal of the American Geriatric Society, 37,* 991–1002.

Help for Incontinent People. (1995). *Guide to resources.* (Available at P.O. Box 544, Union, SC 29379. Phone: (803) 579-7900)

Herfindal, E. T., Gourley, D. R., & Hart, L. L. (Eds.) (1992). *Clinical pharmacy and therapeutics* (5th ed.). Philadelphia, PA: Williams & Wilkins.

Jeter, K. F. (1990). The use of incontinence products. In K. F. Jeter, N. Faller, & C. Norton (Eds.), *Nursing for continence* (pp. 209–222). Philadelphia, PA: W. B. Saunders.

Lowenthal, M., Metz, D., & Patton, A. (1958). Nobody wants the incontinent. *RN, 21,* 82–85, 100.

Mahoney, D. F. (1993). Cerumen impaction, prevalence and detection in nursing homes. *Journal of Gerontological Nursing, 19*(4), 23–30.

Manyak, M. J. (1992, April). Pharmacologic treatment for benign prostatic hyperplasia. *Physician Assistant,* 103–107.

Mayeux, R., Foster, N. L., Rossor, M., & Whitehouse, P. J. (1993). The clinical evaluation of patients with dementia. In P. J. Whitehouse (Ed.), *Dementia* (pp. 92–129). Philadelphia: F. A. Davis.

Nicolle, L. E. (1993). Urinary infection in the elderly. In D. G. Oreopoulos, M. F. Michelis, & S. Herschorn (Eds.), *Nephrology and urology in the aged patient.* Boston, MA: Kluwer Academic.

Ouslander, J. G., Greengold, B. A., Silverblatt, F. J., & Garcia, T. P. (1987). An accurate method to obtain urine for culture in men with external catheters. *Archives of Internal Medicine, 147,* 286–288.

Ouslander, J. G., Schapira, M., & Schnelle, J. F. (1995). Urine specimen collection from incontinent female nursing home residents. *Journal of the American Geriatric Society, 43,* 279–281.

Riehmann, M., & Bruskewitz, R. C. (1994). Management of bladder outlet obstruction in elderly men. In P. D. O'Donnell (Ed.), *Geriatric urology.* Boston: Little, Brown.

Schnelle, J. F. (1991). *Managing urinary incontinence in the elderly.* New York: Springer.

Schnelle, J. F., Newman, D., White, M., Abbey, T., Wallston, K. A., Fogerty, T., & Ory, M. G. (1993). Maintaining continence in nursing home residents through application of industrial quality control. *The Gerontologist, 33*(1), 114–121.

Schnelle, J. F., Sowell, V. A., Hut, W., & Traugher, B. (1988). Reduction of urinary incontinence in nursing homes: Does it reduce or increase cost? *Journal of the American Geriatric Society, 36,* 34–39.

Skelly, T., & Flint, A. J. (1995). Urinary incontinence associated with dementia. *Journal of the American Geriatric Society, 43,* 286–294.

Soybein, S. K., & Awad, S. A. (1982). Behavioral treatment of urinary incontinence in geriatric patients. *CMA Journal, 127,* 863–864.

Chapter 7

Strategies for Eating, Swallowing, and Dysphagia

Judith I. Kulpa and Roxanne DePaul

This chapter provides the caregiver with an overview of normal swallowing in adults, changes in normal swallowing related to Alzheimer's disease, suggestions for identifying eating and swallowing problems, and tips for management. Application of assessment parameters and suggested interventions are presented through a case example.

CASE EXAMPLE

Mrs. Nasticki was a 68-year-old woman with Alzheimer's disease. She had been eating well up until 3 months previously, when her family members noticed that swallowing pills was becoming more difficult. In addition, meal times were becoming longer, and Mrs. Nasticki had lost 4 lbs over that same period of time. Coughing during eating and drinking was noted occasionally. Mrs. Nasticki was also beginning to refuse to eat certain foods, which she used to enjoy. At times, she bit down on the spoon or would not open her mouth to accept a food item. Most recently, Mrs. Nasticki tended to fall asleep toward the end of a meal. Coughing and a gurgly voice quality was heard for about 1 hr after a meal. Mrs. Nasticki continued to maintain eye contact during communication interactions with caregivers and responded best to sensory inputs that were visual, gestural, and tactile (touch). Her verbal expression consisted primarily of social greetings and meaningless vocalizations.

EATING: A SOCIAL PERSPECTIVE

For most people, eating is a pleasurable event and is done voluntarily several times daily. Eating not only provides the body with required nutrients but also creates an environment for socializing with family and friends, celebrating life's major milestones, and experiencing feelings of psychological well-being and nurturing. Eating and swallowing are complex acts that are usually taken for granted when all is going well. However, when there is a change in the normal ability to eat and swallow, the need to eat and drink suddenly takes precedence over the social and psychological aspects of mealtimes. In persons with irreversible dementia, nutrition and hydration play a key role in maintaining maximal functioning of the body's systems, from good skin condition and good bowel and bladder function to optimal cognitive functioning in the face of a progressive disease. Any change in a patient's ability to eat and drink safely and efficiently can have a serious and negative impact for that person, including directly precipitating the death of that person.

NORMAL SWALLOWING AND DYSPHAGIA

Normal swallowing involves approximately 26 sets of muscles of the mouth, throat, and foodpipe, as well as six nerves to these muscles. Normal swallowing is an organized, sequential, and well orchestrated series of events. A disorder of swallowing is called dysphagia. During a typical swallow, food or liquid will take 2 s or less to pass through the mouth and throat. Humans swallow over 1,000 times each day almost without thinking. For most people, if a little food or liquid gets into the airway or trachea, the material can easily be coughed up and redirected to the foodway or esophagus. The airway and foodway share the same tract; breathing and eating in this shared path occurs in a relatively automatic fashion. To help readers understand how to manage feeding and swallowing difficulties, a brief overview of the human anatomy used in swallowing is shown in Figure 7.1 and discussed below.

The food pathway includes all structures from the lips to the stomach and is functionally divided into three sections. As shown in Figure 7.1, the oral cavity is the first anatomical location of the swallowing pathway. The second region is the throat or pharynx (windpipe) and extends downward to connect with the stomach. Thus, the esophagus is located above the stomach and is the entry point for food and liquid substances descending from the mouth and pharynx to the stomach. If a substance is diverted or misled toward the airway (vocal folds and trachea), then an individual becomes at risk for *aspiration*. Aspiration occurs when food or liquid enters the airway through the larynx (voice box) and moves down the trachea and into the lungs. The anatomical relationship between the esophagus and the trachea places humans at greater risk for food entering the airway and lungs in contrast to other animal species.

Note in Figure 7.1 how the airway and foodway share a common space at the level of the throat or pharynx. This illustration shows the anatomy in a static or resting position. However, during swallowing, the airway is closed tightly until the food or liquid passes into the esophagus, and it is safe to take a breath again. Airway closure includes closure of the soft palate (velopharynx), closure of the epiglottis over the airway, elevation of the larynx, and closure of the vocal chords. A miscue in timing or position by any of the muscles involved with swallowing may result in coughing, clearing of the throat, or choking and possible

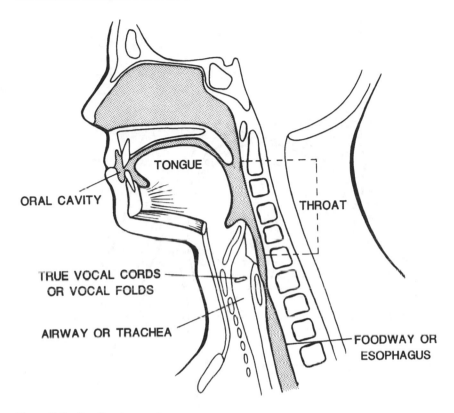

Figure 7.1 Swallowing anatomy.

airway obstruction. If food or liquid enters the larynx and drops below the vocal cords, aspiration has occurred. If large amounts of food or liquid are aspirated repeatedly, a patient may develop *aspiration pneumonia*. In normal persons, if aspiration occurs, vigorous coughing results in eventual clearing of the material aspirated. Persons with dementia may not sense food or liquid in the airway and consequently they may not cough or give the caregiver any indication that aspiration has occurred. This is called *silent aspiration.* Signs of aspiration may include elevated body temperature, positive lung sounds, weight loss, a mucoid or gurgly voice quality, regurgitation through the mouth or nose (or both), and coughing during or after meals. Persons with known gastroesophageal reflux disease or with nasogastric tubes are also at risk for aspiration.

Phases of the Normal Swallow

The normal swallow is typically considered as consisting of three general phases or stages. This scheme is well accepted among health care professionals and provides the rationale for interventions noted later in the chapter. Figure 7.2 illustrates these phases in anatomical cross-section.

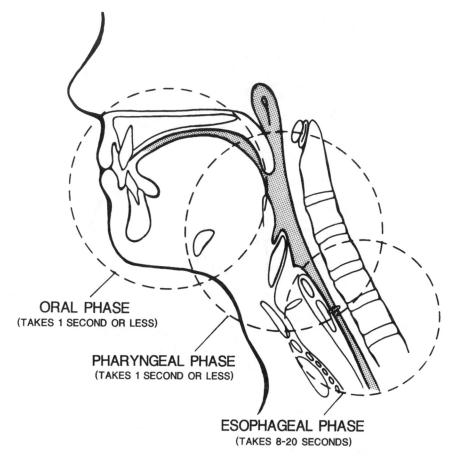

ORAL PHASE
(TAKES 1 SECOND OR LESS)

PHARYNGEAL PHASE
(TAKES 1 SECOND OR LESS)

ESOPHAGEAL PHASE
(TAKES 8-20 SECONDS)

Figure 7.2 Swallowing phases.

The phases of the swallow are further illustrated in Figure 7.3, showing the passage along the anatomical path for swallowing. Oral preparation includes chewing (mastication) of the food substances and mixing the material with saliva. The result of this repetitive chewing and mixing is the formation of a bolus—the material (liquid or solid) that will be swallowed and eventually moved to the stomach. The prepared bolus is brought to the front of the mouth and held (Figure 7.3a), and then the tongue rapidly contracts and squeezes the material to the back of the mouth. When the material reaches the back of the mouth, it triggers the swallow or pharyngeal phase (Figure 7.3b, 7.3c, and 7.3d), in which the bolus is propelled to the top of the esophagus. The final stage is the esophageal phase, during which the bolus is passed through the esophagus (Figure 7.3e).

The preparatory and oral phases of swallowing are under volitional control; that is, people are capable of purposefully governing muscle contraction and resultant movement in these phases. In contrast, the pharyngeal and esophageal

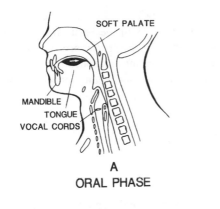
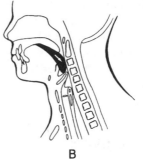

A
ORAL PHASE

B
PHARYNGEAL PHASE

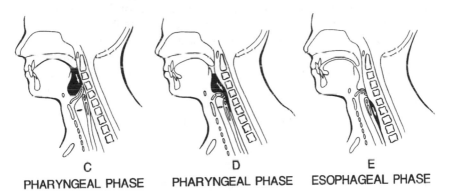

C
PHARYNGEAL PHASE

D
PHARYNGEAL PHASE

E
ESOPHAGEAL PHASE

Figure 7.3 Swallowing phases showing transport of food or liquid (dark area).

phases of swallowing occur more as automatic responses, over which there is no voluntary control. During the phases of swallowing, sensory information about the position of the bolus, taste, and temperature is conveyed by nerves to specific areas of the nervous system.

The process of swallowing is very efficient, with the oral and pharyngeal phases taking 1 s or less for each phase, and the esophageal phase taking 8–20 seconds on average. If a swallow takes 10 s or longer to occur, the patient may be at risk for nutritional compromise. The swallowing system automatically accommodates thin and thick consistencies, small and large bites, varying tastes, and slow and fast rates of intake. However, in persons with a neurologic disease, such as Alzheimer's disease, the tolerance of the swallow system for normal foods and liquids may be altered dramatically, changing individual food and liquid choices.

In dementia, difficulties in eating and swallowing are due to a reduction in the efficiency of swallowing. That is, the critical timing and coordination of movement for producing the phases of swallowing begin to break down as the degree of neurological impairment increases. Although little is known about the specific impairment and nature of the dysphagia in late-stage dementia, it does seem likely that because of the degree of cell loss in the brain in certain areas, swallowing will become increasingly disordered. From a more functional perspective, many researchers and physicians attribute alterations in eating and swallowing patterns primarily to cognitive decline and reduction in the motivation to eat.

RELATED ISSUES IN EFFECTIVE EATING AND SWALLOWING

Oral Hygiene

Recent research on the relationship between poor oral hygiene and an increased risk for aspiration pneumonia has heightened awareness of the need for aggressive oral hygiene programs and dental care in special populations. Maintaining good oral and dental care reduces the risk of bacterial growth and maintains normal viscosity of saliva. The oral cavity needs moisture, and any change in the level of moisture, such as dryness or xerostomia, may affect the taste of foods and reduce swallowing efficiency. This is especially important to monitor if a patient is on any medications that may cause dryness. Oral hygiene can be challenging in a patient with a biting response or other primitive reflexes.

Dentures

In normal healthy elders, consistent wearing and use of dentures contributes positively to proper diet, oromotor and craniofacial stability, and a good appetite. Thus, caregiver efforts include maintaining an individual's use of assistive devices such as eyeglasses, hearing aids, and dentures for as long as possible. Use of dentures through late-stage dementia will vary and can depend on several variables: weight loss and subsequent poor fit of dentures, noted patient oral discomfort or pain, reduced tolerance or gagging with dentures in place, or risk of choking or airway obstruction. If the patient can wear dentures, staff should make every effort to maintain wearing time, especially during meals and waking hours. Routine visits to the dentist for evaluation of the oral cavity and appliances should be scheduled.

INTERVENTION STRATEGIES: MANAGING FEEDING AND EATING IN LATE-STAGE DEMENTIA

Maintaining adequate nutrition and hydration and avoiding aspiration are the ultimate goals of the eating and swallowing process. Unfortunately, many factors can precipitate failure in achieving these goals. According to Groher (1990), several factors can prevent individuals from taking sufficient amounts by mouth: impaired swallowing (dysphagia), type of diet, feeding position, the environmental setting for the meal, changes in health or medical status, medications and possible side effects on swallowing and mental status, and the patient's ability to cooperate with feeding assistance.

In dementia, the functional focus is usually on the progressive changes in cognition (thinking, reasoning, and memory) that these individuals experience. There are no studies of swallowing and changes in sensorimotor control for speech and swallowing in late-stage dementia. Clearly, the severe to profound degree of memory loss makes such study difficult. Late-stage dementia, however, has been associated with changes in speech and language. Many patients with dementia have language changes that are similar to aphasia (language disruption due to focal brain damage) and motor problems similar to apraxia (difficulty programming and sequencing oral movements for speech and swallowing). Notably, individuals considered to be in late-stage dementia may exhibit no volitional speech and appear mute. The breakdown of movement control for speech in late-stage dementia suggests that sensorimotor control difficulties in swallowing are also likely. For example, many individuals with late-stage dementia take more than half an hour to complete their meals; lose weight; cough, choke, and regurgitate during feeding; and have recurrent bouts of pneumonia. As noted previously, these are usually signs indicating dysphagia. Interdisciplinary intervention with the dietitian and occupational therapist is critical for successful management of feeding and swallowing. Both professionals work along with the speech-language pathologist to assist the caregiver in implementing successful feeding and swallowing.

Phase 1: Assessing Eating and Swallowing

Caregivers can assist professionals in evaluating swallowing safety and efficiency by observing the following.

- Is there any observable muscle weakness of mouth, face, or tongue?
- Does the patient hold or pocket food in the mouth?
- Is there drooling or loss of saliva control?
- Is routine aggressive oral hygiene and dental care provided?
- Is the patient's mouth moist or dry?
- What foods and liquids work best?
- Are particular tastes preferred by the patient?
- Are certain consistencies noxious and rejected by the patient?
- Is the patient now refusing foods or liquids previously accepted?
- Is mealtime taking longer, that is, more than 30–60 min?
- Do meals need to be smaller in size, yet more frequent during the day?

Phase 2: Managing External Controls

The first level of management at home or in a facility is to observe and then alter several factors in the environment that may serve to distract the individual from focusing on the meal. Table 7.1 provides several strategies for modifying the mealtime environment to maximize efficiency during feeding periods.

Table 7.1   External strategies for mealtimes

Variable	Strategies
Environment	Reduce distractions—noise, physical activity (e.g., no television or radio)
	Provide good lighting
	Provide small group dining or individual dining in a separate room
	Keep the room temperature comfortable
	Enhance food aromas and reduce other odors, such as cleaning solutions and urine in the dining area
Table setting	Keep setting simple
	Minimize number of items on table (remove salt and pepper shakers, napkin holders, decorations, etc.)
	Use solid color dishes and table cloth
	Use a placemat or tray to provide a cue that the plate belongs in a specific spot
	Provide nonskid placemats, a damp washcloth, or dinnerware with suction cups to prevent dishes from sliding
	Provide a long straw or cups with spouts for liquids
	Use a large lipped bowl rather than a plate
Utensils	Avoid use of plastic utensils
	Provide one utensil at a time (spoon or fork)
	Offer finger foods rather than requiring use of a spoon or fork (e.g., sandwiches, chicken nuggets, tater tots, cheese squares)
	Allow person to drink soup from a cup
Meal schedule	Schedule meals for consistent times every day
	Allow time to prepare the person for the meal
	Offer the food within 5–10 min of seating
	Limit stimulating physical exercise immediately prior to meals
	Make sure person is as comfortable as possible prior to meals (diapers, clothing)
	Seat person in an upright position with the head comfortably forward (not tilted back)
	Provide assistive devices (dentures, hearing aids, glasses)
Time	Provide adequate time for the person to eat or be fed (feeding may take from 45 min to 1 hr)
	Allow a warm-up period for feeding (offer small amount, 1/2 tsp initially and increase to 1 tsp per bite)
	Offer small frequent meals or snacks rather than three large meals
Food	Serve food previously well liked

Phase 3: Managing How to Feed

Specific feeding strategies are listed in Table 7.2. The assumption in the use of feeding strategies is that the individual is capable of eating by mouth without aspiration. These strategies are for the feeder to implement during meals to decrease the risk of aspiration, not for the patient to make modifications.

**Table 7.2   Strategies for maintaining adequate nutrition and
hydration through safe feeding practices**

Role of feeder	Possible strategies
Provide verbal cues	Tell person about the food being introduced Give brief step-by-step instructions: • "Here comes the food" • "Open your mouth" • "Chew" • "Close lips" • "Swallow"
Provide encouragement	Reinforce during the meal: • "Good, keep eating"
Provide visual cues	Demonstrate eating prior to giving food Use word or picture cards

Provide physical assistance	Guide person's hand from place to mouth
	   (if self-feeding)
	Lightly touch areas such as the chin as a reminder
	   to chew food in the mouth and while instructing
	   "Chew"

Phase Four: Managing Special Problems

Many individuals with dementia exhibit reflexes or involuntary motor responses that may interfere with productive eating and swallowing. These reflexes are a result of brain cell changes associated with dementia, other neurologic conditions such as Parkinson's disease, or normal aging (Jacobs & Grossman, 1980). They are often referred to as primitive or infantile reflexes because they appear similar to reflexes seen in human infants. However, the appearance of these responses in elders is due to damage in specific parts of the brain, whereas in infants these reflexes disappear when brain cells mature and prevent lower nervous system centers from responding involuntarily to stimulation (Brodal, 1981).

The most frequent orofacial responses to introduction of food or drink into the mouth observed in adults include chewing, sucking, snouting, and biting. These responses may be elicited by simply entering the patient's visual field as material is brought to the mouth, but they are more typically elicited by touching the perioral area (the lips and the surrounding area) or the inside of the mouth (tongue, gums, teeth, and palate). Table 7.3 provides some possible solutions and management techniques for these problems.

The individual with late-stage dementia may also exhibit some unusual and exaggerated responses in the upper extremities when specific stimulation is provided. A caregiver may inadvertently elicit a forced grasp response. This response is characterized by compulsive grasping following gentle touch to the palmar surface of the hand or fingers. If an object, for example a spoon, is placed in the hand, then flexion of the fingers occurs and the object is held firmly. This involuntary reaction has been described as consisting of two parts: the catching

Table 7.3   Specific methods for special problems

Problem	Possible solution
Holding food in mouth during feeding session	Use verbal instructions and physical prompts • Say "Swallow" while gently pushing head forward and touching chin
Holding food in mouth during or after feeding session	Clear person's mouth of any food particles after feeding Keep individual upright for 15–30 min following the meal or snack
Perseveration (repetitious and continuous involuntary movement). A snout or suckle reflex may be elicited during spoon or straw placement. A biting reflex may be elicited during feeding	If the perseverative movement is successfully allowing for food or liquid transfer, then wait until a reasonable amount of substance passes and then break the perseveration by applying pressure. • For chewing, apply firm pressure under chin • For suckling, apply firm pressure with the fingertips • Avoid plastic utensils that can be broken by a firm bite; avoid fingers in the mouth • Optimal spoon placement puts pressure on the mid-region of the tongue; touching the gums or teeth may elicit a biting reflex • Pulling on a utensil or straw during a suckle may stimulate a bite and engage the feeder in a tug of war • Apply pressure on the jaw and cheek muscles to break the biting reflex
Refusal to eat, paranoia, and bizarre cravings or refusal to eat because of unrealistic concerns	Remove objects that look like foods (plastic fruit, dog biscuits, etc.) Allow person to observe food preparation Respond directly: "Your food is covered by the rent," etc. Use props, such as a meal card that gets punched at each meal
Changes in status • Volume of food or liquid intake increases or decreases • Notable weight loss or gain • Changes in awareness and consciousness • Notable coughing and choking • Regurgitation or reflux through the nose or mouth (or both) • Fever- or flu-like symptoms • Voice sounds gurgly • Noisy breathing or unusual chest sounds	Report changes to the primary caregiver (nurse, nurse practitioner, physician) and in nursing home facilities report changes to the dietitian and the speech-language pathologist

phase, which results from an initial touch, and a holding stage, when the object is held as the particular muscles contract around the object. Apart from the difficulties that this reaction provokes during mealtimes, the same reaction may be elicited when the individual is touched by caregivers or others during activities of daily living or in social contexts. Thus, a simple handshake may be misinterpreted as not wanting a person to leave because the individual will not release the outstretched hand spontaneously. The grasping reaction also needs to be terminated by physical manipulation of the hand or by repositioning the individual (Brodal, 1981).

Phase 5: Establish a Patient Care Plan

Any suspected alteration in nutrition or hydration in individuals with Alzheimer's disease needs immediate attention. The appendix in this chapter provides a sample patient care plan as a framework for assessment and possible intervention. Problems including weight loss, dehydration, food preferences, feeding, and nutritional risk are addressed, along with possible ways to manage the problems. A medical speech-language pathologist, dietitian, and occupational therapist are qualified to assist a caregiver in generating a plan of care.

INSTRUMENTAL ASSESSMENT

In addition to a clinical assessment of swallowing, one of several instrumental assessments available may also be needed. Videofluoroscopy and videoendoscopy are commonly used, and a newer noninvasive technique, swallowing auscultation, may be predictive of aspiration. Instrumental assessments of swallowing are more formal and, depending on the patient, can be frightening or threatening. If an instrumental assessment is ordered by a physician, a caregiver known to the patient should accompany the patient to the procedure and participate in the procedure. Caregivers should also advise the professional who is testing the patient of the foods and liquids the patient likes and tolerates best for optimal study outcomes. However, the prognosis for successful completion of an instrumental swallowing study with a person with late-stage dementia is guarded because of the level of cooperation needed for these assessments.

Assessment of swallowing safety and efficiency is a team process, with input to be gleaned from family, caregivers, and professionals. Questions regarding swallowing behavior and management in persons with Alzheimer's disease can be directed to the physician (geriatrician, neurologist, or otolaryngologist) and to a certified and licensed speech-language pathologist. Speech-language pathologists are trained to identify and manage dysphagia. A referral from the primary physician will be necessary for the speech-language pathologist to evaluate a patient's swallowing abilities.

OPTIONS FOR DYSPHAGIA MANAGEMENT

Research has demonstrated that the ability to swallow efficiently and safely is maintained well into the ninth decade of life in persons without age-related diseases. Because Alzheimer's disease or related dementias are neurological disorders, some general changes in normal swallowing can be expected. As Alzheimer's or related disease progresses, health care providers depend more on observations than on feedback from the patient. It may be difficult to determine whether refusal to eat represents a fear of eating, an inability of the brain to process the incoming stimuli, a will to die, or a combination of these and other factors. When the disease has reached the later stages, it becomes even more difficult to determine the safest and most efficient way of maintaining nutrition and hydration. Because swallowing in late-stage dementia has not been studied scientifically, these unknowns make deciding to feed or not to feed by mouth an ethical dilemma and a quality of life issue for the patient and caregivers.

Caregivers no doubt have heard or read about life support measures, such as ventilators and other biomedical devices. More recently the issue of nutrition and hydration as an ordinary versus extraordinary means of medical care has arisen. The use of advance directives regarding use of ordinary versus extraordinary means of maintaining nutrition and hydration, improved methods of swallowing assessment, and increased knowledge about health care risks related to disordered swallowing, such as pneumonia, facilitates thoughtful decision making for the person with late-stage Alzheimer's disease.

Family and caregivers should be aware that the incidence of dysphagia in chronic care settings is high affecting one third to one half of patients. When feeding problems are also considered, the percentage of elders with eating-related problems increases to 72%. The patients with dementia are represented in these figures, and identifying the presence of aspiration is critical for their health. Furthermore, Langmore, Fig, Terpenning, Schork, and Loesche (1995) recently reported that dependence for feeding is one factor significantly related to aspiration and pneumonia. That is, patients with dementia who are completely dependent on others for meals are at a higher risk for aspiration and aspiration pneumonia.

According to Ciocon (1990) and Ciocon, Silverstone, Graver, and Foley (1988), dysphagia with frequent aspiration is the most common indication for tube feeding elders in long-term care facilities. Tube feeding generally means that a patient is no longer fed by mouth. Occasionally, some oral feeding may continue concomitantly with tube feedings. The term *enteral nutrition* is used to describe the use of tube feeding as the primary source of nutrition. Tube feeding may be viewed as a viable option in the presence of dysphagia with frequent aspiration in neurodegenerative conditions that will only worsen in time. Also to be considered for patients with late-stage dementia who require long-term enteral nutrition are gastrostomy and jejunostomy tubes. Nasogastric tubes may be indicated for patients requiring temporary alteration in oral feeding. However, some patients refuse the insertion of gastrostomy or jejunostomy tubes and a nasogastric tube may be inserted as long as an individual can tolerate it. Patients with dementia may pull out a nasogastric tube, further precluding this tube as a reasonable option.

Proper communication of findings to the patient and guardian is paramount and should include the benefits, burdens, and risks of continued oral feeding. Decisions about whether or not to feed by mouth decisions are difficult at best and pull at the heartstrings of caregivers, family members, and professionals. Development of a plan before a crisis occurs, ongoing communication with the physician and other health care professionals, and family consensus will assist in decisions regarding oral intake and nutrition.

CASE DISCUSSION

Mrs. Nasticki had several behaviors related to swallowing changes, including suspected aspiration. This was signaled by her coughing during the meal, especially on liquids. An option to consider is to thicken the liquids she receives to a nectar consistency. Commercially available thickeners can be used. Another indicator of possible aspiration was the coughing and gurgly quality of Mrs. Nasticki's voice about 1 hr after a meal. This may signal some reduction in esophageal motility (disorganized or incomplete cleaning of the esophagus), gastroesophageal reflux (backward or retrograde flow of stomach contents up through the esophagus), a possible diverticulum (pocket in the esophageal tissue), or failure of the pharynx or throat to clear food and liquid. Staff should keep Mrs. Nasticki upright during the first hour after meals and should discuss the possible medical problems with her physician. More formal testing, such as a videofluoroscopic or videoendoscoic swallow study, may be indicated. During feeding, staff may want to slightly flex Mrs. Nasticki's head and use the facilitation techniques listed in Tables 7.2 and 7.3. Caregivers can also query the physician about changing the form of medication to liquids or about crushing medications and presenting them in applesauce or pudding. Biting the spoon and refusal to accept a food item orally are the manifestations of primitive reflexes. Caregivers can apply tactile facilitating techniques to overcome these responses and maximize oral intake. To reduce fear of the arrival of the food or spoon, caregivers should make sure that Mrs. Nasticki sees the food approaching, take advantage of her response to visual stimuli, and enhance the meal environment (see Table 7.1). Mrs. Nasticki's weight loss is a concern and can be the result of several factors, including the onset of primitive oral reflexes, a suspected slowed and less efficient swallow with prolonged mealtimes, medications (especially if a new drug has recently been initiated), or an undiagnosed medical condition. Mealtime sleepiness may also signal a drug-related disorder. Caregivers should apply several interventions: (a) discussion with Mrs. Nasticki's physician regarding medications and any underlying medical problem; (b) consultation with the dietitian regarding calorie intake, calorie loading, menu planning, and food texture adaptation; (c) consultation with the speech-language pathologist regarding swallowing techniques to apply during mealtime; (d) alteration of the mealtime duration and scheduling; (e) addition of daytime snacks; (f) use of commercially available adaptive foods; and (g) use of positive reward and verbal praise for good eating.

CONCLUSION

Safe and efficient swallowing is pivotal to wellness in the normal aging population and becomes even more important in persons with Alzheimer's disease and related dementias. The challenge to maintain adequate patient nutrition and hydration is great and requires creativity on the part of the caregiver team. Caregivers need to rely on fellow team members, thus garnering the collective advice and expertise available to nurture and support the person with Alzheimer's disease. Caregivers need to keep in mind the complexity of swallowing and airway protection and, most of all, use common sense and do what works best for the patient.

BIBLIOGRAPHY

Brodal, A. (1981). *Neurological anatomy* (pp. 241–240). New York: Oxford University Press.
Ciocon, J. O. (1990). Indications for tube feedings in elderly patients. *Dysphagia, 5,* 1–5.
Ciocon, J. O., Silverstone, F. A., Graver, L. M., & Foley, C. J. (1988). Tube feedings in elderly patients. *Archives of Internal Medicine, 148,* 429–433.
Groher, M. E. (1990). Managing dysphagia in a chronic care setting: An introduction. *Dysphagia, 5,* 59–60.
Jacobs, L., & Grossman, M. D. (1980). Three primitive reflexes in normal adults. *Neurology, 30,* 189–192.
Langmore, S., Fig L., Terpenning, M., Schork, T., & Loesche, W. (1995). *Risk factors of pneumonia in geriatric patients.* Paper presented at the Third Annual Scientific Meeting of the Dysphagia Research Society, Washington, DC.

APPENDIX: SAMPLE PATIENT CARE PLAN

Date: _____   Name: _____   Date of Birth: _____
Current Diagnosis: _____
Allergies: _____
Current Diet/Snacks: _____
    Food/Liquid adaptations: _____ thickened liquids ( ) nectar ( ) honey ( ) pudding
    _____
    _____

    Target Daily Calorie Goal: _____
    [Work with dietitian]
                         _____ % protein
                          _____ % fat
                          _____ % carbohydrates
                          _____ % sodium
                          _____ % cholesterol
                          _____ % fiber
                          _____ % vitamins
Height: _____   Ideal Body Weight: _____   Current Body Weight: _____

ALTERATION IN NUTRITION OR HYDRATION

Problem	Intervention	Follow-up	Resolution
Weight loss	Monitor weight Monitor intake and output Offer between meal snacks Monitor for slowed swallowing Monitor for prolonged mealtimes Monitor for possible aspiration		
Dehydration	Monitor for signs and symptoms 　　of fluid or electrolyte imbalance Monitor oral mucosa moisture Enforce good oral hygiene Monitor skin turgor Note changes in medications Offer water or fluid hourly		
Change in food 　preferences	Review food preferences with 　　family, surrogate caregivers Try alternate food or liquid textures Monitor for primitive reflexes Use feeding techniques		
Change in 　self-feeding or 　feeding 　assistance	Monitor for possible swallowing 　changes Monitor for environmental factors, 　feeding position prior to 　and during meals		
Onset of nutri- 　tional or 　hydration risk	Initiate consults: medical, dietary, 　speech–language pathology, 　occupational therapy, pharmacy, 　other Review nutritional information 　from dietitian Document responses to 　interventions		

EXPECTED OUTCOMES:

Checklist [✔]　　 _____　　 Improved or maintained weight
　　　　　　　　 _____　　 Resolution of nutrition or hydration risk
　　　　　　　　 _____　　 Improved or maintained swallowing efficiency or
　　　　　　　　　　　　 safety
　　　　　　　　 _____　　 Advance directives reviewed with alternate plan of
　　　　　　　　　　　　 care initiated

Chapter 8

A Supportive Environment for People With Late-Stage Dementia

Margaret P. Calkins

It can be—and has been—argued that for people who are truly at the final stage of dementia, the physical environment makes very little difference. They do not appear to be able to respond to visual or acoustic stimuli. They are beyond the point of participating in activities and (some argue) are primarily in need of good care for their physical needs. Yet there is virtually no research to test this hypothesis. Although it may have evolved from clinical observation, it should be recognized that the environment around individuals with late-stage dementia may not have been addressing their needs. Thus, it may be the lack of congruence between these individuals' needs and the environment that has contributed to the apparent lack of impact of the environment.

Although the challenges of caring for someone in the early or middle stages of dementia are significant, there is a substantial body of literature—some based on research and some on clinical knowledge or anecdotal evidence—that provides multiple strategies for developing supportive and therapeutic care. A moderate but growing amount of attention has been directed at the physical environment. There are now several highly regarded design guides, based on comprehensive sets of therapeutic goals developed to guide care for this population, that provide a variety of suggestions for creating a supportive environment for individuals in the early and middle stages of a dementing illness. There is, however, no corresponding body of literature on caring for individuals with late-stage dementia, and there is virtually nothing on what constitutes an appropriate physical environment for this population. Thus, writing a chapter on the creation of supportive environments for individuals with late-stage dementia presents a unique set of challenges. With virtually no research and very little literature, this chapter should be viewed as a starting point—a set of hypotheses based on experience (the author's and others) with this population and interpolation of what might be appropriate at later stages of the disease based on knowledge of the disease process.

SURVEY

To generate more ideas, a survey was developed and sent to members of the Working Group on Research and Evaluation of Special Care Units [WRESCU], a special interest group of the Gerontological Society of America. The close to 150 WRESCU members comprise a broad range of individuals knowledgeable in various aspects of care and research on people with dementia, across all stages. A total of 30 surveys were returned (20% response rate), and the insights provided by these knowledgeable individuals have been incorporated into this chapter. Although the results of the survey are described in the appropriate sections of this chapter, a brief description and summary will help put the results into perspective. The questionnaire consisted of two parts. In the first part, respondents were asked to rate the importance of 35 specific environmental features on a 1–5 scale (1 = *not at all important;* 5 = *very important*). The mean scores for these 35 items ranged from 2.1 to 4.2, with an overall mean of 3.29. This suggests that either the items selected were generally not considered very important or that the physical environment in general is not considered to be very important for this population. The second part of the survey was open-ended and asked respondents to list the three most critical care needs (beyond basic physical needs) and the three most important environmental features of settings for late-stage dementia patients. The majority of items listed were identical or very similar to the items included in the first part of the questionnaire, supporting the notion that the physical environment is not viewed as very important for this population. In general, there was very little overlap in the open-ended section. There were never more than 6 respondents (20%) who listed the same features as important. This suggests either that people with late-stage dementia are very idiosyncratic and that each individual has unique needs (which the respondents were identifying on the basis of their own experiences) or that there is no consensus on what is appropriate for this population. In either case, there is clearly a need for more and better research.

This chapter begins with a brief examination of the justification for the creation of therapeutic environments for people with late-stage dementia. This is followed by an exploration of specific micro-level environmental features which are most tangible to the person with late-stage dementia. Finally, macro-level environmental issues are addressed for both the individuals with dementia and their caregivers (professional and family).

DOES IT REALLY MATTER?

The first question to be addressed is whether it is really necessary to deal with the design of the physical environment for people with late-stage dementia. Some have argued that in the final stages of the disease the individual is on the border of a vegetative state, "awake but unaware," but others have suggested that individuals in late-stage dementia experience more than they can communicate or exhibit (Levy, Knill-Jones, & Plum, 1978, cited in Norberg, Melin, & Asplund, 1986). Unable to control any aspect of their surroundings, which may be continually invaded by well-meaning caregivers, and unable to voluntarily leave the setting, individuals with late-stage dementia may withdraw psychologically.

> There is a risk that, to feel safe, the patient will withdraw further into himself, and thus a vicious circle might start. The patient's ability to react adequately and distinctly to stimuli decreases. . .the stimulation given by caregivers decreases. . .the patient's reactions deteriorate further. . . . All human beings need stimulation to keep their brain functioning in a normal way. Deprivation of stimulation leads to a deterioration of behavior. (Norberg et al., 1986, p. 316)

Norberg et al.'s position is supported by Lawton and Nahemow's environmental docility hypothesis (Lawton, 1975, 1977). The person with late-stage dementia has very low competence, and therefore both the range and amount of environmental press must be quite limited in order to not completely overwhelm the individual. Care must also be taken to avoid understimulation of these individuals, as this can also have negative consequences. In the open-ended portion of the survey, two respondents specifically mentioned the provision of a stimulating but regulated sensory environment as one of the most critical features of settings for late-stage dementia. Beyond the amount of stimulation, its form—whether it is tactile or acoustic or olfactory, whether it is experienced as pleasurable or aversive, and whether the individual can exert any control over the stimulation—is critical.

Additional support can be found in a report by the Office of Technology Assessment (OTA; U.S. Congress, Office of Technology Assessment, 1992), which included a thorough review of the literature on care for people with dementia. OTA identified six theoretical concepts that apply to the care of individuals with dementia, three of which are of particular importance here. These concepts are not limited to the early stages of the disease but should be applied across all stages of dementia to maximize quality of life at all times. The first, and most fundamental, concept is that "something can be done for individuals with dementia" (U.S. Congress, Office of Technology Assessment, 1992, p. 16). Although there is no cure, a variety of symptoms are treatable and should be treated. Another concept is that "the behavior of individuals with dementia represents understandable feelings and needs, even if the individuals are unable to express the feelings or needs. Identifying and responding to those feelings and needs will reduce the incidence of behavioral symptoms" (U.S. Congress, Office of Technology Assessment, 1992, p. 17). Even when, at the end stages of the disease, the individual may not be able to express feelings and needs, one cannot assume the person has no feelings or needs. As long as they are alive, people have feelings and needs that should be met to promote quality of life. The other concept that is important for this discussion is fairly self-explanatory and suggests that "many aspects of the physical and social environment affect the functioning of individuals with dementia. Providing appropriate environments will improve their functioning and quality of life" (U.S. Congress, Office of Technology Assessment, 1992, p. 18). Taken together, these concepts provide a fundamental rationale for why it is appropriate and important to examine what constitutes a supportive environment for individuals with late-stage dementia. Thus, the argument made here is that the environment does make a difference.

It is also important to recognize that these severely compromised individuals are not the only users of these settings. There are also staff who must care for these individuals and families who are still emotionally and practically involved with their lives and their care. There may be others as well—volunteers, administrators, clergy, and more. Each of these users have environmental needs that should be addressed. Although the primary concern of this chapter is the identification of supportive environmental features for individuals with dementia, some basic staff and family needs are also addressed.

MICRO-LEVEL ENVIRONMENTAL ISSUES

Individuals in the final stages of dementia may have only limited awareness of their larger surroundings because the profound cognitive impairment has reduced their ability to perceive and process or make sense of the larger world around them. However, it is likely that they are affected by their immediate surroundings—such as things they can touch or are touched by. This section of the chapter explores some of these influences.

Tactile Stimulation

It has been suggested that people with cognitive impairments retain their ability to react to touch even when they do not respond to verbal communication (Barnet, 1972, cited in Norberg et al., 1986).

> **Case example**   *The woman cried out, almost continuously, in a loud wailing voice. There were no words in these cries, no clues as to what might be wrong. The staff, both well trained and caring, had tried various interventions to calm her down. After ensuring that her medications were appropriate and there was no untreated or undertreated illness, they gave her soft manipulatable objects, had classical music played in her room, or brought her closer to the nurses' station. The empathy that staff felt initially was wearing thin with the constant disruptive wailing, turning into frustration and irritation. Finally, after telling the staff what she was going to do, the clinical nurse specialist got into bed with the woman, lying on top of the covers and cradling the woman in her*

arms. She looked to be sure the woman wasn't more upset by this. With slow and deliberate movement, she began to stroke the arms and forehead of the agitated woman. After several minutes of this gentle massage, the woman began to quiet down. Then, in a clear voice that had not been heard in months, the woman said "Well! How come you're so calm?" The clinical nurse specialist responded, "I'm calm because everything is OK, and I'm going to stay here until you are calm too." (J. Rader, personal communication, 1995)

Case discussion   This scenario describes the therapeutic affect of a calming touch or soft tactile stimulation on one individual. Unfortunately, American society generally does not permit or encourage this type of close contact, certainly not by staff and often not even by family members. Yet 30% of the survey respondents listed soothing touch, rocking and cradling, and appropriate sensory stimulation as one of the three most critical environmental features of a well-designed late-stage dementia unit. Alternative strategies for providing positive tactile stimulation, besides getting into bed with the person, include lightly stroking the body with an angora sock or using a low-power hairdryer on warm to caress parts of the body. Lightly massaging the feet, hands, shoulders, and arms of someone who spends the vast majority of time lying down not only likely feels good but can be essential for maintaining circulation. This healing touch can provide an important way for family members to continue to participate in a meaningful way in the care of their relative. Many masseuses use essential oils when giving a massage and select oils for their calming or stimulating effects (see following section on olfactory stimulation).

The design of the furniture, particularly beds and chairs, is also critical, given the amount of time spent in them. The furniture should be comfortable and provide appropriate support, which may vary with each individual. There are beds that can automatically change the amount of pressure to different parts of the mattress, reducing the potential for developing decubiti. Be aware, however, that many of these products generate a loud and often unpleasant noise every time the pressure changes.

The person with late-stage dementia may still have some independent mobility of the hands and arms. Reaching out and encountering metal, plastic, or vinyl may discourage continued tactile explorations. Covering the arm of the chair or other adjacent furniture with cotton wool or other soft material may serve to promote continued mobility. In the survey, 65% of the respondents said that having soft manipulatable objects was somewhat to very important, but 21% felt this was not very or not at all important ($M = 3.467$). The survey also inquired about having a variety of different textured manipulatables, but the respondents felt this was slightly less important ($M = 3.267$). Although no specific ideas for soft manipulatable objects were given in the survey, possible ideas include fur pieces or a fur muff (this can be real or good quality fake fur); large sponges (natural or synthetic), which are easy to grasp and provide moderate resistance for squeezing; pieces of velvet fabric or velvet-covered stuffed animals; and cotton wool, which is commonly sewn and stuffed into a variety of shapes. Be sure all items are washable.

Olfactory Stimulation

There is increasing research to suggest that the olfactory system is centrally affected in Alzheimer's disease (Doty, 1989; Esiri, Pearson, & Powell, 1986; Kesslak et al., 1988; Pearson, Esiri, Hiorns, Wilcock, & Powell, 1985). Indeed, some researchers have suggested that the olfactory pathway may be involved in the pathologic course of the disease (Esiri et al., 1986; Talamo et al., 1989). Some research suggests that the impairments are global and affect basic ability to detect odors (Doty, Reyes, & Gergor, 1987; Talamo et al., 1989), but other research suggests the impairment is primarily in odor identification and not detection, which may be related to cognitive processing impairments (Koss, Weiffenbach, Haxby, & Friedland, 1988). Despite this limited but growing body of research, the functional impact of these changes is not well known, and increasing emphasis is being placed on the olfactory environment in earlier stages of the disease. It has been hypothesized that the smell of coffee brewing or food baking can not only act as an orientation cue to mealtime but also can stimulate the salivary glands and thereby possibly increase caloric intake (Calkins, 1988; Cohen & Weisman, 1991; Hiatt, 1981). No research on olfactory cues and their impact on individuals with late-stage dementia was found, so it is unknown whether food odors continue to trigger salivary response in this population. Further research on the influence of food-related aromas on people at all stages of dementia is needed.

There is a small but growing body of research on aromatherapy, and although no empirical research could be found on this population, there are references describing the clinical use and impact of essential oils (Buckwalter, 1992; Pounds, 1992). It is known, however, that aromas are more viscerally related to memories and often evoke a stronger response than visual images (Wells, 1990). There is also substantial research to indicate that fragrances affect mood (You, 1994). A number of dementia-specific facilities around the country use aromatherapy as a standard component of the program ("Massaging Will Be Tested," 1989). In one facility, observations of early and mid-stage dementia residents revealed that introduction or diffusion of calming oils, such as geranium, lavender, and marjoram, into the air reduced episodes of irritation between residents and encouraged them to stay in the social spaces longer (M. Carnarius, personal communication, Cleveland, 1995). Aromatherapy and the use of essential oils in massage are in need of more research to understand their potential therapeutic impact for all stages of dementia.

Acoustic Stimulation

The general level of noise in the environment is addressed in the macro environment section of this chapter. The concern here is with the potential impact of acoustic stimulation specifically targeted at the micro level. In one of the few empirical studies on environmental issues affecting individuals with late-stage dementia, Norberg et. al. (1986) found a significant difference in response to music versus therapeutic touch (massage) and object presentation directed at multiple senses (tactile, olfactory, visual, taste). Although the 2 participants in the study had different responses to music, and there are no objective methods available to assess the emotional quality of patients' reactions, the subjective impression of the researchers was that both patients reacted positively to the music. The music was selected to match participants' previous preferences—religious and popular songs—and was played on headphones. Each individual had one song in particular that she or he responded to. Although acknowledging the limitations of this study, which included only 2 late-stage dementia patients, Norberg et al. concluded that it is possible to reach or make contact with individuals in late-stage dementia and that it is possible to assess their reactions. The Hospice of the Western Reserve has had very positive results giving their patients a soft bear with an internal disk that plays several warm and reassuring messages (e.g., "You are special," "Loving you is easy," "Take care of yourself, honey") when squeezed. The executive director indicated that response to the bear has been overwhelmingly positive (E. Petorak, personal communication, Cleveland, 1995).

The similarity in both these examples is that the acoustic stimulation was played immediately adjacent to the individual with dementia, indicating that the use of headphones or devices similar to the bear may have a more direct impact than sounds generated in the macro environment (e.g., music played over the public address system).

Visual Stimulation

There is moderate research indicating that there are substantial changes to the visuo-perceptual system in dementia (Nissen et al., 1985; Sadun, Borchert, DeVita, Hinton, & Bassi, 1987; Schlotterer, Moscovitch, & Crapper-McLachlan, 1984). Although results are mixed on visual acuity impairment, there is some agreement that there is significant dyschromatopsia (color blindness). Results are also mixed on contrast sensitivity—the extent to which there needs to be contrast between foreground and background for the individual to see an object in the foreground. Nissen et al. (1985) and Sadun et al. (1987) found that the contrast sensitivity threshold was higher in patients with Alzheimer's disease, but Schlotterer et al. (1984) did not find this difference. Although research on late-stage dementia is almost nonexistent, in part because of the challenges of conducting any type of visually oriented research with a population this profoundly impaired, (Sadun, 1989) found that patients with late-stage dementia demonstrated severe impairment of vision, including impairments of visual acuity. This suggests that it is unlikely that these individuals are able to process much visual information, particularly when it is more than 2 or 3 feet away. This was supported, obliquely, in the survey by the response to the question about personal possessions. Although personal possessions can provide some tactile stimulation, they are often more visual in nature (art, photographs, knickknacks, etc.). Despite the increasing emphasis on personalization for individuals with early and mid-stage dementia who relocate into care facilities, 40% of the respondents felt that personal possessions were not very or not at all important ($M = 3.26$) for patients with late-stage dementia. However, two respondents indicated "pleasant things to look at" as one of the three most important features of a setting for this group.

Another aspect of the visual environment was identified as important in the survey. Sixty percent of the respondents indicated that it was somewhat or very important to be able to easily change lighting levels, whereas only 16% felt this was not very to not at all important. In addition, in the open-ended portion of the survey, 16% of the respondents identified various aspects of the lighting as one of the three most important environmental features for this population. Even when the mind can no longer interpret and give meaning to visual images, the eye receives and responds to patterns of light and dark, and thus the source and quality of light are potentially important features. All sources of light should be shielded so that patients never look directly at a light source. Of particular importance are overhead lights because much of the time these individuals are lying prone, either in bed or on a chair, and thus are much more likely to be looking directly up at these light fixtures. Fluorescent lamps are prone to flickering, which younger caregivers may not be sensitive to but which may be very disturbing to older visitors and patients. If at all possible, eliminate all overhead fixtures that direct the light downward. For general ambient lighting, use cove lighting. The presence of multiple lamps (with good shades that completely cover the light source) has the added advantage of allowing the lighting levels to be easily changed to suit different purposes and moods. The best way to assess the lighting of a unit is to get into the most typical resident positions—lie in bed or in geri-chairs or sit in other furniture in the same position as the residents and look around. Are there light sources that need to be changed or shielded? The survey also addressed natural light in both bedrooms and activity rooms. Both received very high ratings (means of 4.1 and 4, respectively). It is important to recognize, however, that light from windows can also be uncomfortable. Sheer curtains or translucent folding blinds (one piece of material that unfolds instead of many separate pieces of metal or plastic) provide appropriate control without completely blocking out all the sunlight. Sunlight can reflect off shiny metal blinds, causing glare and visual discomfort, and these blinds should be avoided.

Thermal Environment

Although not mentioned in either part of the survey, it is important to recognize that the thermal environment may play a major role in resident comfort. Because of their relative immobility, and inability to pull up or take off layers of clothing or coverings, people with late-stage dementia have very little control over their thermal environment. In general, older people prefer warmer settings and are more sensitive to drafts. Forced air systems should be designed so that vents do not blow air across the room, particularly to where residents are likely to be sitting or lying for extended periods of time. Although staff, who are physically working hard, may perceive it as uncomfortably warm, efforts should be made to keep the ambient temperature to the residents' liking. Asking other residents whether they are comfortable may be the best proxy.

MACRO-LEVEL ENVIRONMENT

The micro environment that the individual with dementia experiences is embedded within a larger context that has a significant impact on the experience of the micro environment. In addition, other people within the setting, staff and families, are more aware of and affected by this larger macro environment. An environment that supports their needs is likely to have a secondary positive impact on the residents, which is the ultimate goal. Hence, it is important to explore the potentially therapeutic qualities of the environment at this scale as well. This section of the chapter mirrors some of the format of the previous sections, with additional environmental components addressed in the latter portions.

Olfactory Stimulation

Many care facilities have an underlying odor of urine, which has sometimes seeped into flooring surfaces so that it is virtually impossible to get out. Others are characterized by the strong smell of cleaning solutions. Neither of these is particularly pleasant, although increasingly these cleaning products are perfumed with pine or another covering scent. Although the positive benefits of aromatherapy were described above in terms of residents' needs, it should be recognized that staff and visitors are also affected by these scents. Thus, the use of an essential oil to either relax or rejuvenate the residents may have secondary benefits for the staff and visitors. The smell of freshly brewed coffee or popcorn or cookies almost always serves to bring people together in a casual and convivial way, which may also have positive benefits. Too little attention has been paid to the creation of a positive olfactory environment.

Acoustic Environment

People who spend much time within a setting become accustomed to the quality and amount of noise in the setting and gradually become less sensitive to those sounds. Most care facilities are full of a variety of sounds, many of which are irritating or noxious: alarms and call bells, machinery, squeaking wheelchairs and walkers, overhead page systems, televisions tuned to game and talk shows, and staff calling to each other from down the corridors. Also, many people in advanced stages of dementia exhibit frequent, often loud, vocalizations, so units with any number of late-stage residents are likely to be replete with unpleasant noises at least part of the time. Attempts to cover up this cacophony of noise with music are not likely to be positively received by individuals with late-stage dementia. First, they may not be able to differentiate the music from the other sounds. Second, in the research by Norberg et al. (1986) described above, each participant had a distinct piece of music that elicited the most noticeable reactions. Thus, it is unlikely that a single piece of music will appeal to all residents. Instead of covering up other sounds, efforts should be made to eliminate as many of the aversive sources of acoustic stimulation as possible. Changing the call bell and alarm systems so they play a few chimes or a short tune is one strategy. Other facilities are moving toward call systems in which each staff member carries a pager with a quiet signal. Use of overhead paging systems can be limited to emergencies only when staff are given individual beepers. Control of acoustic stimulation was given the highest rating of the 35 individual environmental features, with 80% of the respondents rating it in the top two levels of importance. Acoustic control was also identified as important in the open-ended section by more respondents than any other item.

Visual Stimulation

The survey included several questions about use of color (bright vs. muted) and presence of art. Overall, these were rated as relatively unimportant (mean ratings were 2.76, 2.41, and 2.89, respectively). It should be remembered that the survey was focused on settings for people with late-stage dementia, so the respondents may not have been thinking about other users of the environment. Although the literature is replete with recommendations for enhancing the visual quality of units for people with early and mid-stage dementia, there has been no systematic research to evaluate the impact of a pretty or pleasant-looking setting. In general, given the limited visual capacity of individuals with late-stage dementia, the focus of the macro-level visual environment should be on what is pleasant and supportive for other residents, staff, and families.

Spatial Allocation

The cutting edge of design of long-term care facilities—particularly those for people with dementia—is undergoing a change, with increased emphasis on providing a greater number of smaller spaces for residents. The concept of the single, large, multipurpose day room across from a centrally located nurses' station is now viewed as very clinical and institutional, as opposed to familiar and residential. The new design philosophy was moderately supported in the survey, with items such as private visiting rooms and smaller social spaces being rated as moderately important (receiving mean ratings of 3.3 and 3.5, respectively) and larger social spaces being rated as less important ($M = 2.6$). A kitchen, another feature that is often included in new dementia-specific facilities, was also given only a modest rating ($M = 3.2$). There was, however, moderate support for spaces to support the needs of family members: places for a spouse or child to stay overnight received a mean rating of 3.8, a family education and support area received a mean rating of 3.7, and a private grieving room for families received a mean rating of 3.6. A staff conference room was also seen as important ($M = 3.6$).

Easy access to outdoor space was also included in the survey. It was not rated particularly highly ($M = 3.4$), which suggests that respondents did not feel this was very important for the residents. However, the potential positive impact of a pleasant outdoor space for families and visitors, as well as staff, should also be considered.

CONCLUSION

The goal of this chapter was to explore what features comprise a supportive physical environment for individuals with late-stage dementia. Because there has been so little work to date in this area, much of what was presented was conjecture and should be examined, questioned, studied, and revised. Numerous features were mentioned by only a few of the survey respondents, and there were only a few features about which there seemed to be much agreement. One point that is fairly certain, however, is that it is particularly important to differentiate between negative or aversive stimulation and potentially positive or pleasurable stimulation. Much of the debate thus far has focused primarily on quantity of stimulation and not on quality. As a caring community, we must broaden our perspective.

Moreover, although the focus here was the physical environment, many of the issues identified in the survey related to social environment. Creating a warm and caring, supportive setting for residents and family was mentioned by several respondents. Encouraging contact between the individuals with dementia and other people was articulated in several different ways, from open visiting policies to 24-hr programming. The feature that was identified most often in response to the question about the three most important care goals was a staff that was caring and knowledgeable about the physical, emotional, and individual needs of the residents.

Clearly, the physical environment is only part of a larger system of characteristics that compose a therapeutic care setting. It does not exist in a void but interacts with other dimensions, affecting both residents and caregivers in myriad ways. Despite the severe limitations of individuals with late-stage dementia, efforts should be expended to enhance understanding of how they experience their environment and of what features compose a therapeutic setting.

BIBLIOGRAPHY

Barnet, K. (1972). A theoretical construct of the concepts of touching as they relate to nursing. *Nursing Research, 21*, 102–110.

Buckwalter, K. C. (1992). Confessions of a geriatric nurse researcher. *Journal of Gerontological Nursing, 18*(6), 46–47.

Calkins, M. P. (1988). *Design for dementia: Planning environments for the elderly and the confused.* Owings Mills, MD: National Health Publishing.

Cohen, U., & Weisman, J. (1991). *Holding on to home.* Baltimore, MD: Johns Hopkins University Press.

Doty, R. L. (1989). Influence of age and age-related diseases on olfactory function. In *Annals of the New York Academy of Science: Vol. 561,* (pp. 76–87). New York: New York Academy of Science.

Doty, R. L., Reyes, P. F., & Gergor, T. (1987). Presence of both odor identification and detection deficits in Alzheimer's disease. *Brain Research Bulletin, 18,* 597–600.

Esiri, M. M., Pearson, R. C., & Powell, T. P. (1986). The cortex of the primary auditory area in Alzheimer's disease. *Brain Research, 366*(1–2), 385–387.

Hiatt, L. (1981). Designing therapeutic dining. *Nursing Homes, 30*(2), 33–39.

Kesslak, J. P., Cotman, C. W., Chui, H. C., Van-den-Noort, S., Fang, H., Pfeffer, R., & Lynch, G. (1988). Olfactory tests as possible probes for detecting and monitoring Alzheimer's disease. *Neurobiological Aging, 9,* 399–403.

Koss, E., Weiffenbach, J. M., Haxby, J. V., & Friedland, R. P. (1988). Olfactory detection and identification performance are dissociated in early Alzheimer's disease. *Neurology, 38,* 1228–1232.

Lawton, M. P. (1975). Competence, environmental press, and the adaptation of older people. In P. G. Windley & G. Ernst (Eds.), *Theory development in environment and aging* (pp. 33–59). Washington, DC: Gerontological Society of America.

Lawton, M. P. (1977). An ecological theory of aging applied to elderly housing. *Journal of Architecture and Education, 31*(1), 8–10.

Levy, D. E., Knill-Jones, R. P., & Plum, F. (1978). The vegetative state and its prognosis following nontraumatic coma. In *Annals of the New York Academy of Sciences: Vol. 315,* (pp. 293–306). New York: New York Academy of Sciences.

Massaging will be tested as nursing home therapy. (1989, January 7). *Rocky Mountain News,* p. B3.

Nissen, M. J., Corkin, S., Buonanno, F. S., Growdon, J. H., Wray, S. H., & Bauer, J. (1985). Spatial vision in Alzheimer's disease: General findings and a case report. *Archives of Neurology, 42,* 667–671.

Norberg, A., Melin, E., & Asplund, K. (1986). Reactions to music, touch and object presentation in the final stage of dementia: An exploratory study. *International Journal of Nursing Studies, 23,* 315–323.

Pearson, R. C., Esiri, M. M., Hiorns, R. W., Wilcock, G. K., & Powell, T. P. (1985). Anatomical correlates of the distribution of the pathological changes in the neocortex in Alzheimer disease. *Proceedings of the National Academy of Science, 82,* 4531–4534.

Pounds, L. (1992). Holistic aromatherapy. *Beginnings, 12*(3), 1, 4.

Sadun, A. A. (1989). The optic neuropathy of Alzheimer's disease. *Metabolic Pediatric System Ophthalmology, 12*(1–3), 64–68.

Sadun, A. A., Borchert, M., DeVita, E., Hinton, D. R., & Bassi, C. J. (1987). Assessment of visual impairment in patients with Alzheimer's disease. *American Journal of Ophthalmology, 104*(2), 113–120.

Schlotterer, G., Moscovitch, M., & Crapper-McLachlan, D. (1984). Visual processing deficits as assessed by spatial frequency contrast sensitivity and backward masking in normal ageing and Alzheimer's disease. *Brain, 107,* 309–325.

Talamo, B. R., Rudel, R., Kosik, K. S., Lee, V. M., Neff, S., Adelman, L., & Kauer, J. S. (1989). Pathological changes in olfactory neurons in patients with Alzheimer's disease. *Nature, 337,* 736–739.

U.S. Congress, Office of Technology Assessment. (1992). *Special care units for people with Alzheimer's and other dementias: Consumer education, research, regulatory and reimbursement issues* (Pub. No. OTA-H-543). Washington, DC: U.S. Government Printing Office.

Wells, L. (1990, January 7). Soothing scents. *New York Times Magazine,* p. 7.

You, B. (1994, March 29). Is aromatherapy a cure-all right under our noses? *Chicago Tribune,* Section 5, p. 5.

Chapter 9

Communications and Fundamentals of Care: Bathing, Grooming, and Dressing

Carly R. Hellen

"Help me, help me" rings out from a pleading voice of a resident with late-stage Alzheimer's disease. What is this person trying to communicate? Perhaps the need to feel a person's presence and attention, or maybe these are words found to express the want of food or the desire to be changed to dry undergarments. The call may be trying to tell the caregiver that the perceived world is void of touch and caring and that the resident's position outside his or her room feels empty and vast, lacking in favorable stimulation, and leading the resident to feel very alone.

When a resident has reached the late stages of dementia, cognitive and functional capacities are oriented only to person. Self-care is dependent on others. Verbal communications are experienced in sounds or simple words, sometimes repeated again and again. Occasionally a connection is made, and it seems like a window opens and a totally appropriate sentence or remark is shared with surprised listeners. The ability to read and understand words spoken by others is lost. Conventional language and comprehension are usually nonexistent. The Late-Stage Alzheimer's Communication Profile (see Figure 9.1) can be used as an assessment of the resident's verbal abilities, nonverbal responses, and communication inabilities or problems.

Any discussion of a resident's stage of illness must leave the door open for all who do not fit within the definition of abilities and inabilities for a particular stage. Communicative functions often do not consistently conform to structured symptom descriptions. Staff and family expectations can have a strong influence

113

NAME _____ ROOM _____

HEARING _____ VISION _____

PREFERS TO BE CALLED _____

RESPONDS TO CAREGIVER VOICE:
   ___ LOW   ___ HIGH   ___ SOFT   ___ AUTHORITARIAN

REASSURING WORDS TO USE _____

KEY NAMES OF FAMILY MEMBERS/FRIENDS _____
_____

SUPPORTIVE ENVIRONMENTAL CONSIDERATIONS _____
_____

VERBAL ABILITIES/STRENGTHS

	YES	NO	DESCRIBE
USES SINGLE WORDS			
USES PHRASES			
REPEATS WORDS			
MAKES SOUNDS			
SINGS			

RESPONSE TO:	DESCRIBE
SINGING/MUSIC	
TOUCH/MASSAGE	
ROCKING	
SILENCE	
ENVIRONMENTAL NOISE	
OTHER RESIDENT NOISE	

NON-VERBAL RESPONSES

	YES	NO	DESCRIBE
FACIAL			
POSTURAL			
ARMS			
HANDS			
LEGS			

HOW DOES THE RESIDENT "SAY"

PAIN _____

HUNGRY _____

WET _____

TIRED _____

BORED _____

OVER-STIMULATED _____

LONELY _____

INABILITIES/PROBLEMS

CAN'T MAKE NEEDS KNOWN _____

CAN'T UNDERSTAND SPOKEN WORDS _____

OUTBURSTS/PROFANITY _____

COMMUNICATION GOALS/INTERVENTION AND APPROACH

1. _____

2. _____

STAFF NAME AND DATE: _____

Figure 9.1 Late-stage Alzheimer's communication profile.

on the resident's function. The fascination and joy of caring for persons with dementia comes from the inconsistencies. Just when a caregiver has figured out a patient, perhaps as to what he or she is trying to say or an approach that works, all is once again a conundrum.

Caring touch often speaks louder than words, especially for the resident feeling isolated because of a decreased ability to hear or see. Touch becomes the foundation of shared communications, especially for the dying resident. The knowledge and use of therapeutic massage offers improved circulation, reduced body tension, and overall relaxation responses. Sensitive functional caregiving touch differs from the touch of quiet comfort and acceptance. Considerations for increasing the effectiveness of touch include timing, cultural background, awareness of sexual orientation or gender concerns, and the location of touch. Sometimes a resident will react negatively to touch—this response must be respected. Touch always comes with a message to the resident; compassionate caring and connectedness must be the communication. Chapters 8 and 10 provide an overview of interventions related to tactile stimulation from the physical environment and caregiver interventions.

Communications, verbal or nonverbal, must still remain to be the bridge between the caregiver and the care receiver. Supporting the remaining demonstrations of attempted communications enables residents to stay connected with themselves and the world around them. A resident's life story book, describing significant life celebrations and containing meaningful pictures, will enable the staff to reminisce and communicate using familiar information (see Appendix). A holistic outlook on caregiving surrounds residents with permission to be the best that they can be, to have their personhood upheld and honor bestowed for their uniqueness.

COMMUNICATION CONSIDERATIONS AND SUGGESTIONS

The following are some general suggestions that are useful when communicating with a person who has dementia:

• Use a warm, supportive manner, and think about how the patient perceives verbal and nonverbal messages.
• Touch first to get attention and give reassurance, especially smiles, hugs, and hand-holding. The resident needs to feel acceptance and respect.
• Be sure that the resident's glasses, hearing aid, or both are in place, clean, and in proper working order.
• Talk with the resident in a quiet place, free from distractions, and with good lighting on your face, not from behind you.
• Within the patient's visual field, start a conversation by identifying yourself.
• Speak slowly, use a low voice pitch, say words clearly, and use short, simple sentences.
• Use visual cues or objects. Whenever possible let the resident hold the item.

• Set the mood, perhaps by singing about the task to be done: "Today is your bath day, today is your bath day."
• Use concrete and familiar words.
• Listen to the resident carefully with the intention of being able to understand.
• Close all attempts at communication with positive feedback; "I really appreciate this time of being together and sharing with you."

In addition to general communication strategies, caregivers will find many situations that require new and innovative communication techniques. Underlying all of the strategies is a message of caring, safety, and acceptance. For example, sitting on a couch or on the resident's bed or holding and rocking the resident while humming or singing softly can often communicate caring and provide connectedness between the caregiver and the care receiver. Placing a resident with late-stage dementia in a wide hammock, wrapped in a soft blanket, and gently moving him or her back and forth in a slow rocking motion can facilitate calmness and peace. Recognize verbal and nonberbal signs of frustration while trying to communicate, such as agitation, combativeness, yelling, or withdrawal. If necessary, change your approach or return later. A portable cassette player with the resident's favorite music may reduce screaming or yelling, with the earpiece or headphones providing sensory input and focus.

Whatever communication strategy is used, it is important to create meaningful human interactions to meet the social self-needs of the person with late-stage dementia. Watch for the resident's ability to share feelings and awareness through nonverbal means and body language. Respond to emotional tones and always validate the feelings behind the words or sounds the resident makes; for example, if the tone is upbeat then say, "That sounds good, I'm glad you are pleased." If it sounds sad, say "That really sounds sad, I'm sorry, could I give you a hug?".

Other interventions that may be helpful include

• continuing to offer a choice between two items or asking questions with a yes/no option for the answer. For example: "Would you like to wear your red dress or your blue dress?" [while holding each one up to the resident]. If there is no communication, say "The blue dress is a good choice. It matches your eyes. It will look pretty."
• encouraging verbal responses. With residents willing to participate in singing, sing the same familiar song 4–6 times in a row because each time they will be able to sing a little bit more.
• using gentle massage when appropriate for increased well-being and relaxation.

Communications must surround the person with nurturing strength and fill him or her with peaceful calm. The ability to offer supportive communications becomes the fundamental basis of caregiving during late-stage dementia. The fulfillment of the resident's need for acceptance and respect is spoken through touch, words, and the skillfulness of being able to speak and listen to the person with dementia. Care given, care received, and offered response become symbols and rituals that communicate with unspoken words.

THE COMMUNICATION OF ACCEPTANCE: BATHING

"Let's sing, 'Let Me Call You Sweetheart.' Would you please hold this face cloth for me so we can be together while you bathe?"

Bathing is one of the most personal opportunities for supportive communications. Cognitive, physical, and psychosocial factors often create a challenge to both the caregiver and the care receiver. Issues of modesty, fear of falling, inappropriate responses to water hitting the skin, and decreased understanding of the need for bathing or the process of bathing may increase the resident's anxiousness. The number of staff persons, cultural background, gender, and the age of the caregiver can also affect the success of bathing. The resident's bathing history can create a response of willingness or of fear and combativeness. Having been forced into the shower or tub in the past is usually not forgotten, often resulting in resistant responses in the present that reflect the resident's past fears. There is nothing more personal than the giving or receiving of basic care. The ease with which these tasks are carried out sets the mood for both the caregiver and the resident.

Residents with dementia in the late stages intuitively know whether they are being accepted by the caregiver. Caring touch, gentleness, speed of movement, tenderness of voice, and body posture usually do not escape the sensitive awareness of the resident. For example, holding a resident close to the caregiver's body as the person is raised on the tublift and offering reassuring words may help to reduce the terror often experienced. Cocooning the resident in a bath blanket, gently singing or talking, and making eye contact as he or she is wheeled down the hall to the shower may lessen combativeness.

The process of bathing must let residents know, no matter what their level of cognitive function, that they are OK and that the caregiver is there to keep them safe. In doing this, the caregiver accepts the resident as a person worthy of respect. It is this message of acceptance, when communicated to the resident, that becomes the cornerstone for supporting quality of life.

Certainly one of the keys to communicating the worth of residents is the caregiver's awareness of the symbolism of being dressed. When a patient is dressed, he or she feels put together, having a sense of integration of self and the body. It is important for the caregiver to put him- or herself in the resident's place as clothes are peeled off in preparation for bathing. Residents already know, within their level of awareness, that they are not all put together in relation to their cognitive abilities and life skills. Therefore, undressing the person takes on new meaning. The patient may perceive having clothing removed as an invasion of well-being, as defined by their perceptions. Fear and striking out often results. As an alternative, getting the resident wet with clothing on may precipitate attempts to take his or her own clothing off. This personal choice often bypasses the combative experience of being undressed and sustains the resident's need for dignity and acceptance.

Trained staff, using the care technique of rescuing, can further demonstrate their acceptance of the resident. Rescuing is a distraction technique used when a caregiver is involved with a resident experiencing anxiety, fearfulness, or combativeness as a response to a task he or she does not want to do or cannot understand. A second caregiver enters the situation and tells the initial caregiver to leave the area so that the second caregiver can be with a special friend, the resident. The resident feels rescued from the first caregiver and complies with the second caregiver's daily care activity. For example,

> Sally, the caregiver, is having difficulty getting the resident, Mrs. Weis, into the tub. Mrs. Weis is yelling out, starting to swing her arms about, and pushing the wheelchair backward. Sally tries various distraction techniques, asking the resident to please hold the face cloth or offering a cookie. This does not work. If Sally were to continue insisting on the bath, Mrs. Weis would probably become hysterical, perhaps leading to a fall or someone getting hurt. Mary, responding to the yelling, comes to help Sally. If Mary starts with the same distraction techniques it now becomes two staff persons against one, the resident. But, Mary can say to Sally, "Sally, why don't you find something else to do? Just go away. I want to be with my friend, Mrs. Weis. Sally, why don't you go help Mr. Smith? Mrs. Weis and I want to be together." The result is that Mrs. Weis will feel rescued by Mary and will almost always let her take over the caregiving activity without struggling against it. The feeling of being accepted has been communicated to Mrs. Weis.

Giving care to residents with dementia requires assessing their abilities and inabilities to actively participate. When they are involved, passively or actively, all daily life tasks become their activity at that moment. Redefining or framing activities of daily living as an activity will encourage creative approaches and problem solving when difficulties are encountered.

BASIC GUIDELINES FOR ALL ACTIVITIES OF DAILY LIVING

Timing and consistency are both important when assisting the resident with activities of daily living. Be aware of the best time of the day to schedule activities, and use flexibility in schedules if signs of agitation are observed. Using a familiar caregiver and a routine approach to completing activities of daily living decreases fearfulness and agitation. The caregiver's demeanor should be kind and nondemanding. Use a relaxed, nonthreatening body position and a calm voice. Adult communication standards should be used at all times. Touch must be supportive and caring and never forceful. Use consideration when privacy issues are involved and comply with the resident's preference for the caregiver's gender. Also, as outlined in chapter 6, be sure to use the giving of care as an opportunity for checking the resident's body for bruises, rashes, and other abnormalities.

Involve residents as much as possible by focusing on their abilities in activities of daily living. Just holding an item such as a hairbrush may help the person to feel connected, involved, and safe in the situation. Modify or simplify tasks as much as possible to promote participation and success. Talk with the resident and explain the process as though they understand every word. Be willing to change approaches when what worked yesterday doesn't work today. Also, distraction techniques such as singing, food, talking, or not talking may keep the resident diverted from becoming upset or anxious.

BATHING CONSIDERATIONS AND SUGGESTIONS

Bathing success results from caring approaches and technique. It is important to keep the bath experience as calm and unhurried as possible. Know the resident's likes and fears when selecting a tub, shower, or bed bath. Tub baths are often the most appropriate for supporting skin care needs. Residents usually respond favorably to a tub bath for overall relaxing and soaking. Assess the bathing environment for homelike qualities, warmth, and safety. Suggestions include a fake window with a pastoral scene or colorful beach towels hanging on the walls. Have as few caregivers involved in bathing while maintaining resident safety.

Avoid using the shower chair for rides to the shower. Shower chairs are often cold and wobbly. Residents with late-stage dementia may become very rigid and Parkinsonian during bathing. Wrap the resident in a warm bath blanket for transfer from the bed or chair into the warm tub water. If the tub has a hydraulic chair, use verbal reassurance and touch to decrease the resident's anxiety. Give the resident a bathing-related item to hold, for example, a wash cloth or empty plastic shampoo bottle. This allows the caregiver to thank the resident for helping and also keeps the resident's hands busy and decreases striking out. Be sure to have plenty of towels available, including towels to cover the resident during bathing, if needed, to reduce anxiety. If privacy is an issue, start the bathing with some of the resident's clothes on, for example, a nightie, slip, undershorts, or t-shirt.

Residents with dementia generally respond negatively to the feeling of water splashing or spraying on them. Use a hand-held shower to avoid spray hitting the face. A wash cloth or a sock over the head of the shower may be used to reduce the force of the water hitting on sensitive skin. If needed, wash one part of the body per day. For example, on Mondays wash the neck and shoulders, on Tuesdays wash the back, and so forth. Note this schedule on the resident's plan of care. To involve the resident, the caregiver may place a hand over the resident's hand for washing body parts whenever possible.

Bed baths are appropriate when the bathroom environment precipitates catastrophic reactions. When a bed bath is given, have all the bathing items ready and available so the resident does not need to be left alone at any time. Keep the body covered with towels or a bath blanket except for a small area being washed. Again, use distraction techniques to reduce anxiety: singing, holding items, gentle touch, and talking.

Bathing becomes so much more than just getting the body cleansed. Bathing, a significant personal activity, becomes an opportunity to communicate acceptance of the resident as a valued person. The task then becomes a time of communion between the caregiver and the care receiver. Gentleness, caring, honor, respect, and the gift of nurturing one another becomes the focus of this daily life care activity.

THE COMMUNICATION OF RESPECT: GROOMING AND DRESSING

Case Example

Mrs. Vega was a puzzlement. She had been refusing to get her hair done, something that she had always enjoyed in the past. She either insisted on staying in her room or she would slowly scoot her wheelchair up to the front door and pound on the door, yelling "Get me out of here." She had been asked to leave two nursing homes because of her combativeness during morning care, especially getting dressed. Her daughter tried to help by bring in jogging outfits that were easy to slip over the head or pull up around the waist. Mrs. Vega had always been a finely dressed woman who enjoyed her clothes. These jogging suits were really very attractive.

Case Discussion

In reality, Mrs. Vega had never worn slacks or pant outfits. She loved the many dresses in her wardrobe. Her daughter meant well, but when Mrs. Vega looked at herself in pants she didn't know who she was and she would try to hide or run away. When outfitted in dresses again, Mrs. Vega responded with dignity because her need to be a well-dressed woman, according to her definition, was supported. She felt respected.

The resident in the late stages of dementia needs and deserves the same respect. Supporting dignity through clothing and grooming enables the resident to gain and hold a sense of self-worth. Adding a tie for the executive, simple costume jewelry for the convener of many meetings, and the use of light perfume or shaving lotion for the bed-bound resident communicates regard and willingness to enable self-esteem.

Involving residents in all daily life tasks focuses on doing with the residents, not on doing to or for them. Even the simplest participation calls residents forth from within themselves, connecting them to the outside world. If ways are not found to make this connection, the residents will be more prone to retreating within and making noises, yelling out, using repetitive speech, rocking, and chewing on clothing or fingers.

Respect is communicated to the resident during care by using a technique called bridging. Bridging is a method of sensory connection in which the resident holds the same object as the caregiver while the caregiver carries out the caregiving task. The purpose is to increase the resident's focus on the task, increase attention span, reduce anxiety, and promote respect. The following are examples of bridging:

> *Mr. Schafer is combative during grooming and shaving. He becomes very anxious and his upper extremities become so rigid that hand-over-hand shaving is not possible. Shaving is successful and completed without stress by using bridging. An electric razor is placed in Mr. Schafer's hand so he can feel its shape and vibration. He can also hear the buzzing sound. The caregiver uses another electric shaver to remove Mr. Schafer's whiskers. By his holding a razor, Mr. Schafer is connected to the activity of shaving through the caregiver and back to himself. Anxiety is reduced, and respect is communicated.*

> *Alice, the caregiver, places long strands of yarn on the table in front of Mrs. Brown. They are held in place by masking tape. As Alice braids Mrs. Brown's hair, Mrs. Brown braids the strands of yarn. The activity of daily care is bridged from the resident to the caregiver and back to the resident through the strands of yarn being touched. Defensiveness has been reduced, and Mrs. Brown's increased attention span has facilitated success.*

DRESSING CONSIDERATIONS AND SUGGESTIONS

Continue to dress the resident in bed or in a chair. Use clothing, cosmetics, costume jewelry, and so forth to reflect the resident's previous life roles. Staff should be encouraged to wear a fanny pack around the waist to carry items for distracting an anxious resident during grooming and dressing. For example, staff could carry cookies, scarves, ties, costume jewelry, and simple puzzles cut from the front panel of familiar food boxes such as cereals.

Many residents will have contractures, rigidity, or both, making activities of daily life uncomfortable or painful; do not force joints to move beyond the point of pain. Use large, soft clothing with a loose elastic waist, preferably cotton as it does not retain the odor of urine. Consider clothing or underwear that opens down the back, but do not use these for bed-bound residents if there are buttons or snaps that could rub or create pressure on the skin. Undershirts may be used in place of bras. Use loose fitting socks or stockings to prevent ankle or foot swelling and use washable soft shoes. Residents often feel cold; have available knitted knee socks, leggings, sweaters, and so forth.

SHAVING SUGGESTIONS

Apply pleasant smelling preshave lotion to help orient the resident to the shaving activity. Dressing up an orderly and announcing to the resident that his barber has arrived might facilitate shaving. A reclining geri-chair or a beauty salon chair can be used to help decrease anxiety and possible combative responses to shaving.

If possible, place the resident's hand on the shaver with your hand over his for a hand-over-hand activity. The bridging technique, as discussed in a previous example, may facilitate shaving. Complete the activity with aftershave lotion, again using a hand-over-hand application if possible.

ORAL CARE SUGGESTIONS

Oral care is extremely important for maintaining comfort and hygiene and for preventing infection and dental problems. Using a dental chair for daily care or setting up a reclining geri-chair may ease stress in getting oral care done. Wearing a white lab coat and providing a napkin for under the chin may also be helpful. A child-sized toothbrush may decrease the resident's fears of having a foreign object in his or her mouth, and toothpaste that can be swallowed may be needed.

Removing dentures can be difficult, but the bridging technique can be used. Have the resident hold a denture cup with a generic unused set of dentures while you are trying to remove the resident's dentures. Holding the items often reduces reluctance to open the mouth. Try to mirror the task to the resident: Have a caregiver use her own toothbrush and pretend to brush her own teeth while helping the resident hold his own brush and give his teeth care.

When oral care is resisted, some of the following interventions are often helpful. A resident not wanting to open her mouth might respond to the caregiver's yawning in the resident's face. If the resident yawns back, the toothbrush can go in the mouth while it is open. Pushing up firmly on the resident's chin facilitates the mouth dropping open. Gently squeezing the resident's lips together in the front of the mouth facilitates the lips parting and teeth being exposed. Some residents respond to chaining. The caregiver starts the desired activity (e.g., places the brush in the resident's hand, puts on the toothpaste, and lifts the brush to the mouth), and then the resident takes over. Oral swabs or toothettes soaked in mouthwash can be used if a brush is rejected. On some days, a washcloth soaked in mouthwash may be the only accepted means of oral care.

The communication of respect for the resident shown by participation in these important aspects of care sing forth as a sacrament of dignity. Family members express thanksgiving for the staff's offering of consideration and honor for their loved one. Staff themselves feel pride and fulfillment when they have responded to these opportunities to communicate their tenderness and respect. Unspoken words of worth and personal regard are shared.

CONCLUSION

The responsibility for open, shared communication that enables a climate of acceptance falls on caregivers. The ability to accept the resident's limitations and continue to converse in an adult, supportive way is a challenge. The caregiver's personal feelings of loss and sadness as the resident goes through the late stages of dementia can be overwhelming, complicating the acknowledgment of communication as being a difficult and often exasperating task. All attempts by the resident to communicate are methods to hold up before the caregiver a mirror of inner feelings and attitudes. The challenge for caregivers is to understand communications as a means of being present with residents, providing them with emotional connectedness, acceptance, and respect.

BIBLIOGRAPHY

Hellen, C. (1992). *Alzheimer's disease: Activity focused care*. Newton, MA: Butterworth Heinemann.
Gwyther, L. (1985). *Care of Alzheimer's patients: A manual for nursing home staff*. Chicago: Alzheimer's Association.
Rush Alzheimer's Disease Center. (1994). *Caregiver manual*. Chicago: Author.

APPENDIX: LIFE STORY BOOK

Dear Family Member,

We are asking for your assistance. As we seek partnership with you in caregiving for your loved ones, we wish to know their LIFE STORY. As you know, the person with dementia often lives in the past, in the "world of work." These years often represent a period of time filled with meaningful experiences, many are retained as memories. The staff wishes to have the opportunity to learn as much as we can about the resident's past so we can use the information as a basis of our approach to therapeutic caregiving. A LIFE STORY BOOK offers the staff insights into likes, dislikes, past interests, names of key persons and family members. The LIFE STORY information is then adapted for daily life interests, activities and provides opportunities for companionship and reminiscing. The book can be used to help with the transition from home to his or her new residence because the staff will quickly "know" the new resident and be more able to build a relationship based on memories shared.

Caregiving at this home focuses on the resident's abilities. Often these abilities are enabled and strengthened with information from the resident's LIFE STORY BOOK. We hope that you will consider making a book for your loved one.

Making A Life Story Book

A LIFE STORY BOOK can be made from photo albums, notebooks, or any durable booklet. We suggest using a three-ring binder notebook so pages can be added at any time. Using poster-type stiff paper or cutting up file folders for paper can provide a sturdy page that will survive constant handling. Drawings, writings, pictures, maps, etc. can be used. If you wish to include precious photos please photocopy them and keep the original, placing the copy in the book. Persons with dementia usually retain the ability to read for many years so please write information in short sentences or phrases. Placing names under photos is especially important. Use a dark pen, printing the words clearly and in large print. If you wish to see a completed book or have questions about the LIFE STORY BOOK, please call and ask for Social Services.

Life Story Contents: Suggestions

Genealogy
• Include nationality, heritage, birth dates, family tree, and siblings and their relationship to the resident.
• Use short phrases to note important memories about the family.

Religious or spiritual topics
• Provide background and note interests in organized religion.
• Include pictures of outside, inside, and sanctuary of church, synagogue, or other place of worship.
• Include current participation.
• Note use of or response to ritual, traditions, blessings, and prayers.
• Include words and music for favorite songs and hymns.

Personality
• Is the resident happy?
• Did he or she like people?
• Was he or she a joker?
• What is the resident's favorite joke?
• What are the resident's responses to others?
• What have been the resident's responses to life roles: for example, father, mother, daughter, aunt.
• Provide a general mood description.

Description of childhood
• List friends and clubs.
• List summertime activities.
• What was the resident's work history during his or her school years?

Education
• List grade completed, kind of school, school names, degrees.
• What was the resident's favorite subject, most disliked subject, extracurricular events, teams, clubs, etc.?

Key life events
• Provide dates (year) and describe events.
• Graduations?
• Marriage?
• Children?
• Provide details about the deaths of family members or close friends.

Places lived
• Describe places the resident has lived, perhaps using a map.
• Were the places liked or not liked? Why?
• Talk about specific rooms, outside grounds, distances from school, shopping, etc. Use pictures if possible.

Close friends and neighbors
- Was the resident a helper with others?

Work history
- Did the resident work at home or in the marketplace?
- Alone or with others?
- Describe specific kinds of work and the resident's responses to what he or she liked and disliked.
- Include retirement information.

Military history
- Describe the military history of the resident and significant family members.
- What are the resident's memories of war and peace?

Favorite transportation
- Did the resident drive? Own a car? What kind? Pictures?

Awards received, clubs, groups, positions of leadership
- What groups did the resident belong to?
- Did the resident hold any positions of leadership?

Volunteer experiences or service organizations

Interest in literature
- List titles, passages, verses, poetry, scriptures.

Recreational activities and hobbies
- What were the resident's inside and outside recreational interests?
- Favorite hobbies?

Animals and pets

Travel
- Locations of places visited, favorite places, maps, etc.

Favorite foods, recipes
- Favorite foods?
- Like to cook? To bake?
- Include copies of favorite recipes.

Holidays, seasons of the year
- Traditions, rituals for each holiday, types of decorations used.
- Please include pictures.

Chapter 10

Behaviors Associated With Late-Stage Dementia

Christine R. Kovach

Across the spectrum of caregiving situations, surely one of the most difficult and frustrating involves responding to behaviors associated with dementia. Caregivers new to the person with late-stage dementia express feelings of frustration, inadequacy, and sorrow. How, they wonder, are they to cope with the sight of a person repetitively rocking and grunting? How do they keep their patience when a resident smears stool over him- or herself? How do they not take it personally when someone spits on them? What is the proper response to such behaviors? Can the behaviors be prevented? Where is the guidebook?

Unfortunately, although much has been written about mid-stage dementia, relatively little literature is available about late-stage behaviors. This chapter presents currently recognized explanations for common behaviors associated with dementia. Tips for managing these behaviors in the low-functioning person with dementia are described. Most of what is currently known has come from reports of caregivers who have observed what works and doesn't work in their particular situation. There is a need for more research on all behavior management interventions.

Behaviors associated with dementia are often spoken of as problem behaviors or challenging behaviors. Many of the behaviors are actually an attempt by the cognitively impaired person to cope and an adaptive response to some internal or external stressor or unfulfilled need. Feelings of fear and confusion often precede the behavior. In other words, most behaviors labeled as problems are caused by caregivers' action or inaction or by some stress in the environment or are a positive coping tool the cognitively impaired person feels a need to use.

Behaviors should only be considered a problem when the action interferes or potentially interferes with the health, rights, or safety of the person exhibiting the behavior or other persons such as staff or residents. Remember also that behaviors that seem difficult or unusual are related to a disease process and are not the actions of a person who is trying to be uncooperative or difficult.

PREVENTING BEHAVIOR PROBLEMS

The most useful techniques for treating behavior problems are preventive. Many behavior problems can be prevented by focusing on four main interventions: decreasing environmental stress, meeting primary self-needs, increasing quality and quantity of social connections, and allowing inner retreat times throughout the day that are balanced with more active times.

Decreasing Environmental Stress

The progressively lowered stress threshold (PLST) model has made an important contribution to understanding behaviors associated with dementia (Hall & Buckwalter, 1987). Basically, the model states that people with dementia have less ability to receive and process stimuli from the environment and cannot tolerate as much stimulation from the environment as persons who are not impaired. There is a lowered stress threshold for stimulation from sources such as television noise, crowded rooms, public address systems, housekeeping activities, and multiple sensory experiences such as occur during bathing. Special care units for individuals with mid-stage dementia are therefore designed to be quiet and subdued, and activity programming is scheduled to balance sensory stimulating experiences with sensory calming experiences or downtime. Behavior problems have been reported to be dramatically decreased in the person with mid-stage dementia by focusing on decreasing extraneous environmental stimulation and enhancing the balance between therapeutic sensory stimulating activities and more quiet times (Kovach & Stearns, 1994).

Even though the person with late-stage dementia does not appear to be as sensitive to environmental stimulation as the person with mid-stage dementia, there is still a need to control extraneous stimulation and avoid too much stimulation. Because the person with advanced disease has such a low level of competence, he or she requires both a decrease in extraneous and multiple, competing stimuli and an increase in focused, therapeutic stimulation. Chapter 8 reviewed some features of the macro- and micro-level environment that may be supportive or nonsupportive for people with late-stage dementia. This analysis continues below with a description of specific interventions that may decrease environmental stress and increase therapeutic stimulation.

Auditory stressors   Conduct a noise assessment by listening at various times of the day for sources of extraneous noise. Work with staff to decrease noise:

- Turn off television sets, radios, and so forth.
- Have housekeeping do noisy cleaning one time during the day when the least number of people will be influenced.
- Replace pounding pill crushers with quiet pliers or another type of crusher.
- Have maintenance fix squeaky or noisy drawers, doors, wheelchairs, and other items.
- Consider installing carpeting or drapes to absorb some background noise.
- Avoid background conversations. Make verbal communication focused and deliberate.
- Eliminate echo in areas such as the tub room and bathroom, which are usually heavily tiled and do not absorb sound.
- Decrease staff conferences and interstaff socializing in resident areas

Visual stressors   The environment that is visually accessible to the person with late-stage dementia is often small and circumscribed but will usually include at least a dining room, activity area, tub room, bathroom, and bedroom. Access to both private areas such as the bedroom and social areas such as an activity room need to be available.

- Keep some items that are tied to the familiar and healthy in the visual field, such as pictures and afghans (Cohen & Weisman, 1991).
- Keep colors in background areas, such as on walls and tables, soft and muted, and use contrasting or brighter colors to differentiate items to be used, such as a cup or eating utensil.
- Rid the environment of clutter.
- Eliminate all glare from lighting, and only use subdued lighting during sleep times.
- Decrease the institutional look of concrete walls, ceramic tile, and so on by adding homelike decorations such as pictures, which are smaller scale and familiar.
- Spaces that are too big or too small or filled with too many people or things can be stressful. In general, keep room sizes small and keep the rooms organized.

Tactile stressors   Some people with late-stage dementia are highly sensitive to touch, and their stress threshold is quickly exceeded even by touch that is usually considered soothing and therapeutic. Other people with late-stage dementia, though sensitive to common noxious tactile stimuli, benefit from soothing massage, hugs, and touch as a positive form of nonverbal communication.

- Keep room temperatures comfortable. Many older adults dislike highly air conditioned environments.
- Pad chairs and cover vinyl furniture with a bath blanket for comfort.
- Use flannel sheets and silk pillowcases.
- Keep bedlinens dry, wrinkle free, and odor free.

- Cover bedrails with well-secured bath blankets.
- Always use gentle and slow touch.
- Assess residents for dandruff and other itchy skin conditions, such as dry skin and eczema, and seek treatment.
- Check shoes for comfortable fit and absence of pressure points.
- Eliminate clothing made from rough fabrics, ill-fitting clothing, irritating rubber and elastic in brassieres and waistbands, and clothing that feels constrained.
- Keep skin, hair, and nails clean and dry.
- Transfer the resident using sufficient staff and proper transfer techniques.
- Allow the person a soft special pillow, plush pet animal, or doll if it is comforting to him or her.

Multiple stressors   Nothing seems to exceed the stress threshold of persons with late-stage dementia faster than multiple, competing stimuli. For example, during bathtime the sound of water running, the differing temperatures of the air and water, the feel of the soap and the washcloth, the touch of the caregiver, the raising and lowering of arms, and the movement of tactile stimulation from one part of the body to another often overwhelm the person's stress threshold and lead to agitation, aggression, or catastrophic reaction. Keep stimulation as singular and focused as possible. For instance, during bathing, turn the water from the tub faucet off before the resident enters the tub room. To promote warmth, comfort, and security, cover each unclothed area with a bath blanket as the person is undressed. A couple of bath blankets can be used to cover the resident while he or she is in the tub and then raised only in the area needed to allow a hand and washcloth to do the washing.

Meeting Primary Self-Needs

Behavior problems can result if primary self-needs are not met but can also be triggered by the methods used to meet primary self-needs. Primary self-needs are human beings' basic physical, comfort, and security needs. Several chapters in this book provide useful direction for meeting primary self-needs such as bathing, feeding, dressing, and eliminating. Also, drug interactions and drug side effects can be a contributing or causative factor for the onset of behavior problems. Whenever a behavior problem emerges, a careful review of medications and primary self-needs should be conducted.

Comfort is an important primary self-need. The repertoire of comfort interventions that people are using in dementia care are diverse and expand some traditional views of interventions to decrease discomfort or pain.

Case example   *Mrs. Cohen is an 87-year-old retired piano teacher with a Mini-Mental State Exam score of 3. Mrs. Cohen will feed herself some finger foods with cueing. She is totally incontinent and requires almost complete assistance with bathing, dressing, and grooming. She no longer recognizes many* *family members. Mrs. Cohen enjoys her afternoon cup of tea, continues to respond positively to classical music and pet therapy, and responds with smiles and affectionate touching to meaningful visits from her rabbi, granddaughter, and primary certified nursing assistant (CNA).*

Today Mrs. Cohen is displaying agitated perseverance: she is rocking back and forth in her reclining padded geri-chair, and her muscles are tense. Though Mrs. Cohen often displays rhythmic movements and verbalizations, today her muscles are tense and the movements are more forceful. The CNA notices this change in behavior and checks to be certain Mrs. Cohen's incontinence product is clean and dry. She also checks to be sure the resident's position is in alignment, without pressure points or other obvious sources of discomfort. The CNA notifies the nurse of her findings, and the nurse begins a physical assessment. Mrs. Cohen's vital signs are at her baseline, her heart rhythm is regular, and there are no abnormal lung sounds. Her abdomen is soft and not distended, and Mrs. Cohen was incontinent of a normal bowel movement earlier in the morning. During the next void, the nurse determines by using a leukocyte esterase dipstick that Mrs. Cohen does not appear to have a urinary tract infection. The nurse does a quick assessment of skin and soft tissue for signs of infection but finds nothing abnormal.

Behavioral strategies are initiated: Mrs. Cohen is moved to a quieter environment, and the activity therapist allows her some quiet time and then gives her a soothing backrub. Still, the anxious perseverance continues. The supervisor suggests that Mrs. Cohen may need a chemical restraint such as Haldol, but the nurse knows that she has a past history of tension headaches and currently has osteoarthritis in several joints. The nurse decides to give Mrs. Cohen 500 mg of acetaminophen, which is prescribed to be given as needed. Thirty min later Mrs. Cohen is much more relaxed and observes a Girl Scout troop sing-a-long in the lounge.

Case discussion   This case example demonstrates how involved it often is to identify and treat discomfort in people with late-stage dementia. The nurse carefully assessed for infection—an extremely common cause of change in behavior. Pneumonia, urinary tract infection, and skin and soft tissue infections (e.g. conjunctivitis) are the most prevalent infections in this population (Yoshikawa, 1994) and are discussed in detail in chapter 5. Perhaps Mrs. Cohen had a simple headache or was feeling some arthritic discomfort she could not express. If the staff did not have a systematic and comprehensive assessment and treatment plan, Mrs. Cohen's discomfort could have been left untreated or could have been improperly treated with a chemical restraint. Because people with late-stage dementia are often unable to describe their needs, it is important for staff to be knowledgeable regarding the person's current health status and past medical and health history.

Patricia E. Noonan and Sandra A. Stearns describe many facets of planning an effective late-stage dementia care unit in chapter 4. The protocol used in their mid-stage and late-stage special care units is presented below.

If a change in condition is suspected, the nurse must obtain vital signs, perform a lung assessment, assess urinary output, test the urine for possible infection with a dipstick, and assess the skin, bowels, and soft tissue for infection or abnormality. If normal, behavioral interventions such as distraction, one-to-one activity, or taking a walk are attempted. If the interventions are ineffective in calming the behavior or identifying the meaning behind the behavior, a nonnarcotic analgesic is given for presumptive pain that cannot be expressed. If the analgesic is also ineffective, and the agitated or perseverant behavior persists, an "as needed" psychotropic drug may be administered, if ordered. If there is no order for a psychotropic drug, the physician is notified of the inconsolable behavior. To guide the staff through each of the steps of the process for dealing with behavior changes or agitation, a check-off form (see Figure 10.1) is completed and becomes part of the permanent chart. (Patricia E. Noonan, personal communication, 1995)

Nonpharmacological comfort measures that are often effective include

- positioning for comfort,
- providing a rummage box or busy apron,
- massage therapy,

1. Assessment:			Multistix (Urine)		
	+	-	Test	Result	Adult Normal
Lungs			Urinalysis Leukocytes	____	Negative
Eyes (drainage/irritation)			Nitrite	____	Negative
Skin (rash, lesion, pressure)			Protein	____	Negative
Rectal check			pH	____	5 - 8.5
Multistix (see right)			Blood	____	Negative
* If any of above are +, chart & intervene as needed			Specific Gravity	____	1.000-1.030
2. If all of above are negative, try behavioral interventions, i.e. distraction, 1:1 activity, snacks, walking, audio/video tapes.	% if done		Ketones	____	Negative
			Glucose	____	Negative
3. If unsuccessful, medicate with non-narcotic analgesic per physician order.					
4. If behavior still persists, medicate with prn psych medication per physician order or call physician/psych consult, and chart in nurses' notes.			Signature: _____ Date: _____		

Figure 10.1   Protocol for behavioral changes and agitation.

- flannel bedsheets and silk pillowcases,
- placement of meaningful pictures from the resident's past within view,
- empathetic communication techniques,
- one-on-one interaction,
- hand lotioning,
- decreasing environmental stress, and
- allowing time for inner retreat.

Allowing Regulated Inner Retreat

As noted in chapter 3, the available research (Kovach & Meyer-Arnold, 1996), anecdotal experience, and several theoretical papers (Hall & Buckwalter, 1987; Kitwood & Bredin, 1992; Sabat & Harre, 1992) suggest that people with late-stage dementia do have a need for inner retreat times. This time needs to be balanced with the need for social connectedness and meaningful human interaction. For example, intervening when a resident is repetitively rocking or calmly repeating a phrase such as "mama, mama, mama" often results in increased agitation. Allowing the person this inner retreat will often result in no escalation of the activity, and the behavior will subside without intervention in approximately 30 min. Inner retreat may be serving a function, and thinking of the behavior as possibly useful to the person may make it easier for caregivers to tolerate the repetition because it no longer signals discomfort. If the perseveration is tense and stressed, it often signals discomfort and requires intervention such as those discussed in the case example.

Downtime or inner retreat may take several forms: the need to be physically removed from others in a quiet room; the need to perseverate verbally or through rhythmic movement; the need to display null behavior, in which the person is physically inactive, with eyes open but not focused on a particular event or person, and in which no purposeful activity is apparent; and the need to engage in somnolent behavior, in which the person is not deeply sleeping but will have eyes closed in apparent sleep for short periods of time and is easily aroused. Not enough is yet understood about the dynamic between the apparent need for more inner retreat during late-stage dementia and the notion that too much withdrawn behavior appears to contribute to loss of personhood. It still may be difficult to determine when down time is a therapeutic inner retreat or when it is excessive and contributes to neglect of the person's social needs. Interventions relative to inner retreat are discussed in the Specific Behaviors section of this chapter.

Increasing Social Connections

While making rounds on a unit in a nursing home, the nurse manager was asked why every person who had late-stage dementia was still in bed at 10:30 a.m., in nightclothes, and exhibiting null or somnolent behavior. The nurse honestly replied, "Well, these are the residents who can't complain, so we do them up last."

What a sad testament to the lack of knowledge and effort being given to this needy population. Compared with individuals with mid-stage dementia, individuals with late-stage dementia often need more stimulation to elicit responsiveness and engagement in an activity. As the illness progresses, it does become more difficult to stimulate the person. Even if the person does not acknowledge or respond to the stimulation, there is still a need to make meaningful human connections. The caregiver may need to get into a position where eye contact is possible and use touch and verbal stimulation to communicate. People with late-stage dementia need focused and meaningful human interaction. An example of focused social connection is a quiet conversation in which the words may be poorly understood but the message of safety, caring, and connection is clear. Lotion massages of the hands, back, and so forth should be attempted, though some people with late-stage dementia become more agitated with this intervention. People with late-stage dementia who exhibit affective symptoms such as tearfulness and depressed affect generally respond well to meaningful human interaction. Recitation of prayers that are familiar to the person seems to evoke a cadence and familiarity that yields positive responses. Truly sharing and enjoying a hot cup of coffee, a glass of nonalcoholic wine, a sweet roll, or a musical recording is a pleasurable and social experience. Pet therapy is useful. Bringing toddlers in with their mothers evokes great enthusiasm. Though the response of some of the residents to the toddlers may evoke fear in older children, young toddlers will play on a mat with their parent and are oblivious to the enthusiastic grunts and flailing arms coming from the observers. In summary, make meaningful human connections with the residents every day. This is the most important role of caregivers in maintaining personhood. The person with late-stage dementia is a living person with physical, psychological, social, and spiritual needs who must be assisted to engage in life-affirming activities. If caregivers fail to make these human connections, the patient can indeed lose personhood.

SPECIFIC BEHAVIORS

Alterations in behavior commonly exhibited by the person with late-stage dementia are of three main types: alterations in activity, alterations in perception, and aggression. Most behaviors associated with late-stage dementia are manifested as changes in activity. Increased activity is seen in perseverance, rummaging, active hands, and sundown syndrome. Decreased activity is seen when there is excessive null and somnolent behavior. The dementing illnesses can also cause the person to experience alterations in perception in the form of delusions and hallucinations. Aggressive behaviors usually indicate that the person is either expressing psychological pain or is trying to cope with a perceived threat.

Perseverance

Perseverance is defined as repetitive movement or verbalization. This behavior often occurs during the sundowning time of day. Perseverance may indicate boredom, discomfort, or be used as a coping mechanism. Perseverance may be classified as tense or calm. Calm perseverance is identified by the calm rhythm of the movements or verbalizations, a relaxed facial expression, and relaxed muscles of the arms and legs. There is no escalation in the intensity of the perseverance. Calm perseverance probably does not need to be treated as it may be a coping mechanism. If the person appears bored, try to get the person involved in another group or individual activity that provides some stimulation. Make sure the rhythmic body movements do not cause abrasions or other harm. Perseveration can increase the environmental stress in the immediate area. If this becomes a problem, the resident may need to be situated in an area where he or she can be observed but will not overwhelm the other residents' stress thresholds. If the perseveration consistently lasts more than 30-45 min it may need to be treated as a tense perseveration.

Tense perseveration is identifiable by tense vocalizations, tense muscles, and forceful repetitiveness and rhythms. Tense perseveration often escalates from minimally tight muscles and slow rhythms to strong rhythms and very tight muscles. This type of perseveration indicates physical or psychological discomfort and needs to be treated. Interventions that may be helpful include

- assessing the time of day of occurrence. If perseveration is associated with sundowning, try the interventions listed under sundowning.
- moving the person to a less stressful environment.
- making sure the person's elimination needs have been met. Change incontinence products, put the person on a toilet, and check for constipation or impaction.
- making sure basic comfort needs have been met: Offer a glass of juice, put a sweater on the person, and check for pressure points and good body positioning.
- meaningful human interaction: Talk to the person calmly and soothingly, and use soft touch.
- doing a physical assessment to identify sources of discomfort or illness. Be alert for signs of infection. Test a urine specimen with a leukocyte esterase dipstick as a screen for urinary tract infection.
- checking the resident's health and medical history and current health status to identify possible sources of discomfort.
- giving the person an ordered analgesic.
- consulting with physician, family member, or other health care professional for possible causes of the behavior and treatments.
- giving an ordered chemical restraint (but only after other options have been exhausted).

Wandering and Need for Movement

Even though the person with late-stage dementia often has mobility problems that prevent the wandering behavior often seen in mid-stage dementia, there still can be an enhanced need to move. Research suggests that this need for movement is associated with having been physically active in earlier life and using physical activity as a coping mechanism throughout life (Cohen-Mansfield, Werner, Marx,

& Freedman, 1991; Dawson & Reid, 1987; Thomas, 1995). After eliminating discomfort as a cause for the behavior, the best intervention is to create safe movement areas.

- If the person is able to ambulate, assist the person several times a day to walk. Exercise mats on the floor allow free form physical movement without constraint.
- Specially designed safe rockers are popular with some residents.
- Holding the person's upper body in your arms in a hugging fashion and rocking together with the person may be soothing.
- Active and passive range of motion exercises can still be used and are associated with expressions of pleasure and relaxation even in late-stage dementia.

Rummaging and Active Hands

It is very common for the person with late-stage dementia to have excessive hand activity: picking at a robe, wringing a washcloth, tapping the siderail, fidgeting with bedlinens and clothes, and rummaging through things. After discomfort and other primary care needs have been eliminated, provide the person with safe activities for the hands. Therapeutic-activity sales catalogues contain many interesting manual activity items. Be certain all items used are safe and cannot be swallowed, lead to strangulation, or other harm.

Residents with late-stage dementia may appear to display inappropriate sexual behavior, but the behavior is more likely a reflection of an activity disturbance and overactive hands. The person may undress in inappropriate places, touch his or her private parts so excessively that injury or infection results, or touch his or her genitals in public. Even though sexual behavior between residents is seen during mid-stage dementia and can be appropriate or problematic depending on the circumstances, during late-stage dementia, people generally do not have either the mobility, functional skills, or cognitive awareness to engage in sexual behavior with another person.

- Decrease the stress the person is experiencing if it appears that his or her stress threshold is being exceeded.
- If, on the other hand, the person appears bored, give him or her more activities.
- Provide men with pants without a fly and zipper.
- Use shirts and dresses with buttons in the back so the resident can't easily undress.
- Keep fingernails clean and trimmed.
- Rummage boxes containing a variety of textures such as Velcro, fur, sandpaper, zippers, and so on are very therapeutic. Some rummage boxes can have a theme, such as baseball or Christmas, and may elicit some reminiscence or familiarity.
- Provide busy aprons and busy boards. A busy board with a theme, such as auto mechanics, can be constructed by a volunteer or the maintenance department.

- A variety of interesting tactile and visual handballs are widely available.
- Try to tie activities to something familiar from the past. For example, the former accountant may enjoy folding paper, manipulating paper clips and index cards, and "using" a calculator or typewriter.

Null and Somnolent Behavior

Null and somnolent behavior are more prevalent during late-stage dementia. There is no formula for the correct balance of active time to inactive time. The schedule that has worked well in hospice households is to get residents into the dining or activity room for breakfast. This requires awakening between 6:30 and 7:00 a.m. Residents will have one 30-min quiet period in the morning and then need a 1½ hr nap in bed around 1:30 to 2:30 p.m. Residents will have another quiet time after dinner, and most residents will be in bed by 9:00 p.m. If residents exhibit excessive null behavior or somnolent behavior try these interventions:

- Assess drugs and drug-interaction side effects.
- Assess quality and quantity of nighttime and afternoon sleep. Enhance sleep by eliminating caffeine, offering warm milk, having a bedtime routine, and making sure the resident feels safe and secure through lighting, blankets, pictures, and so forth. Make sure the resident's primary self-needs are met. Make the afternoon nap time-limited.
- Provide more stimulation. Try new and different activities. Try more one-on-one activities. Continually provide cueing and positive encouragement for active behaviors. Add as many social activities as the resident can tolerate without exceeding the stress threshold. Provide a variety of sensory stimulating activities each day to facilitate rementia: smell, touch, taste, listening, seeing. Accept the person and his or her functional limitations unconditionally.
- Change the person's environment. Give the person a new place to be and some new experiences such as pet therapy. Take the resident to the cafeteria or snack shop and enjoy a special beverage or food item.

Sundown Syndrome

As already noted in chapter 3, people with late-stage dementia seem to experience an increase in agitation late in the day more than during other stages of the illness. Though often spoken of as occurring in the evening, late afternoon is also a common time for sundowning behavior. To prevent sundowning, plan a physical activity approximately 2½ hr before the usual sundown period. After this activity put the person into bed for a 1–1½ hr nap. Get the person up and involve them in a one-on-one activity in a low stress environment just before and during their usual sundown period. Other possible interventions to treat sundowning include

- keeping lighting up to daytime levels until bedtime,
- allowing more inner retreat time,

- decreasing stresses from the environment,
- checking for discomfort, hunger, thirst, and other primary self-needs,
- increasing feelings of security by nestling the person in a reclining padded geri-chair with bath blankets and pillows, a soft plush animal, or doll,
- calmly reassuring the person,
- increasing feelings of familiarity through friendly visiting, keeping familiar items close, and establishing a consistent routine, and
- keeping daytime naps time-limited and scheduled.

Delusions and Hallucinations

As the illness progresses there is a greater likelihood that the person will have increased difficulty being oriented to reality, and a variety of alterations can occur. These alterations are a real part of the person's mental life and can be very discomforting.

A delusion is an incorrect idea or belief that persists even when there is evidence that contradicts the belief. A delusion may involve suspicion that the person will be harmed or fear that people are stealing from him or her. If a person is experiencing a delusion, it is important to assess whether the idea is in fact false, especially if it involves suspected abuse or theft. Not all delusions are about negative beliefs. One woman with late-stage dementia was very comforted by the daily sustained delusion that she was pregnant.

A hallucination is an incorrect sensory experience. The person sees, hears, tastes, smells, or feels something without external stimulation and that cannot be verified by someone else. Common hallucinations involve seeing something that is not there, such as vases or bugs on the wall, or hearing voices or sounds that are not apparent to others.

The interventions for delusions and hallucinations are similar. If a delusion or hallucination is not upsetting to the person, it often does not require intervention. It does seem, however, that delusions and hallucinations often are upsetting and are undertreated. Residents are then left to suffer unnecessary fear and discomfort. Pharmacological intervention is often needed when delusions and hallucinations are present and is discussed in more detail in chapter 11. There is often a need to adjust the dosage or change the medication, so if one prescription is not working, continue working with the geropsychiatry staff and do not just ignore these discomforting symptoms.

Some basic interventions that may be helpful when delusions or hallucinations are evident include

- checking to be sure the person's glasses are clean and on,
- checking to be sure the person's hearing aid is in place and functioning properly,
- having the nurse screen for any acute illness or exacerbation of chronic illness,

- determining that the person has had adequate food and fluid intake, and
- making certain that the person's stress threshold has not been exceeded.

Consult with the geropsychiatry staff for persistent delusions and hallucinations. If the delusions or hallucinations worsen or are upsetting to the person, consult with the geropsychiatry staff again for possible medication alterations. Do not allow the person to continue experiencing persistent upsetting hallucinations or delusions without medical intervention. If the person is upset or fearful from a delusion or hallucination, do not agree or disagree that their idea or sensory experience is correct or incorrect. Rather, validate and be supportive of their feelings through a statement such as, "I hear that you are afraid and I will help you. You are safe and we will be sure to keep you safe."

Distraction will sometimes help to decrease delusions and hallucinations. Often, particularly in the case of hallucinations, there is a need to either increase the lighting in the room or move the person from the room for a while. A comforting and frequently effective intervention is to nestle the person securely into a reclining padded geri-chair or bed with warm fabrics such as bath blankets and thermal blankets. Soft pillows, a favorite plush pet animal, and the companionship of a staff member will often decrease feelings of fear and eliminate the hallucination or delusion. It is most imperative for the caregiver to give the person attention. Even taking some comforting intervention such as changing the person's positions, readjusting bedlinens, or sitting with the person for a while may soothe the person's troubled state.

Aggressive Behavior

Aggressive behavior may be verbal or physical and may involve a catastrophic reaction, in which the person's response to an event such as spilling some milk is overly intense and sudden. Aggressive behavior may be self-directed. Remember that the aggression is caused by the person's illness and does not indicate that the person is trying to be bad or that the person doesn't like you. Do not take it personally or let the event hurt your feelings. The person with dementia has lost control over impulses and can therefore act quickly, impulsively, and aggressively when there is a feeling of threat or fear. The aggressive response is actually the person's attempt to cope with or combat a perceived threat. Some basic interventions used to prevent and treat aggressive behavior are

- decreasing the amount of environmental stress,
- anticipating the person's needs to prevent frustration and discomfort,
- increasing inner retreat time and making sure the person has a balance between sensory stimulating and sensory calming experiences,
- assessing what triggers the aggression and preventing the triggering event from occurring in the future, and
- distracting the person from the triggering event by redirecting the person's attention.

Speak to the person in a calm and reassuring voice at all times. Keep the message clear and simple. Do not scold or try to teach the person, as both approaches are ineffective. Involve the person in activities in which he or she can be successful to decrease frustration levels. Try giving the person some more physical activity to release energy and stress.

People with dementia who are prone to aggressive behavior often perceive direct eye contact, touch, and invasion of personal body space as threatening. Keep the person in a calm predictable environment, avoiding new people and places if this is upsetting. Touch the person slowly and gently and allow some distance between yourself and the person. Be aware that the person may be overly sensitive to tactile stimulation and may not tolerate a lot of touching or an invasion of his or her personal body space. Do not use direct eye contact if this is upsetting to the person. Do not approach the person from behind because this may be upsetting and confusing. Do not approach directly from the front as you may be most vulnerable to being struck from this position. Approach slowly and calmly at an angle from a direct frontal approach.

If the person displays self-directed aggression such as hitting him- or herself or picking at skin, in addition to the behavioral interventions listed, be sure to keep the person's nails trimmed, give the person a rummage box, busy apron, or plush pet to fiddle with, and protect the person's skin and body from harm. Finally, if the aggression does not respond to behavioral interventions, consult with the physician or nurse practitioner for possible pharmacological intervention.

CONCLUSION

Many behaviors associated with dementia are not problems in and of themselves but are an expression of an underlying feeling, need, or coping mechanism. A good program for late-stage dementia allows and accepts behaviors that are an expression of feeling or coping and anticipates needs of residents, thereby eliminating or greatly reducing behavior problems. Caregivers who make needed social connections are challenged by the person's need for more stimulation and the muted and lessened responses from the person with late-stage dementia. There is a need to celebrate the small successes in meeting people's needs at the end stage of a difficult illness.

BIBLIOGRAPHY

Cohen, U., & Weisman, G. D. (1991). *Holding on to home*. Baltimore, MD: Johns Hopkins University Press.

Cohen-Mansfield, J., Werner, P., Marx, M. S., & Freedman, L. (1991). Two studies of pacing in the nursing home. *Journal of Gerontology, 46*, M77–M83.

Dawson, P., & Reid, D. W. (1987). Behavioral dimensions of patients at risk of wandering. *Gerontologist, 27*, 104–107.

Hall, G. R., & Buckwalter, K. C. (1987). Progressively lowered stress threshold: A conceptual model for care of adults with Alzheimer's disease. *Archives of Psychiatric Nursing, 1*, 399–406.

Kitwood, T., & Bredin, K. (1992). Towards a theory of dementia care: Personhood and well-being. *Aging and Society, 12*, 269–287.

Kovach, C. R., & Meyer-Arnold, E. A. (1996). Coping with conflicting agendas: The bathing experience of cognitively impaired older adults. *Scholarly Inquiry for Nursing Practice, 10*(1), 23–26.

Kovach, C. R., & Stearns, S. A. (1994). DSCU's: A study of behavior before and after residence. *Journal of Gerontological Nursing, 20*, 33–39.

Sabat, S. R., & Harre, R. (1992). The construction and deconstruction of self in Alzheimer's disease. *Aging and Society, 12*, 443–461.

Thomas, D. (1995). *The effect of premorbid personality characteristics and leisure preferences on wandering behavior among hospitalized patients with dementia.* Unpublished doctoral dissertation, Temple University, Philadelphia.

Yoshikawa, T. T. (1994). Approach to the diagnosis and treatment of the infected older adult. In W. R. Hazzard, E. L. Bierman, J. P. Plass, W. H. Ettinger, Jr., & J. B. Halter (Eds.), *Principles of geriatric medicine and gerontology* (pp. 1157–1164). New York: McGraw-Hill.

Chapter 11

Psychopharmacology and Late-Stage Dementia Behaviors

Ladislav Volicer, Ann C. Hurley, and E. Mahoney

Alzheimer's disease and other progressive dementias are some of the main public health problems in American society. The incidence of dementias increases with age, with one study indicating that 10% of individuals over the age of 65 and 47% of individuals over the age of 85 suffer from probable Alzheimer's disease (Evans et al., 1989). Because the population of people over the age of 85 is the fastest growing segment of American society, the prevalence of dementias is increasing rapidly. Dementia is also one of the most prevalent problem suffered by nursing home residents in the United States. The 1985 National Nursing Home Survey (U. S. Department of Health and Human Services, Public Health Service, Centers for Disease Control, and National Center for Health Statistics, 1989) found that 62% of all nursing home residents were so disoriented or memory impaired that their ability to perform activities of daily living was impaired nearly every day. Other smaller studies have found that the proportion of residents with clinically diagnosable dementia is even higher, reaching 72–78% (Chandler & Chandler, 1988; Rovner, Kafonek, & Filipp, 1986).

The primary symptoms of dementia are memory problems and other cognitive impairments interfering with daily living activities (Corey-Bloom et al., 1995). These include both comprehension problems and functional deficits due to apraxia (Figure 11.1). In addition, most demented patients exhibit one or more secondary behavioral symptoms that can be either disruptive or nondisruptive. The nondisruptive behavioral problem is apathy, which is exhibited by many patients. There is no unified terminology for description of disruptive behavioral problems. Different investigators use several labels for these symptoms, including agitation, aggressiveness, and combativeness. Disruptive behavior is very common in nursing home

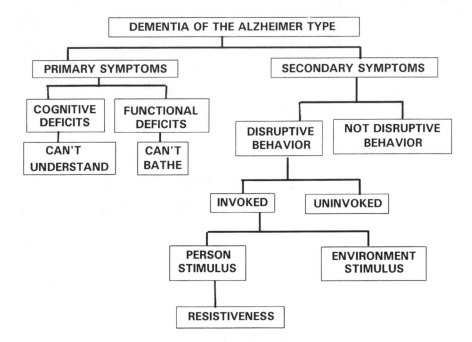

Figure 11.1 Primary and secondary symptoms in dementia of the Alzheimer type.

residents. For instance, Cohen-Mansfield (1988) reported that two agitated behaviors, which included physical and verbal aggression, occurred at least once a week in 87% of demented nursing home residents, and Ryden, Bossenmaier, and McLachlan (1991) found aggressive behavior to be present in 86% of demented nursing home residents. In large probability samples drawn from all nursing home residents (not only those with dementia), estimates of the prevalence of disruptive behaviors range from 26% to 64% (Jackson et al., 1989; Zimmer, Watson, & Treat, 1984). Management of disruptive behaviors is important not only because these behaviors may endanger the safety of the patient, other residents, and staff but also because these behaviors are often reflections of the patient's discomfort. Furthermore, the recent trend toward understanding the perspective of the person with dementia suggests that the behavioral symptoms may be more disabling than the historically emphasized cognitive decline. In a recent review of interventions for treating behavioral problems, Beck and Shue (1994) emphasized the importance of a conceptual framework that encompasses biological as well as psychosocial explanations for understanding and managing disruptive behaviors.

The management of secondary behavioral symptoms of dementia requires a careful evaluation of the patient. It cannot be assumed that the behavior is a symptom of dementia just because the patient is demented. As outlined in chapter 10, the behavior may be a consequence of discomfort caused by a physical illness that the patient cannot report because of speech and cognitive impairments. Conditions such as pain, infections, cardiovascular insufficiency, constipation, dyspnea, and liver or kidney failure may lead to behavioral symptoms that can be readily alleviated by correcting the underlying problem. Interestingly, in qualitative interviews with nursing staff on our dementia special care units, we have found that expert nurses consider change in behavioral symptoms (increase or decrease) to presage overt physical illness (Mahoney, 1996).

However, no reversible medical problem can be found in most cases. These patients have to be evaluated carefully to determine which aspects of the dementing process are triggering the behavioral symptoms. This evaluation is very important because the secondary symptoms can be managed more effectively by treating the underlying process rather than by trying to block the behavioral consequences themselves. Several levels of the processes can be distinguished (Figure 11.2). At the core of the symptoms is, of course, the dementing process itself. This process not only directly causes functional impairment but also may cause delusions, hallucinations, and depression. These primary consequences in turn lead to spatial disorientation, anxiety, dependence in activities of daily living, and the inability to initiate meaningful activities. Behavioral symptoms, such as agi-

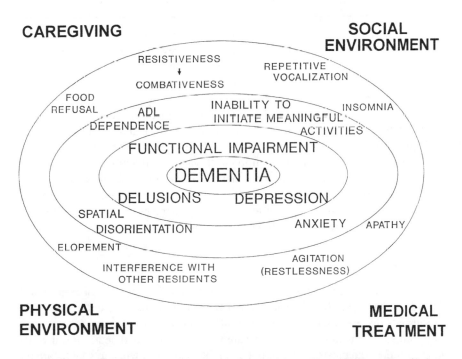

Figure 11.2 Causes of problem behaviors in Alzheimer's patients. (From "Management of behavioral symptoms of dementia" by L. Volicer, A. Hurley, & E. Mahoney, 1995, *Nursing Home Medicine, 3*(12), 300–306. Reprinted by permission.)

tation or aggressive behavior, are peripheral expressions of these more basic processes. All processes at the more basic level influence the next level in a comprehensive way. Thus, delusions may result in spatial disorientation, anxiety, and dependence in performing activities of daily living, whereas depression may lead to anxiety and the inability to initiate meaningful activities. Similarly, spatial disorientation may lead to elopement attempts, combativeness, interference with other patients, and agitation. Inability to initiate meaningful activities may lead to apathy, repetitive vocalization, agitation, and insomnia. Therefore, not only are there multiple possible etiologies for specific behavioral symptoms, but also the scope of therapeutic effectiveness is broader when interventions are directed closer to the core. The relationships of the underlying processes to behavioral symptoms may differ from patient to patient and may differ for the same patient at different times. Therefore, the effective management of behavioral symptoms requires careful and comprehensive evaluation of all possible contributing factors. This conceptual framework emphasizes biological factors, but the role of the physical and social environments also must be considered.

Viewed in this way, behaviors are understood as symptoms of an underlying process or as a meaningful response to disability or an environment that may be perceived as threatening, uncomfortable, confusing, or beyond control (Burgener, Jirovec, Murrell, & Barton, 1992; Gwyther, 1994; Sloane et al., 1995). The basic tenet of ethology, that all behavior has meaning (Eibl-Eibesfeldt, 1989), guides the practitioner to search for etiology as a target for preventive and therapeutic care. Behavior is the outcome of the interaction between personal and environmental systems, which include physical environment, social environment, caregiving strategies, and management of intercurrent diseases (Figure 11.2). Empirical evidence of the contextual nature of behavior is beginning to accumulate in support of earlier theoretical insights about the role of the physical and social environment in shaping behavior in people with dementia (Hall & Buckwalter, 1987; Lawton & Nahemow, 1973). Behavior has been found to vary as a function of setting, activity, complexity of demands, and the nature of caregiver–patient interactions (Beck, 1988; Burgener et al., 1992; Burgio et al., 1994; Cohen-Mansfield & Werner, 1995). Therefore, the first approach to management of behavioral symptoms of dementia should be a well designed behavioral intervention.

DEMENTIA

The most common dementia is dementia of the Alzheimer type (Kokmen, Beard, Offord, & Kurland, 1989). The second most common is vascular dementia. Parkinson's disease, Pick's disease, and diffuse Lewy body disease are less common forms of dementia. In long-term care facilities, a detailed neurological work-up and clinical diagnosis are often not available and, even when available, are not always accurate. Although there are some differences in behavioral symptoms depending on the etiology of dementia, the basic processes underlying these symptoms are similar. This similarity extends even to some nonprogressive dementias, such as those resulting from anoxic insult or subdural hematomas. On the other hand, patients with Korsakoff's disease and chronic psychiatric problems often have behaviors that require different management approaches. This chapter concentrates on caring for elderly patients who have a progressive dementia.

Progressive dementias cause loss of nerve cells and other irreversible brain changes. This leads to development of cognitive impairments that include memory deficit, poor judgment, and other impairments, which are described below. Currently, there are only few pharmacological options for treatment of progressive dementias. Tacrine (Cognex) is approved for treatment of dementia of the Alzheimer type and may be also beneficial in diffuse Lewy body disease. It most likely acts by inhibiting breakdown of acetylcholine, one of the chemicals in the brain that the nerve cells use to communicate with each other. Acetylcholine is important for memory processes, which are disrupted even in healthy individuals who are given drugs that block acetylcholine effect (Beatty, Butters, & Janowsky, 1986). Postmortem examination of brains of Alzheimer patients has shown that the number of nerve cells that use acetylcholine are markedly reduced. This leads to acetylcholine deficit, which may be responsible for the memory problems of patients with Alzheimer's disease. Inhibition of acetylcholine breakdown by Tacrine should enhance function of the remaining cells and may improve memory and other cognitive functions.

However, this effect is present only in earlier stages of dementia when there are still some cells remaining. In addition, many patients do not tolerate effective doses of Tacrine because they develop liver toxicity (Watkins, Zimmerman, Knapp, Gracon, & Lewis, 1994). Even in patients who tolerate the therapy, Tacrine merely delays the progression of dementia, on the average by 6 months (Knapp et al., 1994). Low-dose aspirin therapy may be effective in delaying the progression of a multi-infarct dementia (Grotta, 1987) by decreasing blood clotting but is also not completely effective. Despite these limitations in treatment of the dementing process, there are therapeutic strategies that can be applied to treat some consequences of dementia in the encircling levels.

DELUSIONS AND HALLUCINATIONS

As noted in chapter 10, delusions are very common in all stages of dementia. Paranoid delusions are sometimes the first symptom of progressive dementia observed in a long-term care settings because other impairments may not be detected in a sheltered nursing home environment. In some patients, delusions can be managed by distracting and involving the patient in an activity. It is important to respond to a patient's feeling rather than to argue or correct. Paranoid delusions, for example, beliefs that things being lost or food is being poisoned, usually respond well to low doses of neuroleptics. Neuroleptics have been widely used to treat psychiatric symptoms of dementia, although controlled clinical trials are limited. The framework proposed here may identify relevant outcomes for future study, including behaviors that may improve, as well as those

Table 11.1   Selected drugs used for treatment of behavioral symptoms of dementia

Drug class	Name	Dose range	Frequency
Antidementia	Tacrine (Cognex)	10–40 mg	QID
Antipsychotics	Haloperidol (Haldol)	0.5–1 mg	QD–TID
	Fluphenazine (Prolixin)	0.5–1 mg	QD–TID
	Thiothixene (Navane)	–2 mg	QD–TID
	Perphenazine (Trilafon)	2–4 mg	QD– TID
	Thioridazine (Mellaril)	10–40 mg	QD–TID
	Mesoridazine (Serentil)	10–50 mg	QD–TID
	Risperidone (Risperdal)	0.5–1 mg	QOD–BID
Antidepressants	Sertraline (Zoloft)	50–200 mg	QAM
	Paroxetine (Paxil)	10–40 mg	QAM
	Trazodone (Desyrel)	50–100 mg	TID or HS
	Doxepin (Sinequan)	25–100 mg	HS
Antianxiety	Lorazepam (Ativan)	0.5–1 mg	QD–TID
	Buspirone (Buspar)	5–20 mg	TID
Anticonvulsants	Valproic acid (Depakene)	250–500 mg	BID–QID*
	Carbamazepine (Tegretol)	100–200 mg	BID–QID*

that may decline as a result of side effects such as sedation, anticholinergic symptoms, or muscle rigidity.

All neuroleptics are equally effective in this patient population, although at different dosages (Table 11.1). However, they differ significantly in their side effects. Drugs such as haloperidol (Haldol) and fluphenazine (Prolixin) have a high incidence of extrapyramidal side effects, resulting in blunt affect, muscle rigidity, and dystonia. In contrast, thioridazine (Mellaril) and mesoridazine (Serentil) may cause postural hypotension, cardiac arrhythmias, and sedation. In between are thiothixene (Navane) and perphenazine (Trilafon), which may have both types of side effects but to a lesser extent. The choice of neuroleptics should be guided by the current risk factors for side effects the patient has. A patient with pre-existing muscle rigidity should not receive haloperidol, and a patient with significant cardiovascular comorbidity should not be treated with thioridazine. A new neuroleptic, risperidone (Risperdal) has fewer side effects than the older neuroleptics. It has, however, a very long duration of action, which may lead to buildup of its level in the body and overmedication.

Patients sometimes refuse medications, and that makes the treatment more difficult. Auditory hallucinations, which consist of hearing voices of other patients or staff criticizing the patient, are also common. Hallucinations are more common in patients who have diffuse Lewy body disease. These patients are more sensitive to the side effects of older neuroleptics and may respond better to risperidone.

As the dementia progresses, patients become more confused and often develop delusions regarding their circumstances. Residents may believe that they are working in the nursing home or that they are at a school or in their parent's house. They may also develop delusions regarding another patient or staff, whom they believe is a relative who should obey the patient. Such delusions may lead to spatial disorientation and anxiety; elopement, interference with other patients, and agitation. Demented patients suffering from delusions may also misinterpret staff's caregiving activities and resist such efforts.

Case Example

> Mrs. Vanicelli, a 78-year-old woman with mid-stage dementia lived at home with her husband and 48-year-old developmentally disabled daughter. When her husband died, Mrs. Vanicelli and her daughter were unable to continue to live independently. Mrs. Vanicelli had one brother living in England but no other support systems. Two months after her husband's death, Mrs. Vanicelli was admitted to a mid-stage special care unit, and her daughter was moved to a group home.
>
> Mrs. Vanicelli had multi-infarct dementia and had had two previous major strokes. She seemed to be adjusting well to the move until 2 weeks after admission when she became nonverbal, refused to eat, bathe, dress, or communicate, and would not move from a fetal position in bed.
>
> Over the next 2 weeks Mrs. Vanicelli consumed only small amounts of liquid nourishment and showed no improvement. She had no obvious unilateral weakness, but assessments were difficult because she became violent if anyone attempted to touch her. It was unclear whether Mrs. Vanicelli had had a stroke or was severely depressed because of the multiple recent losses she had experienced. Staff on the special care unit attempted some stroke rehabilitation interventions, but these were responded to with violent outbursts.
>
> Mrs. Vanicelli was transferred to the late-stage care unit, where she was treated for depression with sertraline (Zoloft) and a consistent, supportive caregiving team. Over a period of 3 months she began to consume normal amounts of food, began to enjoy short walks and socializing, and would smile and join activities. She continued to retreat from touch and invasion of her personal body space. As the depression lifted it became clear she was not in the late stages of dementia. She did, however, refuse to return to the mid-stage special care unit.

Case Discussion

Making the diagnosis of depression in a demented individual is very difficult. Several symptoms of major depressive disorder are commonly seen during some of the stages of a progressive dementia, and the assessment is complicated by speech and comprehension difficulties. Therefore, the estimates of depression in demented patients vary from 15% to 57% (Lazarus, Newton, Cohler, Lesser, & Schwein, 1987). Sometimes depression is the first symptom of dementia, and most patients who develop their first episode of depression in old age eventually develop dementia (Emery & Oxman, 1992). The diagnosis of depression in a demented patient can be made by carefully monitoring the patient's expression, obtaining information about episodes of tearfulness and crying from the staff, and evaluating eating and sleeping patterns. Angry affect, which is common even in younger depressed patients (Apter et al., 1990), may be the main symptom of depression. In the case of Mrs. Vanicelli, difficulty making the diagnosis of depression led to some inappropriate interventions and a discharge from the mid-stage unit that was probably unnecessary.

Depression leads to anxiety and contributes to the inability to initiate meaningful activities. As in the case of Mrs. Vanicelli, depression may play a role in food refusal, resistiveness, apathy, insomnia, and agitation. Thus, a large proportion of behavioral symptoms may be caused or worsened by an underlying depression. Behavioral approaches to treatment of depression include using positive feedback and maintaining interaction with the environment. Antidepressant treatment has improved the mood of patients, even those with advanced dementia, and has increased food intake in patients who previously refused food (Volicer, Rheaume, & Cyr, 1994).

Although older trycyclic antidepressants (such as desipramine) are effective in this patient population, they have frequent anticholinergic and cardiovascular side effects. The newer specific serotonin reuptake inhibitors have fewer side effects (e.g., sertraline [Zoloft] and paroxetine [Paxil]) and allow for safe treatment of depression even in very old patients who have other concurrent diseases. Some antidepressants (e.g., trazodone [Desyrel] and doxepin [Sinequan]) have sedation as one of their side effects. This effect could be utilized in the treatment of insomnia in demented patients who also are depressed (see Table 11.1). Mrs. Vanicelli's severe depression lifted in about 3 months with the use of only one medication. Frequently, if symptoms do not improve, there may be a need to consult with the geropsychiatry staff to switch medications or to try a combination of drugs.

FUNCTIONAL IMPAIRMENT

Functional impairment of a demented patient is related to both cognitive and physical impairments. Cognitive impairment includes the inability to use tools (apraxia) or to recognize objects (agnosia) and speech impairment (aphasia). Physical impairment, such as a paralysis due to stroke, aggravates the consequences of dementia. Therefore, it is important to maintain an adequate physical condition even in a patient with dementia. This includes rehabilitation after injury, such as hip fracture or stroke. Rehabilitation is of course limited by the inability of the patient to follow directions and remember instructions. It also may become counterproductive if it leads to discomfort and fatigue. Some strategies that have been found helpful in treating other populations may still be applied. For example, people with apraxia may be able to imitate, even when unable to initiate an activity. Once started, they may be able to continue unaided.

An important function that is lost in late-stage dementia is the ability to walk, followed by the loss of the ability to stand. Residents either develop an unsteady gait or lose the ability to recognize and react safely to objects in their path. Some residents also develop leg contractures, which impair their mobility. To prevent contractures, patients should be encouraged and able to walk as much as possible and should spend limited periods of time sitting in a chair. Kinesitherapy promotes the ability to walk and prevents deconditioning and the development of contractures. It is also helpful to have railings along the walls and an unobstructed path for walking. Functional impairments lead to dependence in activities of daily living and inability to initiate meaningful activities. This can result in apathy, repetitive vocalization, and resistiveness to care.

ANXIETY

Anxiety is a symptom of depression, but it can be also induced by delusions and hallucinations. Functional impairment may also lead to increased anxiety if caregiving activities, such as using a Hoyer lift, frighten the patient. Anxiety in turn can lead to agitation and restlessness, repetitive vocalization, insomnia, and resistive behavior. Several chapters in this book have emphasized that anxiety is minimized by a gentle, calm approach by caregivers, by maintaining eye contact, and by explaining to the resident what is being done. The resident not only must be safe but also needs to feel safe.

The phenomenon of anxiety and fear has been described in a manner compatible with the conceptual framework proposed here. For example, Sloane et al. (1995) described fearful fantasies and beliefs associated with bathing. Ryden and Feldt (1992) identified fear as an antecedent to aggressive behaviors, and nursing staff have attributed behaviors such as grabbing to a resident's fear of falling. In each of these examples, interventions should be evaluated that target residents' feelings. Clinical evidence supports the use of environmental cues and relaxation techniques, such as playing music (Snyder, Egan, & Burns, 1995; Tabloski, McKinnon-Howe, & Remington, 1995).

Trying to correct a patient's delusions seldom succeeds in decreasing anxiety and may precipitate a catastrophic reaction. Gentle distraction and involvement in some activity is usually more effective in reducing the anxiety. If distraction is not effective, short-acting benzodiazepines such as lorazepam (Ativan) may be used to calm the patient. Another antianxiety medication is buspirone (Buspar) which, however, has a delayed onset of effect.

RESISTIVENESS–COMBATIVENESS CONTINUUM

Because residents with late-stage dementia are unable to perform activities of daily living themselves, these activities are imposed on them by the staff. The staff decides when patients go to bed and get up, when they need to be cleaned, and when they need food and liquid. Although demented, patients may not agree with staff timing or goals. Therefore, they may refuse help and impede care. If the staff insist on providing care, the patient may refuse to cooperate or actively resist. This resistiveness could escalate to a combative behavior, which may be a way by which the patient defends him- or herself against unwanted physical contact. This combativeness, which is often called an aggressive behavior, occurs predominantly during hands-on care involving touching (Ryden & Feldt, 1992).

This refusal is often only temporary, and patients may cooperate if the staff repeat their approach after a short period of time, allowing patients to forget that they did not actually want to cooperate. As presented earlier in chapter 9, another effective strategy is distraction of the patient away from the caregiving process. This may be accomplished by having two staff members working as a team. One of the staff members provides distraction by talking or joking with the patient while the other staff member provides the care (e.g., cleaning).

Delusions and hallucinations may also contribute to resistiveness. Neuroleptics are quite effective in preventing resistive behavior, although this is not confirmed by clinical studies (Helms, 1985). This apparent lack of therapeutic effectiveness is most likely due to the poor measurement tools used in these studies, which did not specifically target resistive behavior.

AGITATION–APATHY CONTINUUM

Agitation is an increase of motor activity that does not have an obvious goal. It may express itself as restlessness, repetitive vocalization, and insomnia. However, it is not uncommon for periods of agitation to alternate with periods of apathy, when the patient does not maintain any contact with the environment. Both of these behavioral symptoms may have a similar cause—a lack of meaningful activities. Agitation may be also caused by delusions or hallucinations. Residents may believe that they have to do something or be somewhere and become agitated when this is not possible.

Treatment of an underlying cause of agitation is always more effective than attempts to decrease agitation by sedating the patient. Attempts to reduce agitation by sedatives has the additional problem of side effects from sedatives that last much longer than the behavior the drugs were used to treat. In some cases, an increased activity level may be actually beneficial. This is true especially for pacing, which allows the patient to exercise, improves sleep, and prevents constipation. Repetitive vocalization is the most difficult behavioral symptom to treat. Repeated requests for help may be very disruptive for both other patients and staff. Staff intervention is often not effective in stopping the vocalization, which may be caused by a release of vocal motor activity from the higher brain function, similar to purposeless pacing.

Agitation that is not affected by other treatments sometimes responds to administration of anticonvulsants or mood stabilizers, such as valproic acid (Depakote) and carbamazepine (Tegretol). Used for this purpose, the drugs may be effective in blood concentrations lower that those required for control of seizures. Valproic acid is also effective in decreasing myoclonic movements, which sometimes interfere with feeding of patients and other care.

ELOPEMENT AND INTERFERENCE WITH OTHER PATIENTS

These symptoms may be caused by spatial disorientation but may also be due to delusions and hallucination. Alarm systems that indicate an unauthorized exit are disturbing to other patients and require staff to prevent the patient from exiting. This usually leads to patient agitation and interferes with regular care activities. The best way of securing an outside door is a keypad system. Alternatively, disguising exits by painting them the same color as the wall or by covering up the door handle may be sufficient (Dickinson, McLain-Kark, & Marshall-Baker, 1995), but disguised doors should be combined with alarms for added safety. Another strategy is having the doors locked either all the time or when a patient who presents an elopement risk approaches them. This is more easily accomplished if all patients on a unit are demented. Homogeneous grouping of patients also eliminates problems with intrusion into other patients' rooms, which is upsetting to cognitively intact patients.

Many behavioral symptoms are more easily managed on a special care dementia unit. Such a unit can design programs specific to cognitively impaired patients and can provide special training for the staff. It is easier for the staff to approach patients in a similar way instead of switching to a different approach when dealing with cognitively intact residents. Use of physical and chemical restraints can be minimized if the environment is modified to make it safe for patients who wander, are likely to touch everything, and may put inedible things in their mouths. In addition, the staff can concentrate on assuring patient comfort instead of providing aggressive medical interventions that may not be appropriate in late-stage dementia (Volicer, 1993).

CONCLUSION

Behaviors in the late stage of dementia are consequences of several basic processes. Dementia leads to functional impairment and often to delusions and depression as well. These processes precipitate another level of impairment that eventually results in problem behaviors. Problem behaviors are managed better by treatment of the underlying processes than by symptom control.

Psychopharmacological interventions are an important part of the treatment plan for many people with dementia. They are not prescribed to decrease staff workload but rather to improve comfort and quality of life for the patient. Drugs are only one part of the treatment plan and must be used with supportive behavioral and environmental interventions.

BIBLIOGRAPHY

Apter, A., Van Praag, H. M., Plutchik, R., Sevy, S., Korn, M., & Brown, S. L. (1990). Interrelationships among anxiety, aggression, impulsivity, and mood: A serotonergically linked cluster. *Psych. Res., 32,* 191–199.

Beatty, W., Butters, N., & Janowsky, D. (1986). Patterns of memory failure after scopolamine treatment: Implications for cholinergic hypotheses of dementia. *Behavioral and Neural Biology, 45,* 196–211.

Beck, C. (1988). Measurement of dressing performance in persons with dementia. *American Journal of Alzheimer's Care, 3*(3), 21–25.

Beck, C. K., Heacock, P., Mercer, S., Walton, C., & Shook, J. (1991). Dressing for success: Promoting independence among cognitively impaired elderly. *Journal of Psychosocial Nursing, 29,* 30–35.

Beck, C. K., & Shue, V. M. (1994). Interventions for treating disruptive behavior in demented elderly people. *Nursing Clinics of North America, 29,* 143–155.

Bowlby, C. (1993). *Therapeutic activities with persons disabled by Alzheimer's disease and related disorders.* Gaithersburg, MD: Aspen.

Burgener, S. C., Jirovec, M., Murrell, L., & Barton, D. (1992). Caregiver and environmental variables related to difficult behaviors in institutionalized, demented elderly persons. *Journal of Gerontology: Psychological Sciences, 47,* 242–249.

Burgio, L. D., Scilley, K., Hardin, M., Janosky, J., Bonino, P., Slater, S. C., & Engberg, R. (1994). Studying disruptive vocalization and contextual factors in the nursing home using computer-assisted real-time observation. *Gerontology, 9,* 230–239.

Chandler, J. D., & Chandler, J. E. (1988). The prevalence of neuropsychiatric disorders in a nursing home population. *Journal of Geriatric Psychiatry and Neurology, 1,* 71–76.

Cohen-Mansfield, J. (1988). Agitated behavior and cognitive functioning in nursing home residents: Preliminary results. *Clinical Gerontologist, 7*(3/4), 11–22.

Cohen-Mansfield, J., & Werner, P. (1995). Environmental influences on agitation: An integrative summary of an observational study. *American Journal of Alzheimer's Care, 10*(1), 32–39.

Corey-Bloom, J., Thal, L. J., Galasko, D., Folstein, M., Drachman, D., Raskind, M., & Lanska, D. J. (1995). Diagnosis and evaluation of dementia. *Neurology, 45,* 211–218.

Dickinson, J. I., McLain-Kark, J., & Marshall-Baker, A. (1995). The effects of visual barriers on exiting behavior in a dementia care unit. *Gerontologist, 35,* 127–130.

Eibl-Eibesfeldt, I. (1989). *Human ethology.* New York: Aldine de Gruyter.

Emery, V. O., & Oxman, T. E. (1992). Update on the dementia spectrum of depression. *American Journal of Psychiatry, 149,* 305–317.

Evans, D. A., Funkenstein, H., Albert, M. S., Scherr, P. A., Cook, N. R., Chown, M. J., Hebert, L. E., Hennekens, C. H., & Taylor, J. O. (1989). Prevalence of Alzheimer's disease in a community population of older persons. *Journal of the American Medical Association, 262,* 2551–2556.

Grotta, J. C. (1987). Current medical and surgical therapy for cerebrovascular disease. *New England Journal of Medicine, 317,* 1505–1516.

Gwyther, L. (1994). Managing challenging behaviors at home. *Alzheimer Disease and Associated Disorders, 8*(3), 110–112.

Hall, G. R., & Buckwalter, K. C. (1987). Progressively lowered stress threshold: A conceptual model for care of adults with Alzheimer's disease. *Archives of Psychiatric Nursing, 1,* 399–406.

Helms, P. M. (1985). Efficacy of antipsychotics in the treatment of the behavioral complications of dementia: Review of the literature. *Journal of the American Geriatric Society, 33,* 206–209.

Jackson, M. E., Drugovich, M. L., Fretwell, M. D., Spector, W. D., Sternberg, J., & Rosenstein, R. B. (1989). Prevalence and correlates of disruptive behavior in the nursing home. *Journal of Aging and Health, 1,* 349–369.

Knapp, M. J., Knopman, D. S., Solomon, P. R., Pendlebury, W. W., Davis, C. S., & Gracon, S. I. (1994). A 30-week randomized controlled trial of high-dose Tacrine in patients with Alzheimer's disease. *Journal of the American Medical Association, 271,* 985–991.

Kokmen, E., Beard, C. M., Offord, K. P., & Kurland, L. T. (1989). Prevalence of medically diagnosed dementia in a defined United States population: Rochester, Minnesota, January 1, 1975. *Neurology, 39,* 773–776.

Lawton, M. P., & Nahemow, L. E. (1973). Ecology and the aging process. In C. Eisdorfer & M. P. Lawton (Eds.), *Psychology of adult development and aging.* Washington, DC: American Psychological Association.

Lazarus, L. W., Newton, N., Cohler, B., Lesser, J., & Schwein, C. (1987). Frequency and presentation of depressive symptoms in patients with primary degenerative dementia. *American Journal of Psychiatry, 144,* 41–45.

Mahoney, E. (1996). *Nursing perceptions of behavioral symptoms exhibited by people with dementia.* Unpublished manuscript.

Rovner, B. W., Kafonek, S., & Filipp, L. (1986). Prevalence of mental illness in a community nursing home. *American Journal of Psychiatry, 143,* 1446–1449.

Ryden, M. B., Bossenmaier, M., & McLachlan, C. (1991). Aggressive behavior in cognitively impaired nursing home residents. *Research in Nursing & Health, 14,* 87–95.

Ryden, M. B., & Feldt, K. S. (1992). Goal directed care: Caring for aggressive nursing home residents with dementia. *Journal of Gerontological Nursing, 18,* 35–42.

Sloane, P. D., Rader, J., Barrick, A. L., Hoffer, B., Dwyer, S., McKenzie, D., Lavelle, M., Buckwalter, K., Arrington, L., & Pruitt, T. (1995). Bathing person with dementia. *Gerontologist, 35,* 672–678.

Snyder, M., Egan, E. C., & Burns, K. R. (1995). Efficacy of hand massage in decreasing agitated behaviors associated with care activities in persons with dementia. *Geriatric Nursing, 16,* 60–63.

Tabloski, P. A., McKinnon-Howe, L., & Remington, R. (1995). Effect of calming music on level of agitation in cognitively impaired nursing home residents. *Journal of Alzheimer's Care and Related Disorder Research, 10*(1), 10–15.

U. S. Department of Health and Human Services, Public Health Service, Centers for Disease Control and National Center for Health Statistics. (1989). *The National Nursing Home Survey, 1985: Summary for the United States* (Pub. No. DHHS 89-1758). Hyattsville, MD: National Center for Health Statistics.

Volicer, L. (1993). Alzheimer's disease: Course, management, and the hospice approach. *Nursing Home Medicine, 1*(5), 31–37.

Volicer, L., Hurley, A., & Mahoney, E. (1995). Management of behavioral symptoms of dementia. *Nursing Home Medicine, 3*(12), 300–306.

Volicer, L., Rheaume, Y., & Cyr, D. (1994). Treatment of depression in advanced Alzheimer's disease using sertraline. *Journal of Geriatric Psychiatry and Neurology, 7,* 227–229.

Watkins, P. B., Zimmerman, H. J., Knapp, M. J., Gracon, S. I., & Lewis, K. W. (1994). Hepatotoxic effects of Tacrine administration in patients with Alzheimer's disease. *Journal of the American Medical Association, 271,* 992–998.

Zimmer, J. G., Watson, N., & Treat, A. (1984). Behavioral problems among patients in skilled nursing facilities. *American Journal of Public Health, 74,* 1118–1121.

Chapter 12

Therapeutic Activities for Low Functioning Older Adults With Dementia

Jill S. Magliocco

The role of activity programming has become paramount in the care of persons with dementia. Much is written on the special needs of this population and the importance of reintroducing long established roles of the individual in a new, more simplified manner. However, there seems to be a silence in the literature regarding effective ways to meet the sensory and psychosocial needs of individuals with late-stage dementia.

Activity is defined as a process carried on or participated in by virtue of being alive (*Webster's New Collegiate Dictionary*, 1977). Therefore, all aspects of the person's life become the focus of activities. Yet in most cases of dementia, the ability to participate has deteriorated to the point that task completion may be unrealistic. For this population, the role of activity therapy must shift from traditional recreation to nurturing the strengths and needs within the essence of each individual. "Throughout the course of a dementing illness, feelings and needs continue and when they are nurtured and responded to appropriately, residents achieve a sense of value in themselves" (Hellen, 1992, p. 2).

The focus of activities lies in sensory related experiences. A typical day might include a comfortable blend of sensory stimulating as well as sensory calming activities. Daily scheduling should be based on individual needs and desires, behavioral concerns, and tolerance for stimulation. Sensory stimulation assists persons in overcoming some of the obstacles of their dementing illness, age, and environment by allowing them to experience the pleasures of life through the senses (Bowlby, 1993).

The overall goal of the program is to provide organized, understandable sensory stimulation to increase environmental awareness. This provides a foundation for a happier mood and an improved ability to participate in self-care and relate to other people. According to Bowlby (1993, pp. 282–283) specific goals include

- improving environmental awareness through enhanced sensory cues,
- prompting familiar, functional behaviors,
- improving the general level of alertness,
- enabling appropriate social and environmental responses,
- providing reassuring, orienting information,
- providing pleasurable sensory experiences,
- providing opportunities for emotional expression and communication,
and
- enhancing self-esteem.

Responses to sensory stimulating activities may be as obvious as a verbal comment but will more likely be the establishment of direct eye contact, a change in facial expression, or a change in breathing pattern. Conducting such activities and eliciting particular responses may require some practice. Targeting over-learned or habitual responses are most successful (i.e., smelling when a flower is placed under the nose or smiling at the sight of a baby).

Equally as valuable as the type of stimulation chosen for patients is the length of time they are exposed to the stimulation. For example, turning on a radio or cassette with familiar music as patients sit in their rooms between break-fast and lunch is not therapeutic. Attention spans are brief and often fade in and out within a very short period of time. A given stimulus loses its effectiveness when it has gone beyond the individual's ability to focus and when no leadership is provided to direct it back to the activity.

Activities are only as successful as the person leading them. Knowledge of the dementing illness, communication techniques, and environmental and behav-ioral concerns do not complete the picture of an effective therapist. He or she must possess patience and have compassion for this population. A caring approach offers a message of support to residents and a sense that they are valued. Only when this type of approach is taken and a rapport has been established will there be the opportunity for therapeutic sensory experiences. In addition, the therapist must be persistent. Persons suffering from late-stage dementia may require more prompting and cueing to achieve a response. The therapist needs to exhibit a level of involvement comparable to that of the residents (Lewis-Long, 1989). Careful planning for individual needs along with a supportive approach are key to a suc-cessful experience. The activity should be viewed as an opportunity for the thera-pist and resident to share the experience and each other, not just a task. If the therapist does not present the activity in a positive and supportive manner, the potential for response is greatly diminished. Praise should be given through verbal comments, touch, and genuine gesture because nonverbal communication is often more easily understood by the patient with late-stage dementia.

To achieve responses, patients generally require one-to-one verbal directives, demonstration, and hand-over-hand prompting. One-to-one activity sessions are appropriate for individuals easily overstimulated or distracted by others. This is not to imply that group settings are inappropriate. Small group activities (3–5 residents) offer an additional dimension to the sensory group. For example, one individual may laugh at a given stimulus, which may prompt a similar, spontaneous response in someone else. In music-related activities, 8–10 people in a group is feasible, providing the therapist moves throughout the group redirecting attention to the session.

CASE EXAMPLE

Miss Bunce is a 101-year-old woman admitted to a nursing home in June 1989, with dementia secondary to a cerebrovascular accident. She was born in Poland, had a high school education, and worked as a telephone operator before becoming a homemaker in 1924. She spoke four languages, enjoyed reading and listening to music, and likes plants and animals. She sits in a wheelchair with a tray, has hand splints, and requires total assistance with care and feeding. Prior to her placement in the late-stage dementia program, Miss Bunce was described in recreational therapy progress notes as attending 14–21 activities per month but was "confused and disoriented, as evidenced by her frequent inappropriate verbalizations and inability to attend to tasks. She may not notice others around her even when staff attempts to talk to her on a one-to-one basis."

In the fall of 1994, Miss Bunce entered the late-stage dementia program. On the basis of her score of 1 on the Mini-Mental State Exam (Folstein, Folstein, & McHugh, 1975), present activity involvement, past social history, tolerance for stimulation, and current abilities, a daily schedule (presented in Figure 12.1) was developed.

As touched on in chapter 3, the schedule reflects a blend of sensory stimulating and sensory calming activities consistently implemented by the interdisciplinary team. Flexibility within this schedule should be expected, but that is not to imply that adaptions to the schedule should not be made. Any changes in the schedule should be based on resident need, not staff convenience.

At the time of writing, Miss Bunce has been involved in the program for approximately 1 year. She participates in activities that nurture her roles as homemaker, parishioner, friend, mother, and grandmother. Involvement is fostered by offering her sufficient downtime to renew her energy and ability to engage. Prior to her admission to the program, Miss Bunce displayed a lack of awareness of her environment when she had insufficient rest. With a balanced program of sensory calming and sensory stimulating activity, Miss Bunce can now be described as an active participant who contributes appropriate verbal comments to staff almost daily. She is able to focus on a given activity for up to 20 min, fluctuating between active and passive participation. She actively engages in a task with hand-over-hand assistance and engages in daily 10-min range of motion sessions

TIME OF DAY	ACTIVITY	RESPONSIBLE DISCIPLINE
7:00 - 7:30	Dressed/Cares	Nursing
7:30 - 8:00	Dressed/Cares	Nursing
8:00 - 8:30	Day room, coffee, music	Nursing
8:30 - 9:00	Breakfast	Nursing
9:00 - 9:30	"	"
9:30 - 10:00	Toileted	Nursing
10:00 - 10:30	Range of Motion Exercises 1:1 in room	Recreation
10:30 - 11:00	Rest in room with	Recreation/Nursing
11:00 - 11:30	music/toileted	Recreation
11:30 - 12:00	Activity in day room	Recreation
12:00 - 12:30	Table setting in day room	Recreation
12:30 - 1:00	Music listening in day room	Nursing
1:00 - 1:30	Lunch	"
1:30 - 2:00	"	Nursing
2:00 - 2:30	Toileted	Nursing
2:30 - 3:00	Rest in bed	"
3:00 - 3:30	"	"
3:30 - 4:00	"	"
4:00 - 4:30	"	Nursing
4:30 - 5:00	Toileted	Recreation
5:00 - 5:30	Activity in day room	Recreation
5:30 - 6:00	Social time	Nursing
6:00 - 6:30	Dinner	"
6:30 - 7:00	"	Nursing
7:00 - 7:30	Toileted	Nursing
7:30 - 8:00	Lotion massage Bed	Nursing

Figure 12.1   Daily activity schedule for Miss Bunce.

by moving her arms and sometimes counting. Most recently, staff have been working with Miss Bunce during meals. Hand splints are removed to enable her to sip from a small plastic cup by pinching the rim between her thumb and inside of her forefinger and then raising it to her mouth. At one meal, when the staff member turned to assist another resident, Miss Bunce, who has been fed by staff since her admission, pinched the handle of her spoon and fed herself. As the staff member looked at her in amazement, Miss Bunce laughed out loud in triumph.

The remainder of this chapter offers realistic and practical sensory activities for reaching residents with late-stage dementia. Each of the activities have been implemented on a 24-bed late-stage dementia unit in a long-term care facility. Special considerations for the different types of activities are described. Adaptations in approach or presentation will need to be facilitated by the activity therapist to best meet the needs of each patient.

NORMALIZATION ACTIVITIES

People with dementia often lack a sense of purpose and usefulness, which is contributed to by the loss of old roles, tasks, and responsibilities as the disease progresses. To restore a sense of meaning, "work" based or normal activities should be incorporated into the program, focusing on the resident's current abilities and ensuring success (Hellen, 1992, p. 94). Resident involvement in the task may seem basic, but the value of the activity must be determined by the response. Hellen wrote that normalization tasks combine all the qualities of cognitive, physical, and psychosocial activities. The challenge is to find or develop appropriate tasks for the resident and to achieve a desired and realistic outcome.

> *Mrs. Collins was a homemaker much of her life. At meal times, she is brought to the dining room table and is given a bud vase filled with silk flowers to hold in one hand. While the activity therapist places the tablecloth on the table, Mrs. Collins reaches with the other hand to help straighten the corner. The activity therapist reaches for the vase, and Mrs. Collins meets her half way and says, "Oh that's nice," as the vase is placed on the table.*

The following are descriptions of various other tasks that may be stimulating and enjoyable for Mrs. Collins and for other residents who once were homemakers.

Flower arranging

1 Lay flowers on table in front of resident.
2 Talk about the flowers, have the resident smell them, and direct attention to the flowers and the vase.
3 Encourage the resident to select flowers for the vase.

Scrubbing vegetables

1 Position a basin of water at a level comfortable for the resident to work over.
2 Stabilize or hold the basin to avoid spills.
3 Encourage the resident to scrub and rinse the vegetables. Talk about meal preparation, recipes for soups and stew.

Folding laundry

1 Seat the resident at a surface comfortable for folding.
2 The laundry basket serves as a visual cue—place it in front of the work area.

3   Place towels or baby clothes in front of the resident and encourage folding or rolling.
4   Talk informally about laundry and other household chores.

Baking bread

1   Thaw two loaves of frozen bread dough.
2   Begin baking one loaf of bread prior to bringing residents in so that the smell of bread will fill the room as they are participating.
3   Break dough from the second loaf into small pieces for each resident.
4   Sprinkle flour on the table for kneading.
5   Encourage residents to manipulate the dough and smell the dough.
6   Present the finished loaf to residents and let appropriate residents taste.

> *Mrs. McIntyre, who rarely focuses on a task for more than 30 s squeezed the dough into the flour, opening her eyes wide and focusing on the table for 5 min. Her husband entered the room in delight to see his wife's lap coated with flour and said "She loved to bake, I never thought I'd see this again."*

Afternoon tea

1   Gather residents around a small round or square table, covered with a tablecloth, pretty napkins, and a pretty teacup for each person, and introduce the activity.
2   Reminisce about tea kettles and how they whistle. Have water heating in a kettle so residents have the opportunity to hear the whistle.
3   Offer choices of herbal tea if appropriate and help residents drink.
4   Talk about family and times when families and friends gather.

Social hour   This is most effective when conducted approximately 1 hr prior to dinner or in the midafternoon.

1   Set the dining tables with tablecloths and centerpieces and turn on easy listening or classical music to play in the background.
2   Seat residents in small groups (2–4 residents per table).
3   Offer and pour sparkling grape juice in front of them and assist residents with drinking.
4   Facilitate interaction and social atmosphere.

> *Mr. Moss is typically difficult during caregiving activities and is described by staff as nonverbal during most activities. One evening as the activity assistant was pouring grape juice, Mr. Moss looked up at the two other female residents seated at his table and said, "You girls come here for a date?" Since then Mr. Moss has consistently revealed a more fun-loving side of himself.*

Prayer service   Spirituality and religion remain an important part of most people's lives. Residents for whom religion is important could become involved with singing hymns, reciting bible verses, or saying familiar prayers. Close each group with prayer requests. If a person is unable to make a request, offer to pray for the family and use the family name in the prayer.

Reminiscing and sharing

1   Introduce a topic for discussion and a related object (e.g., if the topic is the changing colors of fall, the object could be a basket of colored leaves).
2   Watch for the resident's response. Is a connection being made through eye contact, gesture, touch, or verbalization?
3   Continue the conversation as long as the resident is able to attend.
4   Close by thanking the resident for the quiet time you've shared.

> *Mrs. Wade has very little intelligible speech left but has many wonderful facial expressions. She chatters on as the therapist listens, offers affirming nods, and smiles. The two exchange "gossip" as the therapist whispers, "Oh, look at that," in Mrs. Wade's ear. Mrs. Wade smiles and laughs, leans her contracted body toward the therapist, and kisses her.*

Reminiscing boxes   Boxes filled with items related to a particular topic or event can be a useful catalyst for reminiscing. Items selected should be from the resident's early adulthood, thereby avoiding modern devices. Items may need to be presented directly to the resident to engage him or her in the activity. Keep in mind that activities are opportunities for sharing experiences and that the involvement of the therapist must be equal to or greater than that of the resident. Support, encouragement, and a sense of sharing will reinforce a sense of belonging and caring to the resident. The following are examples of possible boxes.

Vacation Kit (contained in a suitcase)—shoes, toothbrush, toothpaste, aspirin bottle (empty), slacks, shirts, electric razor, sunglasses, travel brochures.
Baby Basket—receiving blanket, bib, booties, sleepers, cloth diapers, baby powder, rattle, musical toy, bonnet, undershirt.
Car Kit—pictures of old cars, car catalogs from car dealers, chamois cloth, scraper.
Office Kit—pen, pencil, typewriter eraser, typing paper, carbon paper, hole punch, ruler.
Kitchen Kit—eggbeater, scouring pad, old pot or pan, ricer, wire whip, tea ball, vegetable brush, wooden spoon, meat mallet, hot pad, strainer, sifter, rubber scraper, measuring cup, measuring spoon, meat thermometer, canning jar.
Tool Box—folding ruler, level, C clamp, sand paper, cedar block, wrench, masking tape, electrical tape, hand planer, chisel, screwdriver, paintbrush, table top broom, and dustpan.
Ladies' Kit—cosmetic puffs, handkerchiefs, costume jewelry, empty perfume bottles, stockings, sachet, comb, compact, white gloves.

Men's Kit—electric razor, empty cologne bottles, handkerchief, comb, shoe brush, tie, wallet, belt, cap.

Sewing Box—threads, tape measure, pincushion, old patterns, fabric scraps, seam binding, crochet hooks, knitting needle.

MUSIC

Music is referred to as a universal language. When used therapeutically, it can bring some sense of individuality, an experience of caring, creativity, enjoyment, and stimulation. Through music, bridges can be built, which decrease isolation and loneliness, prompt emotion, and elicit reminiscing, and movement in one-on-one or group settings (Bright, 1988).

> *Mr. Palmer, a 95-year-old participant in the late-stage dementia program, often chants the phrase "that way" repeatedly throughout the day. This repetitious sound is disruptive to others on the unit. Mr. Arnold is not easily redirected with the call of his name or use of touch, but when a staff person places headphones on his ears with spiritual music playing, Mr. Arnold folds his hands in prayer peacefully and often begins singing hymns.*

According to Bowlby (1993, p. 156), specific goals for using music as therapy include

- providing an opportunity for expression of emotion through cues associated with particular songs,
- stimulating vocalization and communication,
- stimulating movement through responses, and
- stimulating emotions through association with songs.

The following are possible music activities that residents may benefit from.

Awakenings

Each morning as residents gather in the dining room, brew fresh coffee to fill the room with the scent. Play environmental sounds of birds chirping set to music and have tables set with tablecloths, centerpieces, and place settings to provide resident with auditory and visual cues that a new day is beginning.

Sing-alongs

Sing-along sessions may include up to 8–10 residents seated in a circle so that visual and physical contact may be made with others. Songs should be familiar tunes from the residents' early adulthood. A theme of spiritual, holiday, or childhood songs can also be successful. Cassettes can be used if a musician or music therapist is not available, but an activity therapist is key in keeping residents engaged to their greatest ability.

What's That Tune?

Many residents may not be able to sing a song from beginning to end, but they may be able to complete a phrase such as a refrain. Sing a portion of the song and allow residents sufficient time to complete it. This may also be done by stopping and starting cassette tapes.

Tune Toss

Write the names of various familiar sing-along songs on paper plates, one song per plate. Seat residents in a circle. Place plates on the floor in the center of the circle. Have residents toss or drop a bean bag onto a plate and then sing the song written on the plate.

Pick a Color, Any Color

Prior to the session, create different colored flash cards by writing the name of a song on a 5 in. × 7 in. piece of colored posterboard. Continue until you have a set of 10–12 songs on various colors. During the session, fan the cards out in your hand and encourage the residents to pick one. Have them state the color if appropriate. Read the title and then sing the song. Note that you may need to make choices or limit choices to 2–3 colors for some residents.

Creating a Mood

Music can create a mood or set the tone, providing that factors within the environment are in balance. Upbeat music or music with a prominent rhythm facilitates sensory stimulating activity and movement. Soothing instrumental music facilitates sensory calming activity. Take, for example, the social hour activity listed previously in this chapter. During the late afternoon hours when sundowning occurs, the easy listening music combined with the sparkling grape juice can serve as cues to a time for pleasurable relaxation. The same concept applies in a contrasting situation where strong rhythmic marching music is used to cue residents for movement and exercise.

MOVEMENT AND EXERCISE

Movement is an important part of the daily activity plan for most persons with late-stage dementia. Traditional regimens of exercise are unrealistic because residents are unable to mirror most movements. One-to-one assistance is required and is important at this stage to avoid painful contractures. Physical or occupational therapists (or both) should be directly involved in this program by training both resident assistants and activity staff on a case-by-case basis in the use of range-of-motion techniques.

> *Mr. Rosenthal participated in daily one-to-one range-of-motion sessions. He was wheelchair bound and relied on staff for all activities of daily living and for transport to and from activities. After 4 months in the range-of-motion sessions, Mr. Rosenthal was able to make his own way down the hall by pedaling his wheelchair with one foot.*

To further enhance range-of motion-sessions, add counting to provide rhythm and encourage verbalization. As mentioned earlier, music with a strong beat, such as marching music, can also facilitate movement.

ART

Art is probably the most challenging form of activity therapy for both the resident and the therapist. Traditional use of art processes call on abstract thinking abilities, which no longer exist for the person with late-stage dementia. This section describes spontaneous art techniques requiring the resident to engage in one to two simple steps. Although art will not be appropriate in every case, participants can experience a feeling of accomplishment through having done something on their own and will have a tangible reward for their efforts (Jenny, 1993). No preconceived ideas of what the piece should look like are established. Only nontoxic art materials are used. These materials should not be left unattended by staff. It is recommended that these processes be completed on a one-to-one basis to support and assist residents' efforts. Each of these processes can be completed in more than one session to build a complete piece. Some residents may engage only momentarily. Small sizes of paper combined with large brushes are recommended to foster success and a sense of completion in a short period of time. Appropriate communication techniques of verbal cueing, demonstration, and hand-over-hand guidance should be used to facilitate participation.

The following are descriptions of possible art activities.

Finger Painting

1   Set up a table with 5 in. × 5 in. watercolor paper, tempera paint in various colors, and fine line black markers.

2   Dip the resident's index fingertip into the tempera paint. Offer color choices if appropriate.

3   Gently press the resident's finger onto the paper. Continue tapping the finger on the paper, creating a random design. Let go of the resident's hand to allow him or her to continue the motion. Reengage resident as needed and dip his or her finger in the paint as needed.

4   When the piece dries (in another session), show the resident the picture and ask, "What is this picture of?" Outline their response in black fine line marker. If the resident is unable to respond, outline the image you see and present it to the resident.

Wet-on-Wet Watercolors

1   Start with watercolor paint set, a 1 in. wide brush, and a 5 in. × 7 in. piece of watercolor paper.

2   Dip the paper into a bowl of water.

3   Using the hand-over-hand technique and verbal cues guide the resident's hand with the brush to the paint (offering color choices when appropriate) and then back to the paper. A design is created as the wet color hits the wet paper.

4   In another session, ask the resident, "What is this picture of?" and outline the image in black fine line marker.

Golf Ball Painting

1   Start with 1 golf ball, paper plates, 1 sheet of drawing paper, a gift box, and tempera paint in various colors.

2   Before the session, line the gift box with drawing paper. Tape the corners and pour enough tempera paint in the paper plate (1 color per plate) to cover the plate. Present the box to the resident. Roll the ball into the paint and drop it into the box. Encourage the resident to tilt the box, making the ball roll and creating a design. Hand-over-hand assistance may be required.

3   Dip the ball into paint again as needed.

4   When the paper is dry, remove it from the box.

Blot Painting

1   Start with tempera paint in squeeze bottles and heavy white drawing paper folded in half.

2   Encourage the resident to squeeze colors onto the paper.

3   Close the paper to blend the colors.

4   Open the paper to reveal a dramatic design.

Squirt Bottle Painting

1   Start with plant sprayer bottles (1 per color of paint), watered down tempera paint, a 2 ft × 3 ft piece of muslin or sheet, and a newspaper.

2   Cover a 4 ft × 6 ft area of floor with several layers of newspaper.

3   Lay muslin on top of the newspaper.

4   Fill the spray bottles with tempera paint.

5   Encourage the resident to randomly squirt the muslin, creating a spattered design.

6   The muslin can be stretched across a wooden frame when dry.

OTHER SENSORY RELATED ACTIVITIES

Bird Watching

Use birds in a small enough cage that a staff person can carry it from resident to resident. Place birds at a comfortable distance from the resident, but at eye level.

Direct the resident's attention to the birds and try to get the birds to chirp. Talk to the resident about birds, the colors, and the sounds.

Short Stories and Poetry Reading

Short stories and poetry centered around generations past, holidays, special occasions, seasons, and spirituality can be very calming. Reading is a successful activity for one-to-one contact and can provide the resident with a sense of companionship while stimulating emotions through memories.

CONCLUSION

There are countless other activities appropriate for this population. Therapists are only limited by the boundaries of their imagination and insight into the essence of the individual. Key to the success of the program is the sharing relationship established between resident and therapist. The true value of any activity lies within the connection made between the resident and therapist, not in the quantity or quality of the work. The connection and exchange, even if the resident is only able to participate in a portion of the activity, will offer meaning through the process of sharing. Ongoing evaluation of the program must be made to meet individual needs as abilities decline. The incorporation of activities into late-stage or palliative care truly addresses the whole person and his or her needs for expressing sharing and belonging.

BIBLIOGRAPHY

Bowlby, C. (1993). *Therapeutic activities with persons disabled by Alzheimer's disease and related disorders.* Gaithersburg, MD: Aspen.

Bright, R. (1988). *Music therapy and the dementias.* St. Louis, MO: MMB Music.

Folstein, M. F., & Folstein, S. E., & McHugh, P. R. (1975). Mini-Mental State: A practical method for grading the cognitive state of patients for the clinician. *Journal of Psychiatric Research, 12,* 189–198.

Hellen, C. R. (1992). *Alzheimer's disease activity focused care.* Boston: Andover Medical Publishers.

Jenny, S. (1993). *Memories in the making.* CA: Alzheimer's Association of Orange County.

Lewis-Long, M. (1989). Realistic *Alzheimer's activities.* Amherst, NY: Potentials Development.

Webster's new collegiate dictionary. (1977). Springfield, MA: G&C Merriam.

Part Three

Special Issues in Care

Chapter 13

Working With the Family

Marilyn J. Bonjean and Ronald D. Bonjean

Professional caregivers who have a model of holistic family care understand the impact of Alzheimer's disease on each family and its members, recognize the shift into terminal care and its implications, and minister to the grieving through personal contact and institutional programs. Furthermore, they know their own emotional reactions and needs in working with families when a member is dying.

CASE EXAMPLE

Mrs. Sullivan watched her husband, John, as he lay quietly in his bed. Mercy Manor has been good to both of us she thought, as we struggle through this final phase of his Alzheimer's disease. Married for 50 years, and I never expected it would end like this.

She remembered how angry she was when her husband had to be placed in the nursing home. It felt like losing all control, with those other women taking care of him. Now those feelings are coming back again because he is dying. It has been 10 years since this all started, and it has consumed my whole life. What will I do when he's gone? Funny thing. I've often wished he was gone, and now I'm afraid of the change. I'm accustomed to coming here everyday, and I know everyone. They are sort of my friends. It is all so confusing and painful. I know the children and grandchildren feel it too in their own way and sometimes don't know how to talk to me. I hope the tension of this doesn't separate us too much.

Caregivers like Mrs. Sullivan and her family need assistance from health professionals to sort out the confusion of their feelings and circumstances. This case is discussed throughout the chapter, and a genogram (Figure 13.1) is provided to illustrate the placement of various members in the family structure.

SULLIVAN FAMILY GENOGRAM

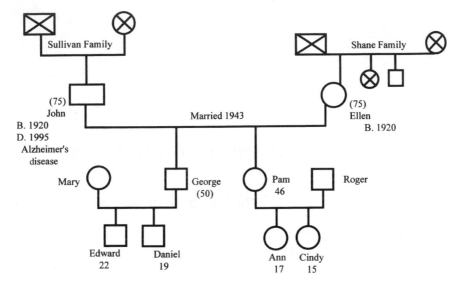

Figure 13.1   Sullivan family genogram.

FAMILY-CENTERED CARE

Chronic illness affects not only the patient diagnosed with a certain disease but every family member and close friend. Acknowledging this reality promotes behaviors from health care professionals and institutions that address family suffering and empower them to be a useful force in the treatment process. Alzheimer's disease has an insidious onset and a protracted course so that as family members enter the terminal phase they have already had long years in the process of caretaking. Because this disease has no cure and eventually reduces the patient to complete dependency, caregiver needs have been emphasized. However, little emphasis has been placed on the experience of the entire family and the terminal phase. The cognitive losses of this disease require family members to react to more than the physical death of a member. Long before physical death arrives, the personality and cognitive presence of the patient are grossly changed. These changes lead family members to a stressful confusion about who is psychologically in or out of the family, sometimes referred to as *boundary ambiguity* (Boss, Caron, Horbal, & Mortimer, 1990).

Spouses often express this ambiguity by stating, "I am not a spouse but I am not widowed. I don't know what I am or how I feel." Children may say, "I am caring for my mother's body, but she has been gone for a long time."

As health care professionals begin to assist families of Alzheimer's patients in the final phase of illness, it will be important for them to understand how the patient is perceived by family members. Some families will have preserved a modified place for the patient by adapting family rituals to include the patient and keeping a psychological presence actively involved in the family. Some families will have separated themselves from the patient and may behave as if the patient is no longer part of the family. Others will have denied the extent of the change in the patient and be trying to function as they did before the disease onset. Families in which ambiguity is highest will have the most stress because they cannot reorganize their boundaries and move on as a group. The final phase of illness may rewaken feelings of grief and loss and stimulate a need for support in all families.

Reiss (1981) emphasized that shared explanations play a crucial role in organizing and maintaining group process and family identity. Health professionals can help families by making explicit the meaning of events that stimulate adaptive behavior. Many families need a context in which they can develop shared situational meanings that promote joint problem solving and consensual decisions. Emphasizing family strengths and resources will increase family capabilities for growing stronger through the chronic illness experience. As the terminal phase of Alzheimer's disease begins, the family faces death as inevitable and even imminent. Although they have known that this disease has no cure since the diagnosis was received, confronting the final loss is something for which most families are unprepared. Issues regarding separation, death, grief, resolution of mourning, and resumption of normal family life beyond the loss become paramount (Rolland, 1994). The role of the health care professional also changes, moving away from medical stabilization and treatment of symptoms toward provision of physical and emotional comfort.

A FAMILY MEETING—BEGINNING THE TERMINAL STAGE

Mrs. Sullivan continued to remember how the staff of Mercy Manor had assisted her.

The meetings they had with us were really helpful—I don't think we would have talked with each other like that without their questions to guide us. Having both children, Pam and George, take time to come and even Pam's children, Ann and Cindy, felt like we were facing this together even if we don't always agree. It certainly was the electronic age: George's children, Ed and Danny, used the speaker phone from school in Seattle!

It helped that the Mercy Manor staff suggested that everyone be asked to participate. I would never have felt comfortable asking for that attention.

The nurse began the meeting by telling the family what was physically happening to John. The Alzheimer's disease had affected so much of his brain that his body could not continue to function for much longer. She let us ask questions, and George asked if his father might get a little better again. The nurse was blunt. "John is moving toward his death. No one can say exactly when that will happen, but it is a matter of weeks or months, not years anymore."

Her directness seemed to help us deal with reality rather than skirting around it, Mrs. Sullivan recalled. People don't often say to you, "He will die," but it does help to hear the words said so we can face the future. After the physi-

cal part was discussed, we all understood death would come soon. The nurse described what it would probably be like and that helped.

"John will be kept as comfortable as possible by positioning him carefully in bed and turning him," she said. "If pain medication is needed, it will be used." She described all the things they would do for John.

The social worker who was at the meeting asked us questions about ourselves, which I hadn't expected. It was good for us. Each of the children and grandchildren were asked what the hardest thing was for them and how the family could help them. When she came to me, I said it was the waiting and that coming to meetings like this was a way the family really helped so I didn't feel I had to do it alone. Pam mentioned how much religious faith meant to the family, and the social worker explained that their chaplain, who was available to all of us, had been visiting John. Our pastor was also very welcome to visit.

Visiting was the final part of the discussion. We discussed how much John was comforted by touch and that even though he did not respond verbally anymore, he probably was comforted by familiar voices and by tone of voice. Just talking to him, reading out loud or praying out loud was useful. The nurse emphasized that we really didn't have to do anything except sit with him a little—our loving presence was a comfort. This seemed to help Danny, who spoke up on the speaker phone. He said he wanted to see Grandpa once more when he came home on school vacation in a few weeks—he'd been feeling nervous about it. Pam just nodded and said this talk made her feel better about visiting too.

As the meeting ended, the nurse asked the children and me how we would like to be notified if John took a really bad turn during the night. I don't drive anymore—I couldn't just come over alone. We decided they would call George, and then he would call me and drive me over to Mercy Manor.

After this meeting, the family went out for a meal and continued to talk about certain parts of the meeting and their feelings. A few days later, each person got a summary of the meeting notes, which also gave them another chance to think things through.

Attending meetings such as the one described above encourages the formation of shared meanings and promotes understanding and tolerance of divergent viewpoints. Each meeting will be unique because the circumstances of each care situation are different, but the following basic outline may be useful.

GUIDELINES FOR TERMINAL STAGE CARE CONFERENCE

Introduction

Introduce the family to all staff members present and explain their function as needed. As many family members as possible should be invited by the facility. Try to scatter staff members around the table so that a visual impression of two groups, family versus staff is avoided. Staff members will feel much more comfortable participating in these conferences if their duties are made very clear and one person is the facilitator who convenes the meeting and moves the discussion from one topic to the next, offering summaries as needed. The social worker will have special training in conducting groups and assisting others with clear communication and may make a good facilitator.

Physical Status

1   The nurse or physician reviews the resident's diagnosis and current status, noting evidence of and reasons for decline.

2   Assess family understanding of the resident's physical status. It is important to use lay terms and to thoroughly explain all medical conditions. Answer questions as needed and be sure to elicit questions from each family member.

3   Relate medications and treatments to the resident's diagnosis and current status.

4   Review the plan of care with an emphasis on what is being done for the resident rather than what is not done. When palliative care is selected it can be easy to inadvertently talk about not doing extraordinary care rather than to describe the emphasis on comfort, hygiene, and dignity.

Prognosis

1   Determine the information given to the family by the physician and any additional need for communication. Encourage the family to call the physician as needed.

2   Review the prognosis as much as possible. Although the exact timing of death is impossible to predict, physical signs of decline become so cumulative that its imminence in terms of weeks or months can be discussed. Use direct language and words like *dying* and *death* rather than *expire* or *pass away*. Caregivers are helped to face the future if they can clearly understand what is happening and have support. When professionals can be direct they set a tone caregivers can follow and model the behavior that the family member's dying can be talked about.

3   Assess the family's understanding of the prognosis by asking them questions about their ideas of what will happen in the immediate future.

Family Involvement in the Care Plan

1   Visits to a dying family member can be so stressful or frightening that some members may stay away and miss opportunities for closure. Suggesting and discussing things to do when visiting can relieve some discomfort. Examples may be physical contact, such as back rubs or holding hands, or giving fluids or small amounts of favorite food if this is still possible. Remind family members that even though the resident may not respond verbally, the sound of familiar voices can be very comforting so that reading aloud, talking to the resident, or praying aloud may be helpful during visits. Emphasizing the comfort of human presence is also important because family members do not have to do anything except be present to have a helpful visit. Remind the family that this is the time to do or say anything not yet completed with the resident so that leave taking can be peaceful.

2   Inquire about the importance of spiritual or religious support and rituals for the resident and family. Describe the chaplain services provided through the facility and invite the family's religious practitioner to conduct whatever ceremonies might be meaningful to them.

3   Determine when the family members wish to be called to the bedside if death is immediately imminent. Some elderly spouses without transportation may not wish to be called in the night.

Promoting Intrafamily Support

1   Ask each family member about the difficulties they may be having anticipating the resident's death and what would be helpful to them from the family and from the staff.

Ask each member what they expect of themselves now and what they think other family members expect of them. This discussion often makes unrealistic expectations explicit and allows for correction and support from other family members.

2   Families are often already doing much to help each other, and reviewing this can promote a sense of mastery in this difficult situation. New behaviors may be more easily added to already existing successes.

Closing the Meeting

Summarize the meeting as a whole. Invite family members to request other meetings in the future, and remind them that staff will probably be doing so. Prepare a written summary of the meeting from notes and mail this to each member as a review. This is especially important for members who could not attend the meeting and for education of all shifts of staff about the needs of each family.

NORMAL GRIEF

After meetings that make the closeness of death explicit, staff will be helping family members with their grief. Comforting families who are anticipating death or have lost a member requires that health care professionals know the characteristics and behavioral manifestations of normal grief. Often family members will ask if what they feel or think is normal. Because the intensity of grief can make the griever feel out of control and overwhelmed, reassurance is needed. Anticipatory grief refers to the process of normal mourning that occurs in anticipation of death and its consequences. Alzheimer's disease develops over many years, so families have been mourning various losses at each illness stage. Many family members will ask whether, after all the mourning of the past, they will still grieve at the death and after. Most family members do. However, questioning about how comfort has come at other stages may help family members remind themselves that they can also manage this.

Grief has as many faces as the individuals who experience it. Some family members may distance themselves emotionally or physically from the dying person or overcompensate with aggressive or demanding actions to hide their vulnerability. Others will openly express feelings and actively grieve with the staff. Keep the following in mind when helping grievers with their responses:

- Encourage and arrange for private places in which strong emotion can be expressed. Do not convey information in the corridor or over the bed of the patient. Take families to private, comfortable places for discussion.
- Name and normalize feelings, which can reduce fear and give a sense of control. Anticipate some feelings so that when they are experienced the caregiver can know they are expected.
- Address terms such as *lose control* and *breakdown* by acknowledging the intensity of this experience, reframing responses as emotional release, and honoring the relationship through grief.

Tell family members that grief can be expressed a little at a time and that the feeling of numbness that often accompanies intense grief is a natural way of slowing the experience of painful feeling and expression of grief. It does not signify lack of caring about the patient. Sensations that come in waves of intensity give the griever a break between painful episodes. Predicting that grievers may experience periods of intense feeling and periods of peace can help them know what to expect and manage the intensity with less fear of being overwhelmed.

Normal grief reactions are composites of many conflicting and confusing feelings, which may rapidly change. Remind grievers that feeling relief and sorrow at the same time often happens. Guilt has been an often experienced feeling for many caregivers, and this part of the illness may stimulate more. Remind them that everything that should be done for the patient is being done; noting the helpful behaviors of the family can ease guilt.

In working with grievers, an attitude of empathy, along with calm reassurance, is very important. If a health professional feels overwhelmed by the strong emotions of the family, anxiety will be heightened and make the whole experience more difficult. Recognizing personal reactions to each family will help the health professional ask for the help needed to manage each situation.

Recognizing personal values around appropriate behavior during the death of a family member is important because it influences the health care professional's ability to give sincere empathy. So that few behaviors will be a surprise, expect that some family members will cry, some will become angry and demanding in the face of helpless feelings, others may clean out the drawers or closets to distract themselves, and still others will seek much attention from the staff. Longstanding individual and family patterns are unlikely to change during the death of a family member. Those who were more open and flexible will be able to take advantage of the opportunities offered by the staff, and those who bring a painful history and negative coping patterns may reenact them now. Health professionals may want to bring the family together for warm, supportive interaction, but if this has not been some part if their history it is probably doomed to failure. Setting some standard for how a family ought to interact around the death of a member risks their being labeled as dysfunctional and makes empathizing more difficult.

An attitude of curiosity about what may be helpful to each family allows professionals to offer meetings and opportunities while realizing that some families will want them and others will not.

Helping Families at the Time of Death

Chronic illness does have the advantage that death is often predictable, and family members can keep a vigil if they desire. For many caregivers who have devoted years to their family member, being present at the time of death is important, and feelings of guilt may arise if they are not. Determining the wishes of family members is very important so that staff members can cooperate. This is a critical time in family care.

Even though caregivers may have taken care of someone for years, they may be frightened of what the death will be like. Explaining the physical responses of the patient and suggesting appropriate behavior for family members may be useful. Reassuring family members that the patient is comfortable and that the staff will remain attentive may be calming. This may be a useful time to involve pastoral care personnel, who will support the family in spiritual and religious practices. Facilities equipped with rooms with comfortable seating or sleeping arrangements for caregivers reflect a commitment to family care.

Support family members, who may feel helpless sitting by the bedside, with comments about the importance of their presence. Even in times of coma, hearing is believed to be the last sense to fail so that a familiar and loving voice can be a comfort to the dying patient.

After death allow adequate time for the family to be alone with the body, to touch it and to speak to it. The realization of death becomes clearer at this time, and encouraging verbalization may help family members process the reality. Although death has been anticipated, expect some shock as normal. Ask the family if they would like time alone or if they would prefer that a staff member stay. Some family members will want privacy, and others may be fearful of being alone with the body. Encourage expression of grief. Give permission for the family to leave when they seem ready. *Only then begin to prepare the body to be taken.*

When family members have not been present at the death but are called with the announcement, offer sympathy and, when appropriate, ask whether they would like to collect the patient's belongings themselves or would prefer the staff to box them. Some family members will want this to be a last ritual for them, and others may be very uncomfortable entering the room with their relative gone.

Helping Families After Death

After losing a family member, some caregivers who have been close to the staff may return for visits and need to process their grief with those who shared the final stages of illness with them. When this happens be prepared to

- listen to repetitive stories or emotions from the caregiver because this helps relieve emotional stress,
- share memories with the caretaker of the last stages and any special memories you have of the patient,
- normalize the grief experience that the caregiver may describe to you and empathize with feelings of loss,
- praise the caregiver for positive behaviors during the last stages shared at the facility, which often helps the caregiver with guilt feelings, and
- recommend grief support groups if this seems appropriate.

Mrs. Sullivan, her son, and her daughter sat around Mr. Sullivan's bed as he was dying. The nurse came in and out of the room frequently, checking Mr. Sullivan's vital signs and explaining changes to the family. Mrs. Sullivan remembered,

> It helped that the nurse explained the sound of his breathing to the family as it changed and encouraged us to talk to him and touch him. We sat together and prayed out loud. I felt a tension over my whole body and a numbness. After a couple of hours, he sighed deeply, and I just knew he was gone. My son, George, called the nurse, and she confirmed that he had died. She asked if we wanted to be alone or wanted her to stay, and I told her to go. I sat beside him on the bed and began to feel more peaceful. My tears came then, and they were a relief. I didn't think I had any left. My children cried too, and we hugged each other a lot and talked to his body. After a while, I knew I could leave. It was like a letting go to say good-bye to him.
>
> As we were leaving, the nurse offered her sympathy again and told us someone from the funeral home would come soon and would contact me at home. She asked if we wanted to return another day to gather John's belongings or if the staff should box them. He had so few personal items by the end, I told her to box them.
>
> I kept feeling numb at times and then waves of sadness and tears. I knew his death was real but still couldn't quite believe it was over. I had devoted so much of myself to him over the past 10 years. My anger would bubble, thinking of that suffering.

Death will affect each family member differently. Pam, Mrs. Sullivan's daughter, cried a little but felt more anxious about her mother. She had cried a lot for her father at one time in his illness and now was more concerned about her mother. She did not want to lose her too. As the daughter, Pam may feel implied caretaking responsibilities for her mother and more protective of her as the remaining parent. Some tension may arise because she has adolescent daughters requiring intensive parenting. She and her brother, George, will now also be more of a focus for their mother.

George periodically brushed tears from his cheeks and tried to support his mother and sister. As the son, he may feel a need to be taking care of them. With two sons in college, some tension may arise between his role as a provider in his own family and concerns for his mother. He may also become more aware of his own mortality because of losing the same-sex parent.

Death of a family member disrupts family equilibrium and requires reorganization to integrate the loss and move forward with family life. Four family tasks have been specified, which are typically sequential and overlapping. They are

1 *shared acknowledgment of the reality of death.* This task is facilitated by witnessing the death, viewing the body, participating in funeral rites, and visiting the grave site. Protecting family members from sharing these reality-testing experiences often leads to unresolved grief.

2 *shared experiences of the pain of grief.* Family members can be most helpful to each other because they share in the meaning of this loss. A special kind of comfort and strengthening of relationship can come from supporting each other during losses.

3 *reorganization of the family system.* This is a process of changing role functions and new awareness of self and other family members.

4 *reinvestment in other relationships and life pursuits.* Mourning may continue for at least 1 to 2 years or longer. Each "first" without the deceased will evoke grief. Individuals are unique in how reinvestment will occur and the time it will take. (Adapted from Walsh, F., & McGoldrick, M. (1988). Loss and the family life cycle. In C. Falicov (Ed.), *Family transition: Continuity and changes over the life cycle*. New York: Guilford Press.)

ASSESSING ABNORMAL GRIEF

Abnormal grief is very difficult to define because responses to loss are so uniquely personal. However, certain general guidelines can help professionals identify problems and make referrals. The inability to grieve normally is often caused less by the present situation and more by profound loss at earlier stages of the family life cycle or other generations. Rosen (1990) described the following signs of complicated grief:

1 Extreme conceptualization of the deceased as very good or very bad.

2 Confusion and argument among family members about the patient's condition or illness.

3 Extreme focus on the patient or almost total avoidance of focusing on the patient.

4 Fixation on perceived poor treatment by the health care community, with insistence that outcomes would have been different with other treatment.

5 Anger and resentment toward the patient that family members cannot explain but know has persisted for a long time.

Caregivers identified with abnormal grief reaction will need a referral for individual or family psychotherapy. Facilities need to have referral sources identified and made known to staff. Caregivers may be successfully referred by empathizing with their feelings, confusion, and suffering and then offering a referral with the hope it may give them a chance to find some peace.

Cultural Issues in Family Grief

Each culture has prescribed behaviors for individual and family behavior around illness, consuming medical care, facing death, and bereavement. It will be impossible for professional caregivers to know the specific values of each culture. To successfully remain sensitive to cultural issues, medical professionals need an attitude of curiosity toward each family. The following questions may be helpful in promoting cultural understanding (Walsh & McGoldrick, 1991, p. 179):

1   What are the prescribed rituals for handling dying, the dead body, and the disposal of the body? What are the rituals to commemorate the loss?
2   What are the group's beliefs about what happens after death?
3   What do they believe about appropriate emotional expression and integration of a loss experience?
4   What are the gender rules for handling the death?
5   Are certain deaths particularly stigmatized or traumatic for the group?

BIOETHICS DECISIONS AND FAMILY GRIEF

The grief families experience will be influenced by how health care decisions have been made over the course of the illness. Their involvement in and consensus about bioethics decisions will make accepting death easier and avoid unnecessary guilt. Chapter 15 provides a discussion of several ethical issues from a legal perspective.

Ethical issues associated with the final phase of Alzheimer's disease focus on the degree of life-sustaining medical care, patient competency, expression of preferences with patient cognitive impairment, the obligations of adult family members, and the degree of obligation imposed on the health care staff by medical indicators. Each of these issues focuses on a single aspect of the ethical contextual setting and is incomplete alone. The most useful care decisions will come from considering them in interaction with each other. Such an approach lifts ethics from an individual level to a process that fulfills goals identified by all members in the caregiving situation.

When ethics serves as means of focusing on process and not simply on individuals, how does one assess needs and prioritize them? Needs may best be prioritized by defining bioethics not so much as legal or physical issues but as an attempt to understand the underlying value system by which individuals try to give meaning to their lives in relation to others. Values are not simply shared cultural ethos or psychological conditioning but an expression of innermost convictions about the meaning of life and death, right and wrong, and ultimate and immediate reality. Bioethics attempts to achieve self-fulfillment of the individual within the defining social context through a facilitation of the awareness of these values. This view does not deny that decisions should be medically sensible, socially responsible, legally permissible, and financially viable. Rather, the priority is placed on value systems that serve as a means of assessing the appropriate-

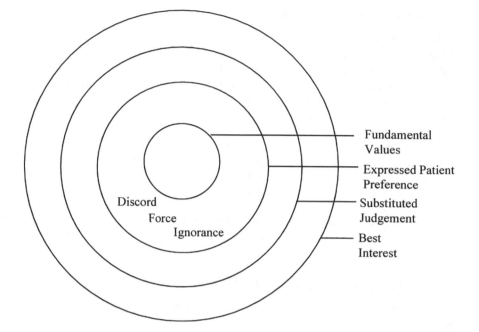

Figure 13.2 Concentric circles signify degrees of familiarity with the individual involved with medical care.

ness of these more tangible components. Through value clarification, consensus may be possible for all parties involved.

Such an understanding of bioethics can be schematically illustrated with regard to standards of decision making. In Figure 13.2, concentric circles signify degrees of familiarity with the individual involved with medical care. Most traditional models identify the innermost circle as the expressed wishes of the patient. The next circle would be substituted judgment, exemplified in medical durable power of attorney, and best interest, which is often defined as an objective, socially defined criterion that considers such factors as relief of pain, risks and benefits of a proposed intervention, and the usefulness or futility of the proposed treatment. However, fundamental values is a deeper circle, a more personal level of self-definition serving in a sense as a yardstick and compass to the expressed wishes of the patient, the creative or spiritual level of understanding which integrates and anchors life patterns. This level of self-definition is often shared with family members because of their intimate association. It guides and measures whether choices foster self-fulfillment.

What is unusual about this inner level of being, fundamental values, is that it may exist but not be explicitly communicated in the immediately expressed wishes of the parties involved because of discord, force, or ignorance. For example, discord can be manifested in rivalry between adult children. Force limits the ability to choose, such as when financial cost makes certain procedures unavailable. Ignorance can be manifested simply through lack of understanding of the medical conditions or limited intervention options available during the end stage of a terminal illness. When values are not clearly communicated, family meetings may help clarify choices and lead to a consensual decision.

Values are found not only in the inner being of the individual but also in groups or families, which are homogeneous to varying degrees. Even in the most homogeneous group or family, diversity of particular choices and goals exists, offering an opportunity for interaction, clarification, and consensus building. In a sense, such an understanding of where values lie necessitates a redefining of the term *autonomy*. Autonomy is not just a reflection of independent self-interest but an expression of an affirming environment that allows exploring of issues, drawing distinctions, and making choices. Relationships underlie the very notion of human autonomy because autonomy means expressing self. The self can only express, and in a sense be found, by reaching out into the group identity and values. Choice is an expression of self-awareness that is a relational process because a shared value system acts as a mirror in the growth of greater self-awareness.

A reflective value system is found in the immediate family structure. Health care systems also possess a value system, which will be expressed overtly or covertly in the treatment process. This value system is not a challenge to family or patient values but rather an opportunity for interaction leading to clarification and consensus building.

Because values are found in a relational context, how can they be prioritized and shared by all parties involved? This becomes even more difficult with a patient lacking the capacity to participate cognitively in the interactive process. When values are viewed as residing in a relational context, family judgment can approximate patient wishes and the value social unit out of which they arise.

Ethical issues arising in an institutional setting can be conceptualized with the diagram presented in Figure 13.3, which identifies four major factors in each

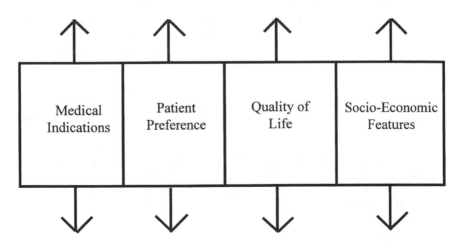

Figure 13.3 Four major factors arising in each ethical decision within an institutional setting.

ethical decision. Which factor will take precedence depends on the stage of illness as well as contextual features such as the family, care environment, and value consensus. This shifting prioritization is indicated by the arrows.

Understanding the medical indications involves more than the anticipated course or expectation of outcome. Nor is it simply a matter of assessing present physiological needs. It also includes defining the responsibilities (role) of health care professionals. What can be done—or will be done?

Patient preference extends beyond legal (e.g., living wills) or psychological (truthful disclosure, competency, etc.) issues to assessing the value basis of decisions. This dimension is not always self-evident, and consequently families may need skilled facilitation in value assessment to increase self-awareness.

Quality of life is a very amorphous term because of its highly contextual dependency. It needs to be defined not simply as the subjective satisfaction experienced by an individual but also that of the family in their current physical, psychological, and social situation.

Socioeconomic features are legal issues, such as standard of care; economic issues, especially those related to justice; and institutional policies and procedures. Caregiver preferences and issues often are categorized under this aspect but should be viewed as integral to all four dimensions. It is the caregiver involvement in each factor that allows for prioritizing them at different stages of Alzheimer's disease.

This model can help staff and families communicate about ethical choice. By this time, many ethical decisions have already been made, as priorities shifted with the progression of the illness. Caretakers struggle with how much substituted judgment to use and when to encourage patient choice. The timing of nursing home placement may have required extensive value clarification with the result that the quality of life for both patient and caretaker has become the dominant factor. Now decisions about hospitalization, pain control, and life-sustaining procedures must be made as medical issues become dominant.

Ethics conferences can be initiated by staff as care decisions are needed. Discussion can center around factors in the diagram as the group decides which is most important at this time. The following questions may be helpful to the facilitation of such a conference.

1   How do the family and patient describe the current medical problem?
2   What do health care professionals wish to add or what questions do they need to answer?
3   What would be a useful outcome of this meeting?
4   What does the family understand the choices to be in this current situation? What are the consequences of these for patient and family members?
5   What does the medical team see as choices and consequences?
6   How does each family member prioritize choices, from best to least preferred?
7   What influences this ranking?
   a   Religious or spiritual belief

      b   Cultural or ethnic background
      c   Family rules, roles, traditions, history, or feelings of responsibility
      d   Expressed preferences of the patient
   8 Where there is conflict—
      a   Is this conflict new or part of larger family history?
      b   What information or feeling is the basis for this position?
      c   Can a both/and, rather than either/or, position be reached?
   9 How will decisions be implemented? What will be the family part of this? (Emphasize what will rather than will not be done for patient.)
   10 How will family members help each other as a group to live with the decision that is made—how can the medical team be of help to each family member? Principles of comfort and dignity extend to the family as well as the patient.

PERSONAL CONCERNS OF STAFF MEMBERS WHO ASSIST GRIEVING FAMILIES

Working with patients and families in the final phases of Alzheimer's disease may influence staff members' awareness of their own mortality, increase apprehension regarding personal losses, and raise anxiety about personal death. Health professionals will move through an adaptation process in developing an ability to work with terminally ill patients and their families. Harper (1977) developed the "Schematic Growth and Development Scale in Coping With Professional Anxiety in Terminal Illness" to describe the maturing of the health professional in this speciality.

   Stage 1. Intellectualization: knowledge and anxiety   At this point the health professional focuses on knowledge and factual issues. The stage is marked by brisk activity, impersonal involvement, and even withdrawal from the patient and family. Death is unacceptable.

   Stage 2. Emotional survival: trauma   Confronting the impending patient death requires confronting personal death. The process of mourning and grieving for self becomes salient, moving the professional from intellectualization to emotional reaction. Guilt and frustration can mount as efforts are made to fight back and the reality of death must be accepted.

   Stage 3. Depression: pain, mourning, grieving   This is the most crucial stage, in which mastering personal frustration leads to accepting death. Caregiving will require experiencing pain and mourning as well as acceptance and peace. The professional will either make this transition or leave the field.

   Stage 4. Emotional arrival: moderation, mitigation, accommodation   A sense of freedom from identification with the patient's symptoms and from preoccupation with personal loss allows professionals to be sensitive to patients but not incapacitated by the dying experience. They now have the ability to grieve but also to recover.

Stage 5. Deep compassion: self-realization, self-awareness, self-actualization Affording dignity and self-respect to themselves enables professionals to give dignity and respect to patients and families. Activities are now based on human as well as clinical assessment of needs. Acceptance that at times it can be more painful to live than to die—that death is a part of life—has brought peace to the professional and stimulated a compassionate participation in this universal human experience.

This model may be useful in helping staff members to reflect on their own experiences and to describe the type of support needed to continue their work. Often staff members on an Alzheimer's unit will need debriefing after a number of losses or a particularly difficult one. Encouragement of emotional sharing and appropriate self-care will be important to maintaining a healthy, effective care team.

FAMILY-CENTERED INSTITUTIONAL POLICIES

The efforts of individual staff members need support from family-centered policies and procedures. Facilities can include families in many activities, for example, by timing placement tours so that as many family members as possible can participate and by planning periodic memorial services for residents who have died. To create a family-centered milieu, staff will need support and education. Facilities can educate staff to

1   Think about the family as an interactional unit rather than a collection of individuals.

2   Appreciate the diversity of family relationships and behaviors around the loss of a member.

3   Recognize normal grief reactions and know methods of supporting grievers.

4   Be comfortable assisting families during highly emotional interactions around death and grief.

5   Facilitate family meetings and offer opportunities for family involvement in care.

6   Know personal values and beliefs about family interaction at times of loss to avoid imposing them on others.

7   Be aware of personal reactions and needs in working with patients and families.

8   Advocate for policies and procedures that help staff feel supported by the facility in their family-centered care.

CONCLUSION

Family-centered policies are guided by the philosophy that the care experience is most important to the family that brings their loved one to the facility, shares the caretaking with the staff, and incorporates the experience into family history. Families should have as much influence and control over their member's dying experience as possible.

BIBLIOGRAPHY

Bommel, H. (1987). *Choices for people who have a terminal illness, their families and caregivers.* Toronto, Ontario, Canada: NC Press.

Boss, P., Caron, W., Horbal, T., & Mortimer, T. (1990). Predictors of depression in caregivers of dementia patients: Boundary, ambiguity and mastery. *Family Process, 29,* 245–254.

Brakman, S. (1994). Adult daughter caregivers. *Hastings Center Report, 24*(5), 26–28.

Cantor, M. (Ed.). (1994). *Family caregiving agenda for the future.* San Francisco: American Society on Aging.

Falicov, C. (1988). *Family transitions: Continuity and change over the life cycle.* New York: Guilford Press.

Figley, C. (Ed.). (1995). *Compassion fatigue—Coping with secondary traumatic stress disorder in those who treat the traumatized.* New York: Brunner/Mazel.

Gatz, M. (Ed.). (1995). *Emerging issues in mental health and aging.* Washington, DC: American Psychological Association.

Greenberg, J. (1994). Family boundary, ambiguity: A new variable in family stress theory. *Family Process, 23,* 535–546.

Harper, B.C. (1977). *Death: The coping mechanism of the health professional.* Greenville, SC: Southeastern University Press.

Henao, S., & Grose, N. (1985) *Principles of family systems in family medicine.* New York: Brunner/Mazel.

Patterson, J., & Garwick, A. (1994). Levels of meaning in family stress theory. *Family Process, 33,* 287–304.

Rando, T. (1984). *Grief, dying and death—Clinical interventions for caregivers.* Champaign, IL: Research Press.

Reiss, D. (1981). *The family's construction of reality.* Cambridge, MA: Harvard University Press.

Rolland, J. (1994). *Families, illness and disability.* New York: Basic Books.

Rosen, E. (1990). *Families facing death.* Lexington, MA: D. C. Heath.

Walsh, F., & McGoldrick, M. (1988). Loss and the family life cycle. In C. Falicov (Ed.), *Family transition: Continuity and change over the life cycle.* New York: Guilford Press.

Walsh, F., & McGoldrick, M. (1991). *Living beyond loss, death in the family.* New York: W.W. Norton.

Wortman, C., & Silver, R. C. (1989). The myths of coping with loss. *Journal of Consulting and Clinical Psychology, 57,* 349–357.

Chapter 14

Making Change Work: Understanding Concepts and Strategies

Janet Wessel Krejci

A discussion is overheard at the nurses' station at a long-term care facility: "There's just too much change here. How can they expect us to take care of patients when everything is always changing? I don't understand why all this environment change is so important. I give good care." Just down the street at the local hospital another conversation ensues: "Now that we are part of this new corporation, I guess everything is going to change. I'm glad I'm only 2 years from retirement."

The end of the millennium has certainly brought many rapid changes to health care. It is easy to become immobilized by our mental models that "there is just too much change." Unfortunately, the change itself is not what is usually feared. In fact, opportunities exist now to make the fundamental quality-of-care changes that health care professionals have long desired. Change is not inherently good nor bad. Changes are usually initiated to improve quality for health care recipients and care providers. This chapter reviews the usefulness of the different change theories, invites a new understanding of important but often unacknowledged variables affecting the complexity of change, and finally offers strategies for successfully initiating and sustaining change to improve quality of care. In this chapter, *change agent* refers to any individual or group responsible for initiating, implementing, and sustaining change.

UNDERSTANDING CHANGE

A lack of understanding of change and its accompanying human consequences often leads to a distorted change process. Being human necessitates gravitation

189

toward change not only to survive but also to thrive. It is the lack of control and perceived threat of personal security, rather than the change itself, that is usually labeled resistance to change.

Unfortunately, efforts at a successful change process are often misguided. There are volumes of classic, innovative, creative, and insightful works on change that can be very helpful (Adizes, 1988, 1992; Argyris, 1985; Argyris, Putnam, & Smith, 1986; Argyris & Schon, 1978; Belasco, 1990; Bennis, Benne, & Chinn, 1969; Handy, 1994; Havelock, 1973; Kanter, 1983; Kanter, Stein, & Jick, 1992; Lewin, 1951; Lippitt, 1973; Senge, 1990; Tichny, 1983; Watzlawick, Weakland, & Fisch, 1974). Although change agents attempt to utilize the basics of change theory, when pressured for time and resources, they are often seduced to force the change rather than develop it in partnership with the recipients of change. By attempting to coerce people to believe that the desired change is in fact desirable, they paradoxically raise suspicion and ultimately sabotage their own efforts. Idealistically but naively, many change agents want a recipe-like approach that will ensure successful change.

It is imperative that change agents reframe their assumptions or mental models about the change process to be successful. The art and science of reframing includes examining assumptions that may sabotage change efforts. Senge (1990) proposed that all individuals hold mental models that unconsciously influence behavior. For example, nurses and nursing assistants are often the indirect recipients of the change process (e.g., changing from an institutional environment to a more home-like environment). The mental models change agents have about staff's inherent expertise, motivations, knowledge, and commitment will clearly influence strategies for change.

In reframing, change agents learn to look at the change from a variety of perspectives, specifically from change recipients' perspectives, to increase success. Change agents become experts in the human response to change rather than exclusively experts in the content of change. In addition to understanding basic theory about the process of change, one must also understand the targets of change, ways in which people change, change as loss, and the concept of organizational anxiety and its influences on change before achieving success.

CHANGE THEORIES

Lewin

The most influential studies on change began with Lewin (1951), with modifications by followers such as Lippitt (1973) and Havelock (1973). Lewin's theory still provides the foundation of change theory today.

Stages of change   Essentially Lewin (1951) identified three major stages of change—unfreezing, moving, and refreezing. According to Lewin, the first stage, unfreezing, is characterized by an initial perception of disequilibrium in an individual, group, or organization. Uncertainty exists, resulting in discomfort and anxiety. People are asked to let go of present security and move to the unknown.

For example, regulations or new research may demonstrate the need for a change in the provision of long-term care (e.g., creating a home-like environment to increase independence and quality of life). When information about these needed changes begins to surface, a sense of foreboding results in those involved in care provision. The change is identified, but the scope, nature, and timing of change is uncertain.

The second stage, according to Lewin (1951), is the moving stage. This is the stage at which the actual change takes place. People begin to see that change is inevitable, and new responses are tried out by individuals, groups, and the organization as a whole.

Lewin's (1951) third stage is the refreezing stage. This is a time of restabalization and adaptation to the change. During this time, many members experiencing change may attempt to engage in behaviors designed to persuade systems to change back to past routines, if adaptation is not successful.

Although Lewin's theory provided the foundation for change theory, conceptualizing current systems as a concrete block does not begin to capture the dynamic complexity of today's change. It is not unusual for many changes to be taking place within a similar time period. Subsequently individuals, groups, and organizations are experiencing all three stages all the time, as well as inevitable day-to-day changes.

Driving and restraining forces   Lewin (1951) offered another important concept in his description of *force-field analysis* and of *driving forces* and *restraining forces*. Driving forces support change, and restraining forces discourage or sabotage change. According to this model, successful change will occur if the driving forces are stronger in quality or quantity (or both) than the restraining forces. Lewin's stages and force-field analysis are revisited below, after other influencing variables of change are described. (See Table 14.1 for a summary of theorists and authors contributing to the study of change.)

Targets of Change

It is important for change agents to discern whether the target of change is an individual, group, or system and whether the target is knowledge, behavior (norms and activities), or attitude (values and beliefs). Most change theorists believe that individuals are easier to change than groups but that the power of a group or system is more powerful than an individual. Therefore, once a group or system changes, individual changes come easier. Knowledge is believed to be easier to change than behaviors (norms and activities) or attitudes (values, beliefs).

Unfortunately, most interventions for planned change are focused on improving group knowledge, with the erroneous assumption that after group instruction is given (e.g., that home-like environments improve quality of life for

Table 14.1   Authors contributing to the study of change

Authors	Contributions
Lewin (1951)	1. Three developmental stages of change
	2. Driving and restraining forces
Benne, Chinn, and Bennis (1969)	1. Planned change theory
	2. Approaches to change
Havelock (1973)	1. Emphasis on building relationship with team
	2. Concentrated on planning phase as most important and time consuming
Lippitt (1973)	1. Utilized a modified problem solving process within Lewin's three stages
	2. Emphasized role of change agent from initiation to termination
Ferguson (1980)	1. Explication of ways people change (exception, incremental, pendulum, paradigm)
	2. Explication of consequences of different ways people change
Rogers (1983)	1. Identification of factors influencing success (i.e., relative advantage, compatibility, complexity, visibility, and trialability)
	2. Five phases of change from awareness through adoption
	3. Identification of stakeholders and levels of change agents (from innovators to late adopters)
Argyris et al. (1986), Senge (1990)	1. Systems thinking
	2. Vision, team learning
	3. Organizational anxiety
Perlman & Tackas (1990)	1. Comparison of change with grief process
	2. Explication of stages of grief

residents), the behavior and attitudes of groups will soon change. This is one of the biggest and most frequent mistakes for change agents. Unfortunately, if the mistake is made and the change fails, the response is often more education, with a renewed emphasis on selling the idea. Paradoxically, as soon as staff members perceive they are being sold an idea, they automatically resist more. When more resistance is experienced, change agents and leaders are often tempted to resort to a more traditional authoritative or power–coercive approach. This in turn may create short-term behavioral compliance but long-term sabotage. A vicious cycle has begun. Although knowledge may be important, it is no guarantee that behaviors (norms and activities) or attitudes (values and beliefs) will be affected.

Not only are there different targets of change, but individuals and groups often change in very different ways. Given that most change theories are described as developmental, change agents mistakenly assume that all individuals change in stages. In reality there are some fairly predictable differences.

Ways People Change

Ferguson (1980) studied transformation and change and described different ways people change, including by exception, incrementally, in pendulum swings, or paradigm shifts. She also identified the varying influences on change depending on the different ways people change.

By exception   When people change by exception, they remain essentially the same with the exception of one or two small behavioral changes. For example, a care provider might ensure a more comfortable water and room temperature in the bathing room, but his or her whole demeanor is still one steeped in an institutional or assembly line approach to bathing and dressing.

When staff members change by exception, they may change concrete behaviors to appear compliant, but their general belief and value system remains unchanged. They identify concrete behaviors to support their compliance, but they remain essentially unchanged but for minor exceptions.

Incremental   When one changes incrementally, the change is slow and gradual, without benefit of insight (Ferguson, 1970). Incremental change can be compared to driving on a road that incrementally and consistently curves several degrees to the right, without the driver's awareness of the turn. In long-term care settings, a once responsible care provider who is uncomfortable with new changes can incrementally become an irresponsible care provider and have no insight into that change. This can be quite destructive and provides another reason to work with recipients of change before they become incrementally disenchanted with the system. Disenchanted providers rarely provide high quality care.

Likewise, care providers can incrementally shift toward new behaviors congruent with the desired change (e.g., providing a homelike environment and individualized and respectful care). It will be difficult to continue to build on learning if there is no insight into the change. However, incremental improvement is often an advantageous alternative over no change.

Pendulum change   Pendulum swings are observed when people wholeheartedly engage in change without thoughtful consideration of intended and unintended consequences. The result is a bandwagon type of effect that is rarely long lasting. This is a common type of process, in which staff members enthusiastically embrace the change without any substantive understanding of the basics of the change. Inadvertently, care providers can do more harm than good if they do not understand the basis for a change. For example, a care provider might misunderstand the basis for environmental change and become patronizing, as if residents were children dining out for the first time, rather than elderly individuals experienced and wise in the ways of life. Although change agents are usually aware of this potential problem, they sometimes inadvertently reward the pendulum swing. Blind enthusiasm is sometimes more welcome than overt or covert sabotage. Pendulum swings should be avoided if at all possible.

Paradigm shift   A paradigm shift is observed when people begin to see the changes with clarity and begin to take thoughtful and focused steps at helping to create the change. It is as if you have given people a new set of glasses, through which they can now see with increased clarity, scope, and distance. The paradigm shift is associated with the normative re-educative approach to change. People may still see the change as somewhat anxiety producing but also as a potential growth opportunity and not a direct threat to their survival. Unfortunately, helping people to experience paradigm shifts is not always easy or quick, but the long-term benefits far outweigh a pendulum swing or mere compliance. Despite the different ways people change, they will almost always experience some degree of loss.

CHANGE AS LOSS

Resistance to Change

Most change agents frame any behavior from team members that is not wholly supportive of the change as resistance to change. Unfortunately, this frame can be destructive. Sometimes the response from team members are valid concerns that should be framed as valuable feedback. If team members have valid concerns that are discounted or discouraged, then true resistance will indeed emerge. Resistance is a reaction to a perception of control. The control perceived is experienced as a discounting and invalidation of one's contribution. This is a very different concept from resistance for resistance's sake. Although realistically change agents cannot individually respond to each and every behavior observed, it is incumbent upon change agents to set ground rules for feedback regarding the change process. More often, the behaviors observed, if not related to valid concerns, are expressions of loss. It is only when loss (or valid feedback) is not addressed and resolved that organizational anxiety and subsequent resistance to change develops.

Grief as Response to Change

Whether individuals are excited, fearful, anxious, tentative, or cooperative about change, change agents must understand that loss is almost always experienced and people need validation of that loss before embarking on change. Perlman and Takacs (1990) equated the process individuals experience during change with the grieving process associated with death and dying. They identified 10 phases, beginning with equilibrium and moving through denial, anger, bargaining, chaos, depression, and resignation before reaching openness, readiness, and eventual reemergence. Although change agents may have difficulty equating the grief associated with personal loss such as death to organizational change, it takes little reflection to realize that staff members do indeed go through a grieving process when confronted with organizational change.

Although not everyone experiences every stage and clearly do not experience the stages in a specific order, it is important to recognize these behaviors as response to loss rather than sabotage. If the anger or chaos is framed as resistance, change agents may respond defensively rather than therapeutically. As most professional care providers know, it is important to validate feelings, actively listen, offer options, and support growth when ready. Unfortunately, when these same care providers are in the role of change agent, it becomes tempting to intervene in ways that are paradoxical to growth (e.g., with false reassurance, by discounting feelings, ordering, offering false praise, etc.). If the feelings of loss are not encouraged but instead are discounted, organizational anxiety can mount and begin to create problems that can distract and sabotage desired change.

RESISTANCE: ORGANIZATIONAL ANXIETY

The concept of organizational anxiety has been described by leaders in systems and organizational change (Argyris et al., 1986; Senge, 1990). Change agents who cannot recognize organizational anxiety as an important variable of the complexity of change almost always risk failure. Organizational anxiety is usually created when there is uncertainty related to (a) personal competence, (b) job security, (c) perceived lack of access to important information, (d) perceived lack of validation from those in power, and (e) general unknown impending changes. The concept of organizational anxiety becomes very important once change agents realize how anxiety gets operationalized in a system. Anxiety gets enacted in one of several ways, including overt or covert conflict (interpersonally or intrapersonally inside or outside of the organization), pathology (actual illness of a system member or general unit demise), or triangulation (Miller & Winstead-Fry, 1982).

Triangulation

Triangulation is a concept identified in systems theory as a vehicle to manage personal or system anxiety. Consider an individual who (a) experiences change as a potential threat (common for a care provider who is not initiating or in control of the change), (b) may have some questions about his or her own personal competency (a care provider who is now expected to interact with residents in a new way), (c) does not necessarily feel able or encouraged to either specifically identify or speak directly about the fundamental issues of anxiety (care providers may feel intimidated by superiors who control their evaluations), and (d) may feel alone or isolated in their experience (e.g., because other newly hired care providers have more education or experience in the new approach). This individual is inevitably experiencing high levels of anxiety.

> **Case example**   *In the case of a long-term care system changing to a more home-like environment, consider a nursing assistant and a nurse who have worked together for years in a very efficient (but not necessarily holistic) manner. They have been highly regarded and rewarded for their efficiency. They perceive the change as a challenge to their skills and are uncertain regarding potential role and power changes. They begin to experience a vague, undefined*

sense of anxiety. It is extremely difficult to directly acknowledge doubts about personal competence, and so direct examination of personal issues is suppressed and free floating anxiety increases.

Case discussion   According to systems theory (Argyris et. al., 1986; Kast & Rosenzweig, 1972; Senge, 1990), this anxiety can be very unnerving and triggers attempts to (consciously or unconsciously) decrease the anxiety. The quickest (not healthiest) way to decrease the uncomfortable feeling of uncertainty or free-floating anxiety is to find someone or something to validate that the problem or enemy lies outside of the individual, not within.

Subsequently, in the example above, instead of acknowledging their uncertainty, the nurse and nursing assistant may begin to make an alliance to validate their own feelings that the upcoming change is idealistic fantasy rather than realistic improvement. They begin to look for problems and quickly contact each other to share their perspectives and get validation for their own feelings. Their free-floating anxiety is now polarized and directed toward a very concrete target. The discomfort of anxiety and uncertainty is controlled and thus decreased, as they are now a team united against an enemy, often the change agent.

In this way, their affiliation needs are met and they no longer feel alone, they no longer have to acknowledge any competency issues, they no longer feel personally threatened because they have shifted the burden to the change agents, and because they believe that the change agent or leadership is wrong, they are no longer intimidated. This is a very powerful reward for their efforts, albeit unconscious, at triangulation. The belief that they now have a common enemy makes the alliance very strong. These triangles are very hard to disrupt, and even when they are disrupted, new triangles tend to form quickly.

Targets of negativity can quickly become other colleagues and even residents or family members. The desire to decrease or control anxiety becomes a leading influence of behavior, although often unwittingly. Other staff members may be included in this dynamic until full-blown scapegoating results. The scapegoat in question usually has some vulnerable point that can be exploited. This vulnerability is sometimes the mere fact that the individual is part of, or represents, an administrative group, thus excluding them from membership in the group considered staff.

Overall System Dysfunction

Absences, incident reports, and turnover may increase. This resulting chaos serves to sabotage the change, and the change fails. Paradoxically, staff begin to believe that indeed the change itself is the cause for problems, because they don't see the intangible triangle formation. If change agents themselves cannot see the underlying dynamic they begin to question the validity of the desired change or begin to blame the resisting members and thus increase the probability of a negative outcome.

This is imperative to understand, because when a system becomes dysfunctional, change agents often act quickly to try and bring order to the unit so that the desired change can occur. Paradoxically, this backfires, as anxiety increases and more, not less, dysfunction results. If individuals are capable and are encouraged to deal with the fundamental issue of anxiety (e.g., uncertainty about personal security) in the very beginning, effective problem solving can ensue. Once change agents understand these basic concepts of change, they will be more successful in initiating and sustaining the desired change.

APPROACHES TO CHANGE

Team Building

Team building is imperative in any approach to change. Team building can be defined along the continuum from formal team building conducted with an outside consultant to a philosophy of day-to-day system management. Team building usually is most effective if it is the latter, a foundation that is the basis for all decisions and system operations. Although outside consultants can be most helpful, their role in the change and team building needs to be clearly identified and clarified or efforts can backfire.

Team building is not something that can be accomplished in a 1- or 2-day workshop. It is an ongoing process. Senge (1990) emphasized team learning, rather than team building, as a learning discipline that any organization needs along with vision, systems thinking, and personal mastery. Team building can often fail as it is a temporary solution to a crisis. Team learning, in contrast, is an emphasis on teaching teams to dialogue with each other to create understanding of the value of diverse views.

Teams must have a clear idea of the vision and be invited to share and co-create the vision of the system to whatever degree possible. Teams that have shared vision and believe that every team member has a valuable contribution initiate, implement, and sustain a more innovative and effective change than ever originally designed. Attending to Rogers's (1983) characteristics of change (discussed below) will facilitate team building because they underscore the important values and norms of the team.

Three Approaches to Change

Some of the most critical work accomplished in approaches to planned change was accomplished by Bennis et al. (1969). They articulated three approaches to change that are instrumental to change agents. These approaches are power–coercive, rational–empirical, and normative–reeducative. All approaches are needed for different strategies. Approaches for specific situations and potential outcomes are summarized in Table 14.2.

Power–coercive The first and most recognizable approach is what Bennis et al. (1969) termed power–coercive. This approach is used frequently in American

Table 14.2   Approaches to change

Approach	Situation and approach	Potential outcomes
Power–coercive (rules, laws, mandates)	When a change or mandate is not negotiable (e.g., OBRA): 1. Communicate honestly and openly to staff or team. 2. Identify rationale explicitly. 3. Elicit ideas from team members about implementation.	1. Staff or team members may show initial compliance but sabotage larger change issues. 2. If staff or team are informed early and understand rationale, members can respond to the change very effectively.
Rational–empirical (educational, informational)	When team members need information: 1. Provide it in a variety of ways to increase success (audio, visual, imagery, written) 2. Evaluate team members' learning related to understanding change	1. Knowledge may or may not be understood. 2. Although knowledge may lead to behavior and attitudinal change, it is not guaranteed.
Normative–Reeducative	When norms, values, beliefs will be affected: 1. Use team-building and decision-making techniques to explore congruence of present norms, values, and beliefs with desired change. 2. Experiential exercises (imagery, role play, sensory awareness) are often helpful. 3. Attend to the influence of Rogers's (1983) characteristics on successful change (compatibility, complexity, trialability, visibility, relative advantage)	1. If norms, values, and beliefs of present system can be articulated and understood, more effective change strategies can be designed. 2. Team members are more apt to take ownership of change if it is integrated with norms, values, and beliefs. 3. Rational–empirical strategies need to be used in conjunction these strategies to be successful.

society and consists of laws, rules, policies, procedures, job descriptions, and other approaches that clearly communicate an expectation, with a subsequent negative consequence if the expectation is not met. Therefore, power–coercive approaches can be successful when behaviors are concrete, measurable, reducible, tangible, and nonnegotiable (e.g., stopping at a stoplight, making sure residents are fed).

Although this can be a successful approach to encourage behavior compliance, it does not ensure a concurrent change in attitude or more intangible behaviors and interactions. This is very important when dealing with environmental and patient care issues. In the example of changing a dining environment from institutional to homelike, a power–coercive approach might ensure that place settings are on tables and that no more than four residents sit at a table. It will not ensure, however, that care providers will facilitate healthy interaction that might approximate a home environment.

Rational–empirical   The second most common approach is one called rational–empirical (Bennis et al., 1969). This approach is the most common approach to change in organizations and includes the basic assumption that humans arc cognitive beings that are motivated by rational thought. Unfortunately, this is not always true.

For example, it is rational to stop smoking once one understands the relationship between smoking and disease. It also appears to be rational that all individuals want to be treated with basic dignity and respect. It is clear, however, that knowledge does not lead to smoking cessation nor to respectful and quality care. Unfortunately, change agents frequently believe that in-servicing in a rational–empirical mode will (and should) create not only knowledge but also behavioral (norms and activities) and attitudinal (values, beliefs, etc.) change. The more a planned change requires staff members to give up a comfortable routine with which they are competent (or least comfortable), the less chance a rational–empirical strategy (e.g., written or oral in-servicing) will be successful. Information doesn't necessarily motivate change.

Normative–re-educative   The third approach is the normative–reeducative approach. This approach emphasizes a recognition of the complexity of human response to change and highlights the powerful influence of internal and external norms on human behavior. The focus in this method is to change norms by helping individuals see and value the situation from a different perspective. This does not imply that change agents need to sell their goal, nor does it imply that one should simply reeducate individuals. Rather, it directs change agents to first understand the current norms and values of a system (e.g., shift, unit, department) and then link current norms and values with the desired change. Rogers's (1983) model of innovation diffusion offers some important insights into recognizing current norms and values as a precursor to change.

Rogers: Characteristics of Successful Change

An extensive summary of Rogers's (1983) theory is beyond the scope of this chapter. However, some of his concepts are extremely helpful in understanding norms and values as they apply to a normative–reeducative approach.

Rogers (1983) identified five characteristics of change that increase probability of success—perceived relative advantage, level of complexity, compatibility, trialability, and communicability. Analyzing the desired change according to these characteristics will facilitate a deeper understanding of the staff members' norms and values. Change agents can then see the change from the perspective of the staff members and should be able to better design effective strategies.

Relative advantage   If the desired innovation is to create a homelike rather than institutional environment, then care providers must see it as a relative advantage. In other words, if the change can be framed or conceptualized as an advantage for staff members, successful change is more likely. Some advantages include decreased confusion, falls, moaning, and resident requests, which would decrease workload on staff. Other advantages might include increased meaningful interaction with residents, more aesthetic surroundings, and development of relationships with staff and family, which increase job satisfaction. The crucial issue is that the advantage needs to be seen through the eyes of the staff rather than the exclusive world view of the change agent.

Complexity   The next question to address is the level of complexity of the change. Higher complexity will make change more difficult. Is new information, different priorities, or different or more difficult responsibilities associated with the change? This necessitates a dialogue with staff to identify the level of perceived complexity. Staff can then be asked to brainstorm ideas to either introduce the complexity in stages or decrease or simplify the complexity.

Compatibility   Compatibility needs to be discussed with staff. Is the innovation compatible with the work structure as presently designed? (For example, do lunch breaks coincide with resident dining, thereby decreasing staff availability? Are meals delivered in a manner compatible with serving residents at smaller tables or rooms?) Is the vision of a homelike long-term care facility compatible with the values and norms of the staff? If the staff do not believe that the residents are capable of interacting differently, then they will see the change attempt as proof that the change agent or administrative team is out of touch with the reality of providing care. Although these issues may seem to be minor details, it is often these details that are understood by staff as pivotal in making the change work.

Communicability   Communicability is the next characteristic. Although this characteristic seems most obviously important, it is overlooked most frequently. Is the innovation something that is easily communicated to staff in an understandable manner? Once staff move beyond understanding the innovation and begin to clearly communicate the goals to families, residents, and new staff, successful change is more likely.

Trialability   The last characteristic is that of trialability. Attempting to pilot or trial the innovation is helpful in several ways. It decreases anxiety to try something rather than experience it as final. Allowing time for trial and error gives groups more time to adjust. Staff can make valuable contributions during the trial period before decisions and plans are finalized. Once staff become involved at this level, change agents no longer have to sell the change. Members have made a personal commitment to success. Utilizing these characteristics can facilitate a successful normative–reeducative approach. Equipped with the knowledge of change theories, targets of change, ways people change, change as loss, organizational anxiety, and approaches to change, change agents can more successfully initiate and sustain successful change.

PUTTING IT ALL TOGETHER

The previous issues were articulated because they are all potentially powerful influencing variables. However, in the reality of today's dynamic complex health care system, not all issues will be addressed in all change endeavors. The change agent must be an expert at systems thinking. Systems thinking is a way of assessing dynamic complexity and discerning the important system relationships that affect change (Senge, 1990). Understanding the issues outlined will help change agents focus on points of leverage for successful change. With the new knowledge provided regarding the important variables influencing the complexity of change, it is helpful to revisit Lewin's (1951) stages of change.

Initiating Change

Unfreezing Lewin's first stage of unfreezing is the most time-consuming and crucial stage. The important role for the change agent at this stage is to accurately frame or diagnose the problem and to begin to build a relationship with staff members. Change agents need to clearly listen to staff expertise at this stage. Usually proposed changes are in need of major modifications if they are to be successful. Care providers who work closely with residents often have greater wisdom about needed changes than a change agent who may be somewhat removed from direct care. Needed resources need must be identified for the change process as well as ongoing needs for training and development after the change is instituted.

At this stage it is important for the change agent to clearly articulate the need for change. Sharing any relevant information is crucial. The rational–empirical approach to change is used quite extensively during this time, as much information will be new. The recipients of change should be queried as to the best way to identify and disseminate needed information, to allow for clear, accurate information sharing and an avoidance of escalating rumors that fuel anxiety.

The normative–reeducative approach is also important at this stage to identify system norms and values. For instance, consider a unit that is going to change to a more homelike setting, which will bring physical changes (e.g., in furnishings, room construction, colors, and flooring) and care delivery changes (assignments, meal times, increased family input). A brief guided imagery exercise could be highly effective to assist the staff in visualizing an ideal, homelike setting where residents and staff are treated individually with dignity and respect. The staff could begin to see how shifting their own values and norms could be beneficial to providers and residents.

Imagery can also be used to elicit recipients' responses to proposed changes. Experience with guided imagery has supported the notion that many care providers have negative images of change (tornados, fires, hurricanes, lightning). Reframing change through imagery can decrease negative reactions. Decision-making and idea-generating techniques such as nominal process, delphi technique, and brainstorming could be used to identify advantages and obstacles of present norms (staffing patterns, break routines, daily schedule). These approaches are very successful during the heightened anxiety of the unfreezing stage and help to identify and increase the perceived relative advantage, complexity, and compatibility of the change process (Rogers, 1983).

Power–coercive approaches are usually present at this stage (e.g., OBRA, state surveys). Change agents need to be honest if some change is not negotiable. Most recipients of change can accept a power–coercive approach to change if they understand its origin. For example, federal or state regulations may mandate change. It is important to identify which part of the change is not negotiable and which part is open for creative adaptation. Often during the unfreezing stage, change agents report mandated changes in a negative, almost victim-like manner. If change agents present change in this manner, it fuels the perception that there is an external enemy preventing quality care. As identified in the discussion of triangles, an identification of an external enemy reduces anxiety but does not encourage personal responsibility and growth. In the example of changing to a homelike environment, staff can be told that changes are not negotiable (power–coercive approach) but that a work group will have influence on approaches to the implementation and the resources needed for implementation.

The unfreezing stage is crucial for identification of rising organizational anxiety. Change agents are most productive if they acknowledge the potential for anxiety as a normal response and offer vehicles for support (open forum, log entries, an open-door policy with the change agent during realistic time frames). As indicated by Perlman and Takacs (1990), denial and anger will be initial reactions, which may turn into anxiety and subsequent triangles if not handled appropriately. Staff need honest information, options, and acknowledgement, not judgment of feeling. The change agent does not have to serve as a counselor or therapist during this period, a common temptation with professionals who work as caretakers. This reinforces dependency rather than growth. Rather, the change agent needs to offer support but also communicate a belief in the staff's ability to make good decisions, access needed resources, and contribute value to the overall change process.

Moving   This is a strategic phase for change agents, as the old rules no longer apply, and new ones are not quite set. Although many perceive this time to be a time of chaos, this is when the most leverage can be found because rules and norms are undefined. A change agent may be able to initiate change much more easily during this period.

It is a time when new behaviors are most easily developed and trialed. If the general change movement relates to creating a homelike atmosphere, many different changes can be supported under that general movement (e.g., changing wall colors, putting centerpieces on the table, visiting hours, meal choices, etc.). Without this general direction for change, these smaller changes may seem irrelevant, peripheral, and thus nonsupported.

At the moving stage, the change agent must be acutely aware of any developing resistance to change and work on partnerships with the recipients of change. Problems encountered must be identified in a timely manner. Piloting (congruent with normative–reeducative approach) is utilized most successfully during this time, with latitude for making modifications in the change when necessary. Unintended consequences of the change often occur during this period. For example, some residents may regress rather than progress with the new changes. Family members and residents may protest the change as harmful. These unintended consequences can be adequately confronted during the pilot stage, before permanent changes are made.

There may be need for a power–coercive approach during this time as well. It is during this time of potential chaos that staff members may begin to bargain or test the limits. Consequences may need to be delineated if rational–empirical and normative–reeducative approaches are not sufficient. It should be stressed that initiating any punitive reactions to staff during this stage can easily increase organizational anxiety to intolerable levels.

In Perlman and Takacs's (1990) conceptualization, this would probably be the time for bargaining, chaos, depression, and resignation. It is important for the change agent to see these attitudes and behaviors as normal, not as an indication that the change is failing. It is imperative during this stage for change agents to separate reaction to the change itself from reaction to potential loss and threat. There may be some loss of personnel during this time, but as the change begins, new personnel will begin to get interested in working in an area that is moving toward change.

According to Rogers (1983), visibility of any successes during this stage should be honestly and appropriately encouraged. Visibility of modifications made as a result of staff contributions are also important at this stage. Communicability, another of Rogers's characteristics, should be assessed at this time. The staff members, residents, and families should be able to begin to articulate a description and rationale for the change related to improving care. If they are not able or willing to articulate the change as related to quality care, there is a clear gap between the desired change and the evolving change. If handled during this stage, problems can be adequately addressed and solved.

Refreezing   Change agents must realize that the change has to be reinforced and modified to maintain growth and renewal for all. During this time, if change has been primarily successful, you might see individuals and groups at the stages of openness, readiness, and reemergence (Perlman & Takacs, 1990). Although not all individuals or groups will reach this point, it is important for change agents to help individuals make healthy choices. As indicated earlier, there may be staff who resist the change and incrementally shift to become care providers who are no longer providing quality care. All the issues of evaluation are enmeshed in these situations. It is worth pointing out, however, that change agents will do well to be prepared for some staff members to truly blossom with the changes and others to incrementally begin to drift into lower quality care. If this probability is known ahead of time, the change agent may be more successful in supporting valid choices for all involved.

The main goal during this stage is to reinforce what has been successful, ensuring visibility of the success, and to modify what is not working. Ensuring visibility is often ignored by change agents at this stage as they sometimes erroneously believe their work is finished once restabilization sets in. Unfortunately, as unintended consequences of the change evolve (clear need for additional education or a need for different assessment processes for those in homelike environments), organizational anxiety can be triggered. Making success visible and assuring staff that problems will be confronted, not minimized nor hidden, is an effective strategy.

It is not uncommon for a new change to arrive on the toes, rather than the heels, of a previous change during this stage. Change agents must recognize their role within the larger system as well as the role of new change agents who are developing the next wave of change. At this point, the change agent relationship begins to be terminated or renegotiated as a new role within the new change.

CONCLUSION

In summary, although change theories can guide change agents, there is no recipe for success. The ability to see the dynamic complexity of important variables is crucial for successful application of change strategies. All approaches to change (power–coercive, rational–empirical, normative–reeducative) can and will be utilized at different times. The significant issue is to attempt to identify intended and unintended consequences of each approach given the situation variables.

Change agents have an exciting yet challenging role. They need to understand human and system complexity, change theories, ways people change, approaches to planned change, the grieving process, and the significance of organizational anxiety. Above all they need to be creative and open, yet driven by a vision to improve quality of care in collaborative partnerships, tapping the wisdom and energy of both recipients and providers of care.

BIBLIOGRAPHY

Adizes, I. (1988). *Corporate lifecycles*. Englewood Cliffs, NJ: Prentice-Hall.
Adizes, I. (1992). *Mastering change*. Santa Monica, CA: Adizes Institute.
Argyris, C. (1985). *Strategy, change, and defensive routines*. Cambridge, MA: Ballinger.
Argyris, C., Putnam, R., & Smith, D. (1986). *Action science*. San Francisco: Jossey Bass.

Argyris, C., & Schon, D. A. (1978). *Organizational learning: A theory of action perspective*. Reading, MA: Addison-Wesley.

Belasco, J. (1990). *Teaching the elephant to dance*. New York: Crown.

Bennis, W., Benne, K., & Chinn, R. (1969). *The planning of change* (3rd ed.). New York: Holt, Rinehart & Winston.

Ferguson, M. (1970). *The Aquarian conspiracy*. Los Angeles: Tarcher.

Handy, C. (1994). *The age of paradox*. Boston: Harvard Business School Press.

Havelock, R. (1973). *The change agent's guide to innovation in education*. NJ: Educational Technology.

Kanter, R. M. (1983). *The changemasters*. New York: Simon & Schuster.

Kanter, R. M., Stein, B. A., & Jick, T. D. (1992). *The challenge of organizational change*. New York: Free Press.

Kast, F., & Rosenzweig, J. (1972). General systems theory: Applications for organization and management. *Academy of Management, 15*, 447–465.

Lewin, K. (1951). *Field theory in social science: Selected theoretical papers*. New York: Harper.

Lippitt, G. (1973). *Visualizing change: Model building and the change process*. LaJolla, CA: University Associates.

Miller, S. R., & Winstead-Fry, P. (1982). *Family systems theory in nursing systems practice*. Reston, VA: Prentice-Hall.

Perlman, D., & Takacs, G. (1990). The ten stages of change. *Nursing Management, 21*(4), 183–191.

Rogers, E. (1983). *Diffusion of innovations* (3rd ed.). New York: Free Press.

Senge, P. (1990). *The fifth discipline*. New York: Doubleday.

Tichny, N. (1983). *Managing strategic change. Technical, political, and cultural dynamics*. New York: Wiley.

Watzlawick, P., Weakland, J., & Fisch, R. (1974). *Change*. New York: W. W. Norton.

Chapter 15

Legal and Ethical Issues

Alison Barnes

Health care providers are increasingly aware that they work in a legal environment that prescribes the extent of disclosure to patients and the need to weigh treatment recommendations with knowledge of the needs and preferences of patients and their families. This awareness has arrived more slowly in long-term care, where—except for end-of-life cases beginning with that of Karen Anne Quinlen in the 1970s—most decisions to provide or withhold procedures have remained longer in the medical sphere, outside the spotlight of legal rules.

This is particularly true for patients with advanced dementia. The use of legal guides to informed consent are complicated by reliance on advance directives and surrogate decision making. Often, such legal doctrines seem to lack a fundamental recognition of the complexity of treatment decisions in cases such as late-stage dementia. The law has not fully integrated the implications of medical technology that can keep a patient alive when allowing a quiet death might be truly humane. Conversely, critics assert that long-term care providers have withheld treatment that could avert death and improve quality of life to an acceptable level even given the inexorable progress of the dementia. The law is developing to protect the interests of both the patient and the provider by establishing some fundamental guidelines for providing and withholding care.

This chapter provides an overview of the legal rules, with specific examples provided by law cases. The text first examines the legal capacity to make health care decisions, a standard that is relevant to all but the most debilitated or uncommunicative patients, and the standards by which substitute decision makers should make decisions on the patients' behalf. It then contemplates four paradigmatic decisions: whether painful treatment or treatment with a low likelihood of success is appropriate for patients with late-stage dementia; whether to treat the underlying disease, generally an experimental procedure; whether to provide cardiopulmonary resuscitation on an individual or policy basis; and whether to consider nutrition or hydration as subject to withholding or withdrawal on the same basis as other life-prolonging procedures. The discussion concludes with a case narrative that illustrates legally sound responses to some of the dilemmas that most frequently confront practitioners. The chapter is intended to serve as a ready resource to help clarify the choices before the health care provider, the patient with late-stage dementia, and surrogate decision makers.

THE CAPACITY TO MAKE HEALTH CARE DECISIONS

Early in the 20th century, the courts articulated the right of individuals to give informed consent to any health care procedure, derived from the right of every legally competent person to bodily control and integrity.

General Legal Standards: The Patient's Right

An understanding of legal rights to self-determination in health care choices is useful as a foundation for more complex decisions for patients of doubtful, marginal, or absent capacity for decision making. Unless a patient has been declared legally incompetent by a court and a guardian appointed, that patient retains his or her legal right to refuse treatment and may in some instances demand care that providers deem less than optimum. Even if the patient is legally incompetent and has a guardian or responsible family member acting as a surrogate decision maker, it is possible for the patient to retain sufficient capacity to express an opinion about proposed treatment—about fear of changing environment and routine or fear of pain and dependency, for instance. Such a patient should be consulted with patience and care, even if the moments of capability, termed in law a *window of lucidity,* are few and inconveniently timed.

Each state determines the extent of disclosure a health care provider must make to obtain a patient's consent as well as the measure of comprehension the patient needs. Most states require disclosure that would be provided by a reasonable practitioner in a similar situation. A minority of states require that a physician disclose the information that should be considered material to the decision making of a reasonable patient.

Generally, the health care provider must consider a number of factors in choosing the information disclosed, including (a) the diagnosis, including test options; (b) the nature and purpose of the proposed treatment; (c) the risks of the treatment; (d) the probability of success; and (e) treatment alternatives, including those which are generally acknowledged in the medical community to be feasible (Appelbaum, Lidz, & Meisel, 1987, pp. 13–14) The provider must also disclose any conflicts of interest or ulterior motives, such as research or other financial interests in the procedures recommended (see, e.g., *Moore v. Regents of the University of California,* 1990).

A competent patient generally has the right to refuse any treatment, including nutrition and hydration, even if the result is death (e.g., *Satz v. Perlmutter,*

1978). It is irrelevant to the law whether the treatment has begun and must be withdrawn or is withheld. On the other hand, treating without consent is seldom the basis for a successful suit if the outcome is entirely positive. For example, a patient might assert that the health care provider should have known the patient had refused resuscitation and therefore negligently proceeded to improve health and continue life. Courts generally will hear the patient's claim but refuse to award damages because "life is not a compensable harm" (e.g., *Anderson v. St. Francis-St. George Hospital,* 1993).

Legal Standards for Decision-Making Capacity

Most determinations of competency are made by health care providers, with the ultimate responsibility on the attending physician. The case that moves into a legal forum is rare. There are, however, two strong reasons to know and observe legal competency standards in addition to accepted medical tests intended to yield a gross determination of the patient's mental capacity: (a) to utilize the thinking of the legal system in attempting to define capacity and incapacity fairly for all similarly situated patients, including those with late-stage dementia and (b) to anticipate the rare case that results in legal proceedings.

A legal determination of the patient's capacity generally turns on the patient's ability to comprehend the specific need for the treatment, the purpose of the treatment, the treatment alternatives, and the consequences of refusing treatment (Mishkin, 1989; Roth, Meisel, & Lidz, 1977). Two similar cases, *Lane v. Candura* (1978) and *Department of Human Services v. Northern* (1978) illustrate the nature of comprehension required. Each involved an elderly woman with advanced necrosis of the feet due to diabetes. Mrs. Candura, when interviewed by the judge, acknowledged that her feet were in poor condition and that she understood the doctor's advice that the necrotic feet might cause her death if not amputated soon. The court observed that Mrs. Candura was otherwise less than fully competent, with a distorted view of time and wandering train of thought. In addition, the court called her decision irrational. Nevertheless, given her "high degree of awareness and acuity . . . regarding the proposed operation" and her refusal of surgery even if she were to die, the court found her competent to refuse. In contrast, Mrs. Northern was apparently "lucid and apparently of sound mind generally. However, on the subjects of death and amputation of her feet, her comprehension is blocked, blinded or dimmed to the extent that she is incapable of recognizing facts which would be obvious to a person of normal comprehension." The court observed that Mrs. Northern looked at her "dead, black, shriveled, rotting and stinking" feet and refused to acknowledge their condition. She asserted that she wanted to keep her feet and live, refusing to consider that such a goal might be impossible. The court appointed a guardian for Mrs. Northern and empowered the guardian to give consent to the recommended surgery.

The President's Commission for the Study of Ethical Problems in Medicine and Biomedical and Behavioral Research (1982), in its seminal document *Mak-*

ing Health Care Decisions, stated that the competent patient must have (a) pos-session of a set of values and goals; (b) the ability to communicate and under-stand information; and (c) the ability to reason and deliberate about choices. Of course, a person with late-stage dementia will not meet these requirements regardless of the care taken to cultivate communication. The patient's right to choose must be filled by advance directives and surrogate decision makers.

SURROGATE DECISION MAKERS

Health care decision makers everywhere look to family members to decide about treatment for patients who cannot make their own choices. However, statutory authority for the professional custom is relatively recent in the United States and may be limited or absent in some states.

Designation of Surrogate Decision Makers by the Patient: Advance Directives and Living Wills

State and federal law includes provisions permitting individuals to leave written instructions appointing another person to make health care decisions in the event of incapacity, including dementia, in *an advance directive,* also sometimes called a *health care power of attorney* or *health care proxy.* The individual may also leave instructions regarding particular decisions. A separate writing with such instructions directed to anyone, particularly the health care provider, is called a *living will.*

A significant problem in the use of all types of advance directives is the indi-vidual's reluctance or practical inability to identify what treatments are rejected and when the patient's condition warrants such rejection. Generally, form living wills reject "extraordinary means" or a similar—and vague—description of treat-ment. Liability might result; for example, a recent case not yet finalized may require a nursing home to absorb the cost of care incurred after the staff inserted a nasogastric tube to treat a patient with Parkinson's disease for pneumonia. The patient's wife sued for removal after the tube came to be used for nutrition and hydration as well. Little is clear except that there is no consensus on the meaning of "extraordinary measures." The greater precision and detail reached by the patient in consultation with the health care provider, family, and legal counsel, the better.

The Federal Patient Self-Determination Act (PSDA)

The PSDA requires hospitals, nursing homes, and other health care provider organizations that participate in Medicare or Medicaid to maintain a written pol-icy on advance directives, which must include the following: (a) a statement of the right to make advance directives; (b) policies on implementation of advance directives; (c) a statement of any limitations on implementation of directives based on conscience; and (d) a statement of the individual's right to accept or refuse medical or surgical treatment.

Every facility must provide the policy in writing to every resident or patient on admission and must receive a written acknowledgement from the individual. The medical record must include information on whether the patient has executed an advance directive. However, the facility may not condition the provision of care on whether or not the patient has an advance directive.

Under the PSDA, a legal surrogate can exercise the patient's right to make an advance directive (42 C.F.R. Sec. 483.10(a)(3)). This recognizes authorized, legally appointed guardians, authorized health care surrogates in some states, and nonstatutory traditional practices (such as family consultation) in other states.

State Statutes

It is sometimes very confusing, in this era of frequent travel, that each state can make very different laws about the health, safety, and welfare of its citizens. Though some health care laws are to some extent made uniform by the requirements of federal health benefits programs, the health care provider practicing in more than one state must be acquainted with any significant legal standards in each one.

Regarding the authority of relatives to make health care decisions for their family members with late-stage dementia, American law traditionally was silent. In the past 25 years, the lack of law sometimes restrained health care providers from providing nonemergency treatment to incompetent patients without family or court appointed surrogates. Currently, a substantial number of states have statutes that authorize a hierarchy of relatives to make decisions for an incapacitated patient. Some provisions are found in so-called family consent statutes enacted specifically to provide legal authority for common professional consent practices. A greater number of such prioritized lists are included in living will and health care surrogate statutes, as a fallback position for patients who have failed to designate a surrogate decision maker. Typically, the list prefers the spouse, adult children, and parents, after which any designated relatives vary considerably. Though the preference for traditional family is clear, at least one state (Alaska) permits decisions by a cohabitant as a last resort.

The Uniform Health Care Decisions Act of 1993

Over the next few years, the variety of statutes may be simplified. States are likely to adopt some version of the Uniform Health Care Decisions Act of 1993 (a model law offered as guidance for legislatures). The act permits the competent patient to name a health care surrogate (termed a *proxy*) by a writing, which need not be witnessed or notarized. Clearly, this must take place before late-stage dementia. The proxy has authority to make health care decisions whenever the patient is determined to be incapacitated by the primary physician. This significantly simplifies procedure under current state laws, which typically require at least one additional physician.

Standards for Substitute Decision Making

The law recognizes two standards by which decisions might be made by a health care surrogate: the best interests standard and the substituted judgment standard. Substituted judgment attempts to reach the decision the incapacitated person would make if he or she were able to choose. It has become the standard most often used by the courts whenever there is evidence tending to reveal the patient's preferences, either by statements or life-style choices. It is clearly inappropriate only when an individual was never legally competent or able to express a choice. Thus, it is generally appropriate for patients with late-stage dementia.

The best interests standard, in contrast, tries to promote the patient's objective well-being in terms of health, safety, and security from risk. The decision maker concentrates on such tangible factors as physical deterioration, pain, or anticipated length of life. It places the decision maker in the role of caretaker and has largely given way to the value of individual autonomy represented by substituted judgment.

Recently, it has become apparent that the best interests standard is no longer always at odds with substituted judgment. A growing number of cases—some of more questionable reasoning than others—recognize that nontreatment and comfort care leading to death are a recognizable best interest for some patients. Hence, there is some confusion or blending of the two standards that may be relevant in late-stage dementia.

In any case, a surrogate must be guided by any applicable state statutes on guardianship or health care decision making. According to the Uniform Health Care Decisions Act of 1993, decisions by the proxy are to be guided by substituted judgment—that is, on directions by the patients or inferences from the patients' general statements, which indicate how they would choose if they were able. States set the burden of proof the surrogate must meet if a court is to determine whether the patient would have chosen nontreatment. See, for example, *Cruzan v. Director, Missouri Department of Health* (1990), which held that a state can require clear and convincing evidence. If the patient's wishes are unknown, decisions must be made in the patient's best interests. Therefore, the substitute decision maker for a person with late-stage dementia must determine that person's best interests. Generally, the standard favors health, but at extremes of disability, case law affirms the "best interest" of comfort care and peaceful decline.

SPECIAL CONSIDERATIONS

The most difficult decisions by or for a patient are those that cause pain or decline and death. Decision making is still more complicated when the contemplated treatment is intended to stabilize or improve the patient's condition but offers a low likelihood of success. Generally, this dilemma arises in late-stage dementia because of age or generally deteriorated health.

Allowing death to take place in some circumstances is clearly acceptable to the law. The individual's right to choose, which usually may be exercised by a surrogate decision maker, generally supersedes the state's interests in (a) the preservation of life; (b) the protection of innocent third parties; (c) the prevention of suicide; and (d) maintaining the integrity of the medical profession. See, for example, *Superintendent of Belchertown State School v. Saikewicz* (1977). Regarding the first and third considerations, the preservation of life is weighed with the interest of an individual in rejecting trauma or indignity in prolonging that life. Regarding the second, the only real impediment to individual choice has been the existence of dependent children—not a concern for a person with late-stage dementia as, even if such a child exists, the ability to provide and care for the child has gone. Regarding the fourth, prevailing medical practice is recognized by law as not demanding without exception that all efforts toward life prolongation be made in all circumstances (*Superintendent of Belchertown State School v. Saikewicz*, 1977).

Admittedly, some courts can be criticized for undervaluing the lives of individuals who have less than their full physical or mental faculties, generally citing poor quality of life as reason for destructive health decisions. See, for example, *Satz v. Perlmutter* (1978) and *Bouvia v. Superior Court* (1986). Health care providers who encounter decisions they believe are inappropriate for a patient are morally justified in protesting within the institution and to the justice system if necessary. In assessing the likelihood of ultimate success, one should consider carefully the nature of the decisions that can be made for an incapacitated patient under state law.

Painful or Speculative Treatments

An important part of legal consideration of poor quality of life has been recognition of pain or intrusion on the body, particularly for the individual who cannot comprehend the purpose or anticipate the time limitations on the discomfort. In the Saikewitz case, for example, the Massachusetts courts found that a profoundly retarded man has the right, through his guardian, to refuse the indignity of treatment that offers only a limited extension of life without recovery (*Superintendent of Belchertown State School v. Saikewicz*, 1977). In the case of John Storar, by contrast, the New York courts allowed health care providers to continue treatments and transfusions over the objections of his mother to a profoundly retarded 52-year-old man with bladder cancer (In re *Storar*, 1981).

Great differences in the facts of the cases are not apparent. Logically, however, a poor prognosis for a reasonable interval of comfortable existence after treatment weighs against the negative experiences of treatment (e.g., *Rasmussen by Mitchell v. Fleming*, 1987) The courts have not found a single satisfactory theory for comparing the cases and so tend to decide each one on its unique facts, including the nature of the disability and treatments, the prognosis, and the persuasiveness of proponents and opponents of treatment.

Treating Alzheimer's and Related Dementias: Experimentation and Incapacity

The possibility of using unproven treatment raises sharp questions about the fundamental doctrine of individual autonomy (albeit exercised by a surrogate decision maker for a person with late-stage dementia). It is critical that health care providers make full disclosure of all facts regarding the experimental treatment and the likelihood of benefit to the patient. Further, the incapacitated patient's past values and goals should be carefully examined and documented to determine whether a decision in favor of treatment is acceptable under the doctrine of substituted judgment. If it is not, it is unlikely to be acceptable to the courts because the best interests of the patient cannot unquestionably support the affirmative decision. The least acceptable possibility is that a significant purpose of the experimental treatment is to produce knowledge beneficial to others. The health care provider in such circumstances has a conflict of interest, which might not be cured by disclosure to the surrogate decision maker. Indeed, if that is the principal or sole reason for the treatment, it is very likely that only a competent patient can consent to participate (see, e.g., *Moore v. Regents of University of California,* 1990). Thus, the patient with late-stage dementia is almost never a candidate for prolonged or peaceful treatment with speculative results and little chance of success.

Do-Not-Resuscitate and Do-Not-Treat Orders: Health Care Providers as Surrogates

Beginning with an Institute of Medicine study more than a decade ago, some long-term care facilities have been sharply criticized for maintaining facility-wide do-not-rescuscitate (DNR) orders or allowing physicians to unilaterally enter a DNR order on a patient's chart. Such practices deprive the patient of the right to choose, either personally or by authorized proxy. Though prohibited by federal law, such de facto policies still exist in some facilities (Commission on Nursing Home Regulations, 1986).

Courts more often approve of a guardian's authority for nontreatment orders. In the Rasmussen case, for example, the court approved of DNR and do-not-hospitalize orders for a 64-year-old patient (with 3 nonresident siblings) found by the court to be in a "chronic vegetative state" (*Rasmussen by Mitchell v. Fleming,* 1987). The patient had never stated a preference. Similarly, in the often-cited Severns case, the Delaware court, acting on a husband's request and the patient's expressions of preference as a member of the Delaware Euthanasia Education Council, recognized the authority of the courts to enter life-shortening orders (*Severns v. Wilmington Medical Center,* 1980).

For such orders, as with other treatment and nontreatment decisions, patients with late-stage dementia are well served by the closest, caring persons who can decide, as similarly as possible, as the patient would have decided.

Nutrition and Hydration as Treatment

The courts have universally recognized artificial nutrition as a medical treatment that can be refused like another medical treatment. Most of the case law contemplates the circumstances of patients in persistent vegetative states. In the Corbett case, for example, the court rejected the distinction between forced sustenance and forced continuance of other vital functions for a 75-year-old woman in a persistent vegetative state for over 2 years (*Corbett v. D'Allesandro*, 1986). The use of a gastrostomy tube has been termed "intrusive as a matter of law," that is, regardless of the facts in the case (see *Brophy v. New England Sinai Hospital*, 1986).

However, a particular health care provider or facility may not be forced to withdraw artificial nutrition and hydration. Rather, the patient must be transferred to a facility and provider willing to comply with the surrogate's request (*Brophy v. New England Sinai Hospital*, 1986).

ETHICS CONSULTATIONS

Institutional ethics committees entered the sphere of chronic care because of new high-technology care options to prolong physical function; the emergence of hospital ethics committees—generally heavily weighted with physician and administration risk-management input; and the response of chronic care facilities, who increasingly received patients for whom the hospital's decision was "Don't leave off yet."

In an important New Jersey case (In re *Conroy*, 1985), a judge writing independently to concur with some of the majority decisions and to dissent from others examined the differences between hospital ethics committees and nursing home ethics committees. *Conroy* is relevant to the circumstances of advanced Alzheimer's patients because the elderly patient, Claire Conroy, was in a state sometimes termed *PVS* (persistent vegetative state), despite documentation of responses untypical of such a diagnosis. The judge wrote that elderly chronic care patients are a particularly vulnerable and isolated population; hence, decision making may not have the benefit of opinions from involved family members, as suggested by the model of surrogate decision making for the young woman Karen Anne Quinlan. The judge noted that nursing home ethics committees are seldom dominated by physician input and are therefore more egalitarian in their decision-making processes. Generally, such committees also have more time to anticipate decisions regarding patient needs, allowing a more reflective and global view of the decisions, which is appropriate to committee members who know the patient's needs on a daily basis. This suggests that staff members consulting a sound chronic care institutional ethics committee can anticipate involvement—to the extent appropriate to the expertise of various members—and a response of consensus from the committee as a whole or from a subcommittee of several members with particular knowledge of the problems or the patient.

    This distinction between acute and chronic care committees generally avoids a number of potential problems, such as resistance by the principal caregiver to an intrusion on his or her decision-making authority; the tendency in acute care to exclude the opinions of relatives and friends of the patient; and the steep ethical cliffs of high-cost, low-success procedures.

    On the other hand, some decisions may be weighted with the fiscal concerns of the administration or with failing regard for any preferences of the now-inarticulate patient discernable through past decisions or a values inventory. In sum, the ethics committee process tends to become a forum of last resort in cases of confusion or outright disagreement when neither family nor professional caregivers care to go to court. If the family for any reason has difficulty participating, the process becomes the forum for discussion of institutional caregiver ethical quandries. Although none of the possibilities is inherently bad, the broader view encompassing patient choice must be preferable.

    The caregiver seeking clarity from an institutional ethics committee is well advised to take an interest in both the substance of the information before the committee and the process by which decisions are reached. A most significant criticism of institutional ethics committees is that the lack of uniformity and completeness in either or both of these areas leads to inconsistent—and therefore unfair—decisions about patients similar in terms of needs or prognosis. Such inconsistency erodes the confidence of all who depend on the committee's deliberations.

    It is therefore appropriate to assure that, to the greatest extent possible, all the relevant facts about the decisions have been presented and noted by listeners. Further, it is a great advantage of chronic care that each member of the committee can usually participate independently in a bedside consultation appropriate in content to the member's special areas of expertise. In the discussion arising from this basis, it is preferable to review the values on which the committee's decisions will be based, weighing patient choice in a balance with continued life and objective measures of physical well-being such as pain and pleasure. In some cases, the most important concern is to avoid cultural contamination of a decision by considerations of race, gender, or economic status.

    Finally, however, institutional ethics committees differ in their perception of the purpose to which their decisions should be put. Most, it seems, appreciate the nature of the caregiver and family consultation in search of clarification of principles by which difficult decisions can and should be taken. Others, apparently influenced more by a legal or adjudicative model, foresee the implementation of the committee's decision without the possibility of modification for factors that found no place in the committee process. Clearly, developing an effective and helpful ethics committee depends on professional advice and participation in advance of decision making on behalf of an individual patient.

PARADIGM CASE EXAMPLE

The example presented below represents no individual living or deceased. Rather, it is contrived to illustrate specific principles and policies raised in the chapter.

Mrs. Mobley had lived for 6 years in a nursing home because of advancing symptoms of Alzheimer's disease when she was admitted to the hospital for removal of a benign cerebral tumor. Unfortunately, because consent to the surgery had been delayed, complications developed. After 33 days in the intensive care unit, she remained comatose, dependent on a respirator and feeding tube.

Mrs. Mobley was returned to the nursing home, where after 4 weeks she developed pneumonia and renal failure. The attending physician was reluctant to initiate dialysis or transfer her back to the hospital. The neurologist confirmed that Mrs. Mobley would never regain consciousness. Dr. Johnson recommended withholding further treatment and withdrawal of the respirator and feeding tube. Dr. Johnson did not personally know Mrs. Mobley, having been her physician and seeing her occasionally only after the initial years in the nursing home.

Mrs. Mobley's family consists of her son, John, age 42, who lives on the opposite coast of the United States, and a granddaughter, Anne, who lives in the region. When contacted, John says he cannot be present and, in any case, feels unable to make decisions for Mrs. Mobley, with whom he has had strained relations for years. Anne, on the other hand, lived with her grandmother recently while she found work in the vicinity.

Mrs. Mobley's close friend, Miss Thomas, is a frequent visitor in the nursing home. She asserts that Mrs. Mobley often said, "When it's time to go it's time to go," and favors only a vigil of comfort care for her friend. Anne, on the other hand, arrives in an agitated state and threatens legal action if health care providers "kill" her grandmother.

CASE DISCUSSION

Professional Judgment and Substitute Decision Making

Under the law, the attending physician is not authorized to unilaterally enter a DNR order unless it is clear that all efforts at resuscitation are futile, that is, completely inappropriate and virtually certain to be unsuccessful. The concept of futility is not well developed in the law because it has only a short and controversial history as a significant factor in health care choices. One might consider whether the extension of life is for a significant period of time, but the importance of a month or a year is in this case muddled by Mrs. Mobley's diminished perceptions. There is good, but not perfect, justification for categorizing further interventions to extend Mrs. Mobley's life as futile.

The Rights of Family Members and Others to Choose

For many, the statements of Mrs. Mobley's friend might be persuasive as an expression of the patient's true feelings, which she might not have wished to share with her granddaughter. However, the law favors the traditional family, a significant problem for same-sex couples and close friends who fill the role of family in emotional matters and intimate confidences.

In this situation, it would be risky to withdraw or withhold treatment without the acquiescence of the granddaughter, Anne. Her statements are particularly significant because she is in recent and reasonably frequent contact with the patient, giving credibility to any claim she might make to decide for her.

Family members would be able to bring suit. However, because the family generally must show that Mrs. Mobley wanted treatment (and therefore any surrogate decision maker should have decided in favor of it), it appears unlikely that the facility or health care providers would be found liable for damages to Mrs. Mobley's life and health.

In such sensitive circumstances, facilities can seek to carry out nontreatment policies by obtaining a court order to discontinue or decline to start the treatment requested by a family member. However, to avoid ultimate liability, it is necessary only that the facility and providers follow established procedures for making and recording such decisions, documenting the appropriateness for the patient given the impairment of health, poor prognosis, and ultimate futility of imposing invasive treatment.

Evidence of the Patient's Choice

Evidence of the patient's reluctance to undergo intensive medical intervention to prolong her life might be built on the hesitation of surrogate decision makers to authorize her surgery. If that consent was delayed by Anne, it is somewhat more persuasive that her current viewpoint is irrational and might soon turn to consent to discontinue treatment or even that some emotional burden makes her unable to endorse actions that will naturally lead to death.

Some practitioners utilize some type of values inventory for incapacitated persons such as Mrs. Mobley, to gather from the patient's history and reports of family and friends any information on which one might build an inference about what Mrs. Mobley would have wanted.

If Mrs. Mobley had executed a living will, it would very likely be one that calls for no life-sustaining care in the event of terminal illness. This illustrates the failure of many advance directives, because of vague definitions and still vaguer instructions regarding desired care, to provide much help toward carrying out the patient's wishes. Indeed, the very vagueness of the instructions sometimes raises questions about the understanding and intent of the patient at the time the advance directive was signed. Generally, the law considers Mrs. Mobley to be in a terminal condition if she cannot live without artificial life supports for breathing and heart function. Although artificial feeding is definitely an extraordinary measure and a medical treatment under the law, the patient cannot (obviously) be deemed terminal because of decline when feeding is discontinued.

CONCLUSION

Health care providers for patients with late-stage dementia who are almost universally elderly face more challenges from their consciences than from the courts. Too great a proportion of the cases litigated to determine the right to treat or withhold treatment from marginally competent or incapacitated patients involve younger people; the fate of the old is more often accepted quietly.

Nevertheless, a basic familiarity with the law is essential in the milieu of discordant families in a litigious society. Health care providers who are familiar with legal thinking on these sensitive matters can feel more confident in their own choices and can better advise families about the delicate balance of values in health care decisions for people with late-stage dementia.

BIBLIOGRAPHY

Anderson v. St. Francis-St. George Hospital, 610 N.E. Second 423 (1993).

Appelbaum, Lidz, & Meisel, (1987). *Informed consent: Legal theory and clinical practice.* New York: Oxford University Press.

Bouvia v. Superior Ct., 225 Cal. Rptr. 297 (Cal. App. 1986).

Brophy v. New England Sinai Hospital, 497 N.E. 2d (Mass. Sup. Ct. 1986).

Canterbury v. Spence, 150 U.S. App. D.C. 263, 464 F. 2d 772 (D.C. Cir. 1972), cert. den. 409 U.S. 1064 (1972).

Commission on Nursing Home Regulations, Institute of Medicine. (1986). *Improving the quality of care in nursing homes.* Washington, DC: National Academic Press.

Conroy, 486 Atlantic 2nd 1209 (1985).

Corbett v. D'Allesandro, 487 S. 2d 368 (Fla. Ct. App. 1986).

Cruzan v. Director, Missouri Department of Health, 497 U.S. 261 (1990).

Department of Human Services v. Northern, 563 S.W. 2d 197 (Tenn. App. 1978, cert denied S.Ct. 1978).

Lane v. Candura, 376 N.E. 2d 1232 (Mass. App. 1978).

McCloskey, E. (1991). Between isolation and intrusion: The Patient Self-Determination Act. *Law, Medicine and Health Care, 19,* 78.

Meisel, A. (1979). Exceptions to the doctrine of informed consent. *Wisconsin Law Review, 1979,* 413.

Mishkin, B. (1989). Defining the capacity for health care decisions. *Advances in Psychosomatic Medicine, 19,* 151.

Moore v. Regents of the University of California, 51 Cal. App. 3d 120, 271 Cal. Rptr 146, 793 P. 2d 479 (1990).

Natanson v. Kline, 350 P.2d 1093 (Kan. 1960).

N.Y. Public Health Sec. 2960 et seq. (setting explicit standards for entry of DNR orders).

The Patient Self-Determination Act, 42 U.S.C. Sec. 1395cc(a)(1)-(2), 1395cc(f), 1395mm(c)(8) (Medicare); 1396a(a)(57)-(58), 1396a(w) (Medicaid); 42 C.F.R. Part 417 (1990).

President's Commission for the Study of Ethical Problems in Medicine and Biomedical and Behavioral Research. (1982). *Making health care decisions.* Washington, DC: Government Printing Office.

Rasmussen by Mitchell v. Fleming, 741 P. 2d 674 (Ariz. Sup. Ct. 1987).

Roth, L. H., Meisel & Lidz, (1977). Tests of competency to consent to treatment. *American Journal of Psychiatry, 134,* 279.

Satz v. Perlmutter, 362 So. 2d 160 (Fla. App. 1978).

Severns v. Wilmington Medical Center, 421 A. 2d 1334 (Del. Sup. Ct. 1980).

Scott v. Bradford, 606 P.2d 554 (Okla. 1980).

In re Storar, 52 N.Y. 2d 363, 438 N.Y.S.2d 266, 420 N.E. 2d 64 (Ct. App. 1981).

Superintendent of Belchertown State School v. Saikewicz, 370 N.E. 2d 417 (Mass. 1977).

Superintendent of Belchertown State School v. Saikewicz, 373 Mass. 728, 370 N.E.2d 417 (1977).

Tomlinson, T., & Brody, H. (1988). Ethics and communication in do-not-resuscitate orders. *New England Journal of Medicine, 318,* 43.

Chapter 16

Program Evaluation

Marilyn J. Rantz and Mary Zwygart-Stauffacher

As strategic planning is done to develop a late-stage dementia program, an important consideration must be deciding process and outcome measures to be used to determine the quality of services delivered. People with late stage dementia have a variety of needs, which are met by many different disciplines. Having interdisciplinary input in the planning process of the program will facilitate both program development and evaluation. This chapter suggests both process and outcome measures and discusses related issues for administrators, directors of nursing, or other program planners to consider when developing a late-stage dementia program.

ESTABLISHING MEASUREMENT CRITERIA

Fundamental premises of quality measurement activities require that those items chosen to measure quality are consistent with the mission, goals, and objectives; that items are appropriate for the population served; and that outcomes are predictable. For outcomes to be predictable, there must be some degree of predictability to the usual course of the chronic illnesses experienced by the patients. If the interdisciplinary group can agree that there is some degree of predictability, outcomes can be measured. Determinations can then be made regarding whether an outcome is one that is predicted or one that indicates that there is a problem with care delivery.

Determining predictability of chronic illness has been challenging in long-term care. Because residents have multiple chronic diseases and because the trajectory of the illnesses are diverse, establishing predictable standards of what can be expected at certain points in time has been difficult. For example, when can exacerbation of a chronic illness be expected or when can a plateau be expected? Is death an appropriate outcome, or is it an indicator of substandard care? Is skin breakdown an inevitable outcome to be expected in the course of a resident's chronic illness, or is it an indicator of inadequate care delivery? Is weight loss an inevitable outcome to be expected, or is it an indicator of substandard care (Miller & Rantz, 1991)? These are the challenges that the interdisciplinary team must address in determining the process and outcome measures used to evaluate the program. Using the mission, goals, and objectives for the program as a guide, the interdisciplinary group can identify outcomes that they believe are consistent with the needs and disabilities of people with late-stage dementia.

Understanding the Person With Late-Stage Dementia

To establish process and outcome criteria for evaluation, the interdisciplinary team should thoroughly understand the residents who are the focus of the program. With a clear understanding of the characteristics of residents, ideas for measuring the processes of care delivery and the outcomes of care delivery can be generated by the team. Some positive outcomes could be related to skin, aspiration pneumonia, contractures, infections, bowel elimination, aggressive behavior, and hospitalizations. These are further explained as specific outcome measures based on resident characteristics:

- Skin remains intact.
- Residents do not develop aspiration pneumonia.
- Residents do not develop contractures.
- Residents do not develop infectious processes such as pneumonia, urinary tract infections, or septicemia.
- Residents do maintain bowel evacuation and do not develop constipation.
- Episodes of aggressive behavior are minimized.
- Residents do not require hospitalization.

Family and Staff Satisfaction

Family satisfaction with the care delivered and staff satisfaction delivering the care are both important components of an evaluation plan. Family interviews and surveys should be conducted throughout the length of the resident's stay in the facility. Family should be involved in a planning meeting when the resident's care plan is established at the time of admission to long-term care. A member of the interdisciplinary team could interview the family 2 weeks after admission, 6 weeks after admission, and every 3 months during the resident's stay to discern their satisfaction with the care. Additionally, an interview could be conducted after discharge or death of the resident to obtain a reflective account of the family's satisfaction with care when they have no reason to fear sharing negative perceptions. Interviews should be conducted in a private place on the unit or by telephone. Interviews should be open ended, allowing family members to discuss not only their satisfaction but also potential dissatisfaction with care. Using this approach, family input could be useful to staff in making adjustments in the plan of care. Additionally, interviews are often a good source of information for individualizing care and for generating ideas for evaluating the services offered.

Periodic staff satisfaction surveys should be conducted to assure that staff are satisfied with working with these special residents and their families. Content of the survey should include questions about satisfaction with care delivery, working conditions, and leadership support. Additionally, there should be open-ended questions soliciting suggestions to improve care delivery. It will likely be beneficial to separate the components of satisfaction and suggestions to assure staff anonymity for the satisfaction questions. However, names of employees should be submitted with their suggestions for improving care delivery. Identifying staff who make specific suggestions will enable administrators to ask for further information about ideas and will facilitate involving employees in planning for implementing appropriate changes.

Sources of Other Evaluation Data

The interdisciplinary team should carefully examine existing data that the facility is collecting for other program evaluation purposes or data that are generated within care delivery processes. Many times there is no need to develop new or additional instruments for collecting information to evaluate a program. Many times data are already being collected for other purposes and can be used for program evaluation. For example, staff and family satisfaction may be routinely assessed by a facility.

Another existing source of evaluation data is the minimum data set (MDS). All licensed nursing homes are required to collect and report MDS assessment information. The MDS is a potentially rich source of evaluation data, especially when analyzed with the quality indicators (QIs) from the Nursing Home Case-Mix and Quality Demonstration Project (NHCMQ). It is feasible for a facility to track QIs for this population. Residents in a late-stage dementia program can be compared with themselves over time or with other groups of residents in the facility. They can also be compared with residents in other facilities. The QIs from the NHCMQ include such items as the prevalence of injuries, falls, problem behavior toward others, indwelling catheters, urinary tract infections, weight loss, dehydration, physical restraints, little or no activity, Stage 1–4 pressure ulcers the incidence of contractures, and the use of psychotropic drugs (Ryther, Zimmerman, & Kelly-Powell, 1995). For details on how to use the QIs in program evaluation, several resources are available. Regulatory agencies in all states will have access to this data and the latest directions to calculate the QIs in 1996. Information about the QIs are available via the Internet at the Center for Health Systems Research and Analysis at the University of Wisconsin—Madison, in Wisconsin. Additionally, many computer companies are offering services to analyze facility MDS data using the QIs.

EVALUATING PROCESSES OF CARE

Processes of care can be evaluated in a multitude of ways. For example, the team may want to establish standards for behavioral management documentation. Criteria for evaluating the documentation completed by nursing and other interdisciplinary staff could include items such as:

- a specific description of the actual behavior exhibited by the resident,
- the frequency of the behavior,
- the length of time the resident exhibited the behavior for each occurrence,
- the intensity of the exhibited resident behavior (i.e., mild, moderate, severe),
- a description of the environment when applicable (i.e., activity in the area),
- a description of specific staff behavioral management intervention,
- a description of the resident response to the staff behavioral management intervention,
- a description of any revision in the staff behavioral management intervention as indicated,
- whether the care plan has specific behavioral management interventions, and
- whether the care plan has specific behavioral management goals for each specific resident. (From Miller, & Rantz, 1992, pp. 4:3–4:4. Copyright © 1992 Aspen Publishers, Inc. Reprinted by permission.)

The purpose of auditing behavioral documentation such as this is to evaluate staff compliance with resident behavioral management documentation policies or procedures, to identify any areas of deficiency or concern in compliance, to propose feasible alternatives for revision in the documentation procedures, and to improve compliance with associated documentation practices (Miller & Rantz, 1992).

CASE EXAMPLE

You have been contacted by your corporate headquarters to develop the pilot project for a late-stage dementia program. This program will be implemented in each of the corporate facilities on the basis of the model developed in your facility. You wisely decide to use an interdisciplinary committee and realize that there must be quality outcome measurements. However, at the first meeting the group looks to you for direction about how to precede in developing the program. They are especially concerned about how to establish outcomes for measuring the effectiveness of the program. You decide to have them review the latest information about clinically managing late-stage dementia clients and invite an expert in the care of these people to visit your facility and help educate committee members. After the group reviews the educational materials and spends time with the expert, they establish their own program mission, goals,

*and objectives. They agree on outcome measures and methods for data collec-
tion. The group is continuing to meet on a biweekly basis as program planning
continues, and implementation is targeted within your facility within the next
6 months. By using the principles of continuous quality improvement, you will
have the opportunity to evaluate your program effectiveness, modify your program, and then share your successful model with your corporate peers.*

CASE DISCUSSION

The intent of quality improvement activities is not to identify problem individuals delivering care but to identify problems in the processes of care delivery. The
problems are systems problems, not people problems. "The focus on quality
improvement is always on improving the process, not the people. Breakdowns in
quality are caused by a weakness in how services are delivered, not in who deliv-
ers them" (Ryan, 1993, p. 44). Quality improvement is not to be used in a punitive way in employee performance reviews. The thrust of quality improvement
activities is to use interdisciplinary teams to help design systems that cross disciplines and facilitate the processes of care and subsequently improve the quality
of care.

Data gathering and evaluation provides the foundation for the team to examine the aspects of care that they are doing well and those that need further
improvement. Many times people focus only on the aspects that need improving.
However, it is equally important to evaluate what the team believes are reasons
for the successes they are achieving. For example, when the team identifies outcomes that they are able to achieve at an expected level, they need to examine
what processes of care are helping them to achieve those outcomes. Perhaps there
are processes of care delivery that can be applied to other outcomes the team is
struggling to achieve. The team must take the time to evaluate, analyze, and
understand why they are able to achieve success in certain areas. Focusing on
successes helps motivate team members to consider that they can achieve excellence. As Atchley (1991) so clearly pointed out, "There must be incentives from
within individual caregivers, provider organizations, and/or the long-term system
before there is motivation to go from acceptable (minimum) standards of care all
the way to excellent" (p. 22). Quality improvement activities look at both what is
being done well and what needs to be revised. It helps focus energies to achieve
excellence.

Another concern is that changes in practice need to actually occur when data
from quality information activities indicate that a change in practice is necessary.
To facilitate such changes, it is necessary to formalize action strategies and stabilize innovations within the organization (Miller & Rantz, 1989). It is important
that organizational structures be designed to implement and ensure that practice
changes occur. A quality information team can make decisions about how the
processes of care may need to change, but they will need organizational structures to assure that staff follow through with the needed changes. One approach

is to use a participative committee structure for decision making and dissemination of decisions. Follow-up quality measurements are essential to determine whether or not practice changes are actually implemented. This can be a team effort and involve all disciplines and groups of employees within the facility. Nursing assistants are integral to quality information because they are the majority of the caregiving staff within a long-term care agency. They should be part of the planning process as well as part of the quality information measuring process. Nursing assistants can participate as quality information team members and they can participate as data collectors (Rantz & Miller, 1987).

CONCLUSION

Continuously improving quality requires that employees must view quality as a process, not a program. This requires a long-term commitment of the organization to the changes that are required to successfully use continuous quality improvement. The benefits of quality management, according to Bowe (1992), are that customer expectations are consistently exceeded, that clients are satisfied, and that clinical outcomes, market share, financial strength, and team work are all improved. Additional benefits of quality management are that job satisfaction increases, absenteeism and employee turnover declines, the ability to recruit improves, policies and procedures leading to cost reductions are enhanced, and progress can be measured and monitored.

BIBLIOGRAPHY

Atchley, S. J. (1991). A time-ordered, systems approach to quality assurance in long-term care. *Journal of Applied Gerontology, 10*(1), 19–34.

Bowe, J. (1992). Total quality management. *Contemporary Long-Term Care, 15*, 59–60.

Miller, T. V., & Rantz, M. J. (1989). Management structures to facilitate practice changes subsequent to QA activities. *Journal of Nursing Care Quality, 3*(4), 21–27.

Miller, T. V., & Rantz, M. J. (1991). *Quality assurance for long-term care: Guidelines and procedures for monitoring practice.* Gaithersburg, MD: Aspen.

Miller, T. V., & Rantz, M. J. (1992). *Quality assurance for long-term care: Guidelines and procedures for monitoring practice* (Suppl. 1). Gaithersburg, MD: Aspen.

Rantz, M. J., & Miller, T. V. (1987). Change theory: A framework for implementing nursing diagnosis in a long-term care setting. *Nursing Clinics of North America, 22*(4), 887–897.

Ryan, M. J. (1993). The future is continuous quality improvement. *Quality Management and Health Care, 1*(3), 42–48.

Ryther, B. J., Zimmerman, D., & Kelly-Powell, M. L. (1995). Update on using resident assessment data in quality monitoring. In T. V. Miller & M. J. Rantz (Eds.), *Quality assurance for long-term care: Guidelines and procedures for monitoring practice* (pp. I:28–I:30). Gaithersburg, MD: Aspen.

Chapter 17

Future Challenges and Considerations

Christine R. Kovach

As one century comes to a close and another begins, care of people with dementia poses a great challenge to the health care system. This book underscores the multi-faceted nature of health care for people with late-stage dementia and provides general guidelines that caregivers can use now. It must be recognized, however, that this is only the beginning of attempts to address the needs of persons with late-stage dementia. The planning and delivery of long-term health care services occurs within the context of public policy and the prevailing social climate. This chapter attempts to look toward the future of late-stage dementia care and outlines some of the challenges, needs, and opportunities that are likely to lie ahead.

A critical and compassionate analysis of an array of issues that affect dementia care is needed. Too often, this type of analysis degenerates into opposing positions: community versus professional care; nursing competence versus medical gatekeeping; regulation versus innovation. Little is served by these polarizing stands. Open dialogue that acknowledges and merges the strengths of multiple viewpoints and options, while avoiding the temptation to wallow in blind idealism, will likely lead to more progress in preparing to meet the needs of a growing segment of the population.

THE STRUCTURE OF CARE

Chapters 3 and 4 presented strategies for opening a late-stage dementia care unit in a nursing home. Many of the changes that have occurred in environment, programming, and physical care as a result of opening both mid- and late-stage special care units (SCUs) would also be highly desirable for people who are not cognitively impaired. Homelike rooms and furniture, varied activity programming, meals served family style, and enhanced health promotion and physical assessment are generally viewed as desirable for all. The movement to open SCUs is perhaps the beginning of a broader reform of nursing homes away from a medical "sick role" model of care to a more holistic, supportive, and homelike model.

Clearly, there isn't only one right structure for operationalizing concepts of palliative care for people with late-stage dementia. At this point the SCU model seems to be working, as evidenced by improved staff and family satisfaction and some limited research that supports positive outcomes for residents (Kovach & Stearns, 1994; Maas & Buckwalter, 1990; Rovner et al., 1990). It is also possible for some long-term care facilities to serve the unique needs of the person with late-stage dementia on a general unit.

Also, there have been some problems implementing the SCU model. The rapid proliferation of SCUs has lead to major changes on paper but little fundamental change in services provided at some facilities. SCUs have become marketing tools to attract new residents, and some facilities do little more than install chandeliers and carpeting to impress family members. Research has not demonstrated that merely segregating residents with cognitive impairment together in a pretty environment is therapeutic. Until evidence to the contrary is boldly presented, however, family members will probably continue to be overly impressed by elegant furnishings and other accoutrements. Perhaps the environmental accessories symbolize dignity, normalcy, or doing the right thing for one's loved one. The elegance of a unit may, therefore, be important for symbolic reasons, but elegant surroundings are not requisite for an SCU.

In consulting with many long-term care facilities opening mid- and late-stage SCUs, it is evident that the unique cultural environment of each facility is an essential resource for creating the new unit. All SCUs should have some fundamental characteristics, which have been presented throughout this book. But attempting to create a template, especially when there is still so much that is poorly understood about optimum care, is premature. The culture of the facility, especially good facilities with a long history, is an essential context that must be considered and incorporated into new programming.

Visiting-nurse hospices and several other Alzheimer's family-care hospices have been opened to meet the needs of people with late-stage dementia who will be cared for at home. As noted in chapter 2, however, most families prefer nursing-home care to home care when the dementia reaches the end stage. Efforts at home care should be continued and expanded to allow access to these services in more geographical locations. If care is given in the community, it must include strong support for family caregivers. Too often this is not the case, either because of a lack of services in a specific area, funding constraints, or the persistent underuse of community services by caregivers. Family caregivers often need respite services, help with physical care and household chores, psychological support, ongoing education, and assistance accessing resources. The person with late-stage dementia living with a family member needs to receive adequate attention to symptom control, including prevention, assessment, and management of physical problems, as well as attention to quality of life needs.

The trend in current public policy is to encourage movement of long-term health care for many chronic illnesses out of the institution and into the home. This movement, it is argued, affords people better quality of life, an ability to "age in place," and does not sever family ties dramatically. These arguments may mask the reality that underlying these noble pursuits is an effort to diminish allocation of funds to meet the needs of people with certain chronic illnesses. Care may essentially end up being given by an unsupported elderly caregiver who also has several chronic health problems. The person with late-stage dementia requires total or almost total help with all activities of daily living. Communication impairments, physical problems, and behaviors associated with the illness all require a lot of time and effort on the part of caregivers. Caregiver stress is well documented. When cognitive ability is severely limited, the person may be much less aware of who family members are and may also lose his or her attachment to place. The emergence of women in the work force, changing family structures, and geographic mobility of families will continue to mean that family caregivers will often not be available to provide home services. At any rate, assessments should be made so that the burdens of caregiving don't outweigh the benefits of remaining at home.

CARE PROVIDERS

The medical profession continues to have difficulty attracting physicians into the field of geriatrics. As people age, the complexity of care increases. People with late-stage dementia need geriatricians to assist with symptom control, prevent physical iatrogenesis, and manage chronic and acute conditions. Also, physicians working in family practice and internal medicine need more training in dementia care, family counseling, and services available.

In the past, nurses have looked more favorably on positions in the acute care setting. Decreased numbers of acute care beds, frustration over becoming a "techno" nurse, and more opportunities outside of acute care are moving more registered nurses into the community and long-term care positions. The complex needs of people in late-stage dementia mandate that more registered nurses work in community and long-term care settings than do currently. Because nursing homes are so highly regulated, nurses who are comfortable with regimen and regulation have been attracted to administrative positions in nursing homes. More professionals are needed in long-term care who are creative thinkers and can see the possibilities while not being deterred by the many obstacles in the current long-term care system.

Certified nursing assistants (CNAs) continue to be undereducated, underpaid, and devalued in the current health care system. Late-stage dementia care demands heavy physical care from CNAs but also necessitates a rudimentary understanding of psychology, family dynamics, and psychosocial interventions for a person with a severe debilitating brain illness. The need for a large cadre of CNAs will continue. Stress and burnout from the heavy demands of this type of work can be moderated, as discussed in chapter 4, by planning reasonable workloads, providing adequate depth and breadth of education, instituting formal and informal support systems, and initiating a system of positive feedback and rewards for work well done.

Social workers, activity therapists, speech therapists, and nutritionists also play a large role in meeting the needs of this population. Services from all of the disciplines must be coordinated. Family caregivers and trained volunteers are important members of the health care team. Family members need a lot of flexibility in the amount and type of care they personally provide to a loved one or in volunteer efforts on a late-stage dementia unit. Often, as the feelings of loss and actual and anticipatory grief become acute, family members may need to pull back from participation or, conversely, may have a more intense need for closeness and formal ties to caregiving and the unit activities.

ISSUES OF QUALITY

In truth, little of what is known or believed about quality of care for this population has been subjected to rigorous clinical trials or other evaluation studies. The definition of quality in late-stage care remains ambiguous, ill-defined, and variable. There are, for example, cultural differences in views of death and the dying process and of family obligation during this period. These differences must be respected and accommodated, making a standard for quality of care relative to these factors more difficult to delineate.

Complicating quality indices further is the awareness that the inevitable outcome for people with late-stage dementia is death. Quality indicators for this population need to be identified. Traditional measures of quality (i.e., patient satisfaction, decreased length of stay, return to work) are inappropriate. Other outcomes of care, such as physical and mental comfort, or positive affect, are exceedingly difficult to measure in a minimally verbal group with severe cognitive impairment. These outcomes are also difficult to quantify. Public policymakers and health care administrators often distrust and devalue "soft" outcomes. Evaluations of structure and process variables are also needed but will continue to be hampered by amorphous notions regarding what constitutes quality relative to late-stage dementia care.

Quality measures will need to address equity in accessing care and in distributing resources for dementia care. In reference to accessing services, the interventions that have been presented in this book reflect a fundamental change in philosophy or paradigm. This indicates that people with late-stage dementia will not have access to a range of late-stage dementia services until a massive educational effort is launched. Equity also involves distribution of limited resources with more than a modicum of justice. Public policymakers who pit one group with a health care need against another (e.g., we can't give money for dementia care because it will take money away from prenatal care) are using tactics that

are dishonorable. The problem or question needs to be reframed. It has been estimated that $200 billion a year could be saved if much of the current waste, fraud,
and profiteering were eliminated from the health care system (Consumer Reports,
1992). A person with late-stage dementia is a conscious human being deserving
quality care. Until more progress is made in uncovering possible cures or treatments for the underlying disease process, comprehensive palliative care is the
optimum mode for delivering services.

The acute care setting is increasingly a place for intensive, short-stay admissions. Long-term care will be the preferred setting for treatment of many nonin-
tensive needs. The optimum timing for moving a patient with dementia away
from acute care services to a less intensive effort at cure is an important and
unanswered question. Currently, symptom control, such as pain and dyspnea
management, is more sophisticated in hospitals. Long-term care must increase
the sophistication and array of services offered for symptom control. More attention needs to be given to prevention of physical problems during late-stage
dementia, such as pneumonia, pressure sores, constipation, impaction, contractures, and infections. These problems lead to discomfort and are costly to treat.

The health care system is designed to treat and cure illness. Indeed, the U.S.
mindset on competition, success, and intellectual ability makes chronic illness,
disability, and death particularly unpalatable. The health care system, if for no
other reason than a demographic imperative, must move to more holistic, multi-
focused delivery systems. All persons are both healthy and ill, and both concepts
involve physical, psychosocial, and spiritual components. The goals of care—
cure, prevention, promotion, rehabilitation, and palliation—need to be operationalized into more formalized and empirically validated clinical protocols.

For too long, nursing home regulations and Medicare reimbursement rules
for use of hospice services have thwarted innovation. Regulation should not con-
strain ideas or put blinders on those who are in positions to change care practices
and standards of care. When an innovation violates or contradicts a regulation,
work with regulators should begin to get a waiver or to modify the regulation.
Innovative ideas are sorely needed in long-term care. These ideas must be subjected to research and evaluation. Innovating continuously is also undesirable,
and stabilization and refinement of dementia care should follow any major
reform effort.

SOCIAL VALUES AND CARE

The challenges discussed in this book will test the moral fabric of society. In a
society that expects magic bullets to eliminate problems, no such solution
appears likely to emerge in the near future. The strategies that are generated to
meet the needs of the growing population of people with late-stage dementia will
clearly reflect societies values and priorities.

Changes in experience with death, as well as societal views regarding pain,
illness, and death all constitute important contexts for the care that is delivered to
people with late-stage dementia. The latter half of this century has seen a move-

ment of death and dying out of homes and into institutions. Death has become foreign, marginalized, and denied. Concomitant with this compartmentalization of death, much of Western society no longer believes that suffering is an inevitable part of living (Crowther, 1993). People go to huge lengths to avoid discomfort. Society also generally views illness and death as unnatural and despicable. When families are confronted with the inevitability of illness and death, the psychological pain and desire to disengage can be great. Caregivers are concerned with easing the discomfort of families and patients. A societal expectation of complete absence of physical and psychological discomfort does, however, conflict with what is known about the processes of grief and coping and what it is to be fully human.

CONCLUSION

Fear of death, disability, and cognitive decline looms large and hampers efforts to provide compassionate care. People in Western society need to become more comfortable with death and acknowledge bereavement as a natural process. Sadly, much of what is known about environmental design, dementia care, and palliative interventions has not been implemented in health care systems. Fundamental to providing enhanced care to people with late-stage dementia is acceptance of the palliative model of care and allocation of resources for dementia services. Education, dialogue, and continued research are needed.

The journey with patients and families through late-stage dementia, death, and bereavement is a privilege that can epitomize compassion, efficient use of resources, quality health care, and human connectedness. Changes in dementia care and in the health care system each present both an opportunity and a challenge—the opportunity provided by the increased demand for specialized dementia care services and a challenge to rigorously develop and test therapies and interventions that will make effective and efficient use of resources. Dementia care is optimally interdisciplinary, so it is appropriate for multiple disciplines to herald the next century by working together to enhance therapies and services from early to late-stage dementia.

BIBLIOGRAPHY

Consumer Reports. (1992). *How to resolve the health crisis: Affordable protection for all Americans.* Yonkers, NY: Consumer Reports Books.

Crowther, T. (1993). Euthanasia. In D. Clark (Ed.), *The future for palliative care: Issues of policy and practice.* Philadelphia, PA: Open University Press.

Kovach, C. R., & Stearns, S. A. (1994). DSCU's: A study of behavior before and after residence. *Journal of Gerontological Nursing, 20*(12), 33–39.

Maas, M. L., & Buckwalter, K. C. (1990). *Final report: Nursing evaluation research: Alzheimer's care unit.* Iowa City: University of Iowa College of Nursing.

Rovner, B. W., Lucas-Blaustein, J., Folstein, M. F., Smith, S.W. (1990). Stability over one year in patients admitted to a nursing home dementia unit. *International Journal of Geriatric Psychiatry, 5,* 77–82.

Index